Contents

Also available from Osborne Books...

Workbooks

Practice questions and assessments
with answers

Student Zone

Login to access your free ebooks and
interactive revision crosswords

Download **Osborne Books App** free from the App Store or Google Play Store
to view your ebooks online or offline on your mobile or tablet.

www.osbornebooks.co.uk

Management Accounting: Decision and Control

Tutorial

Aubrey Penning

Published by Osborne Books Limited
Tel 01905 748071
Email books@osbornebooks.co.uk
Website www.osbornebooks.co.uk

Design by Laura Ingham

Printed by CPI Group (UK) Limited, Croydon, CR0 4YY, on environmentally friendly, acid-free paper from managed forests.

British Library Cataloguing in Publication Data
A catalogue record for this book is available from the British Library

ISBN 978 1909173 873

Introduction

Qualifications covered

This book has been written specifically to cover the Unit 'Management Accounting: Decision and Control' which is a mandatory Unit for the following qualifications:

AAT Professional Diploma in Accounting – Level 4

AAT Professional Diploma in Accounting at SCQF – Level 8

The book contains a clear text with worked examples and case studies, chapter summaries and key terms to help with revision. Each chapter concludes with a wide range of activities, many in the style of AAT computer based assessments.

Osborne Study and Revision Materials

The materials featured on the previous page are tailored to the needs of students studying this Unit and revising for the assessment. They include:

- **Workbooks:** paperback books with practice activities and exams
- **Student Zone:** access to Osborne Books online resources
- **Osborne Books App:** Osborne Books ebooks for mobiles and tablets

Visit www.osbornebooks.co.uk for details of study and revision resources and access to online material.

1 Management accounting techniques

this chapter covers...

This introductory chapter provides a summary of some of the main techniques that are applied later in the book. Most will be familiar from your earlier studies. They are all important to your studies throughout this Unit.

We will start by reminding ourselves of the key differences between management accounting (which includes this area of study) and financial accounting.

Next we will examine the three main management accounting systems, absorption, marginal and activity based costing. We will learn about their impact on reported profits and how they have strengths and weaknesses that influence the situations where they are most useful. We will also remind ourselves about the principles of cost behaviour that are utilised in marginal costing, and learn how to analyse semi-variable costs using the 'high-low' method.

We will then remind ourselves how the functions of the organisation are managed, and how this links to responsibility accounting.

Finally, we will examine discounted cash flow.

MANAGEMENT ACCOUNTING TECHNIQUES

decision and control

In this book we are going to learn how to use management accounting techniques to monitor performance, to help to control operations and to inform decisions. This builds on the skills and knowledge gained in the costing units studied at the lower levels.

In this first chapter we will consolidate our understanding of a range of concepts and tools that are fundamental to management accounting. Although most (or all) of the topics will be familiar to you from your earlier studies, it is vital that you study this chapter carefully, so that the techniques can be applied where appropriate.

FINANCIAL ACCOUNTING AND MANAGEMENT ACCOUNTING

financial accounting

Financial accounting is concerned with recording accounting information so that accounts can be published and used by those outside the organisation. It is governed by legislation and accounting standards, and focuses on the needs of stakeholders from outside the organisation, like shareholders, suppliers, and prospective investors. Strict formats and timescales are imposed on organisations that determine exactly how and when the information is produced.

management accounting

Management accounting is the general term used for the production of accounting information for those inside an organisation. Because it is an internal system there are no external rules about how or when the information should be produced. Management accounting exists to help managers plan, monitor, control, and make decisions about the organisation. Its emphasis is on providing information that can help with the future of the organisation. The guiding principle for management accounting information is that it should be **useful** to its readers. If the information fails that simple test, then it has been a pointless waste of time producing it!

financial and management accounting compared

The table on the next page sets out a summary of the main differences between financial accounting and management accounting.

financial and management accounting compared		
	Financial Accounting	Management Accounting
Users	External Stakeholders	Internal
Format	Summarised	Specific
Governed by	Legislation & Standards	Usefulness
Frequency of Information	Annual (& possible six-monthly)	As required
Time Focus	Past	Future

MANAGEMENT ACCOUNTING SYSTEMS

methods of costing

Management accounting is the branch of accounting that deals with providing internal information within an organisation. Providing costing information is an important area of management accounting, and you will be familiar with the principles of costing from your earlier studies. Just as management accounting has no external rules governing how it should be carried out, cost information can also be developed in various ways. Although costing systems should always be tailored to the needs of the organisation and its managers, there are three general approaches to costing which you will need to become familiar with. They all attempt to calculate a cost for the units that the organisation produces. These 'units of output' could be bicycle wheels made by a bicycle component manufacturer, or specific operations carried out in a hospital.

- **Absorption Costing**

  This is a system that attempts to determine a 'full' cost for each unit of output. It therefore includes both direct and indirect costs, and uses the mechanisms of allocation, apportionment and absorption to incorporate the indirect costs.

- **Marginal Costing**

  This costing system categorises costs according to their cost behaviour, and divides them simply into variable and fixed costs. This system uses a cost for each unit of output based purely on the variable (or 'marginal') costs. All fixed costs are regarded as time based and are therefore linked to accounting periods rather than units of output.

- **Activity Based Costing (ABC)**

  This is a development of absorption costing, and uses a more sophisticated system to deal mainly with the indirect costs. This involves examining the costs to determine what causes them, and using this information to charge the costs to the units of output in an appropriate manner.

You will need to understand the working and implications of these three systems, so we will now examine how each one works in more detail.

ABSORPTION COSTING

You will probably be familiar with the absorption costing process from your earlier studies, but the following will enable you to recall firstly the terminology, and then the steps involved.

terminology:

- **Direct Costs**

  Costs that are directly attributable to the units of output. They can be divided into Direct Materials, Direct Labour, and Direct Expenses.

- **Indirect Costs**

  Costs that cannot be directly attributed to the units of production. They are also referred to as overheads. In a manufacturing environment only the indirect costs relating to production are usually absorbed into the product cost.

- **Cost Centres**

  Parts of the organisation where it is convenient to gather costs. It could be a department or section, or an area where a certain activity is carried out. 'Production' cost centres are where the unit of output has some activity carried out on it, whereas 'Service' cost centres provide a service to other cost centres rather than do anything directly to the units of output.

- **Absorption Bases**

  The methods available to absorb cost from the production cost centres into the units of output (or products). All absorption bases use expected (or budgeted) costs and activity levels to work out an absorption rate. Examples of absorption bases are Direct Labour Hours, Machine Hours, and Units of Output.

steps in absorption costing

1 Costs are divided into direct costs and indirect costs. The direct costs can immediately form part of the cost of the units of output known as 'prime cost', while the indirect costs (overheads) will need to be absorbed into the cost of the units via the next stages.

2 Indirect costs are either allocated to one cost centre (if the cost relates to only one cost centre), or apportioned to several cost centres by some fair

system (if the cost relates to several cost centres). For example rent costs might be apportioned using the area of the building used by each cost centre.

3 If costs have now accumulated into service cost centres, the total cost of each service cost centre is shared amongst the production cost centres that benefit from the service provided. This is carried out using secondary apportionment. For example, the total cost of running the stores service cost centre could be shared out by using the numbers of requisitions from the various production cost centres as a basis for secondary apportionment.

4 The costs that have been gathered in the production cost centres can now be absorbed into the units of output by using a predetermined absorption rate based on the expected activity level. The indirect cost is absorbed from the cost centre into the units of output as they pass through the cost centre. A common basis for this absorption is direct labour hours, so that the longer a product is worked on in the production cost centre, the greater the amount of cost is absorbed.

Case Study

THE ABSORPTION COMPANY: ABSORPTION COSTING

The Absorption Company manufactures several products, one of which is the Sorp. Its factory is divided into two production cost centres (Assembly and Finishing) and one service cost centre (Maintenance). 80% of the activity in the Maintenance cost centre benefits Assembly, while the remainder benefits Finishing.

Before the financial period started the expected indirect costs for the forthcoming year were:

	£
Assembly	208,000
Finishing	72,000
Maintenance	40,000

Each unit of Sorp uses direct material that costs £42. It takes five direct labour hours in Assembly and two direct labour hours in Finishing to make one unit of Sorp. Indirect costs are absorbed from the production cost centres using a direct labour hour rate. The expected direct labour hours for the year were 120,000 in Assembly and 25,000 in Finishing. All direct labour hours are paid at £8.

required

Calculate the following:

1 The indirect cost absorption rate in each of the two production cost centres.

2 The absorbed cost of one unit of Sorp.

solution

1   the indirect absorption rate

	Assembly	Finishing	Maintenance
Expected Indirect Costs:	£	£	£
Allocated / Apportioned	208,000	72,000	40,000
Secondary Apportionment	32,000	8,000	(40,000)
Total	240,000	80,000	
Expected Direct Labour Hours	120,000	25,000	

Absorption Rates:
Assembly   £240,000 ÷ 120,000   = £2.00 per direct labour hour
Finishing   £80,000 ÷ 25,000   = £3.20 per direct labour hour

2   the absorbed cost of one unit of Sorp

		Cost of one unit of Sorp:
Direct Materials		£42.00
Direct Labour:		
Assembly 5 hours @ £8.00	£40.00	
Finishing 2 hours @ £8.00	£16.00	
		£56.00
Prime Cost		£98.00
Indirect Costs:		
Assembly 5 hours @ £2.00	£10.00	
Finishing 2 hours @ £3.20	£6.40	
		£16.40
Total Absorbed Cost		£114.40

MARGINAL COSTING

Marginal costing accepts that there is a fundamental difference between costs that are based, not on the origin of the costs, but purely on the behaviour of the costs when the activity level (or output level) changes. There are several main ways that the costs could behave within a range of activity levels:

Variable Costs   Costs where the total amount varies in proportion to the activity level when the activity level changes. Variable costs are also known as marginal costs when using marginal costing.

Fixed Costs   Costs that do not change when the level of activity changes (within certain parameters).

Semi-Variable Costs   Costs where a part of the cost acts as a variable cost, and a part acts as a fixed cost.

Stepped Fixed Costs   Costs which are fixed within an activity range, but change to another (higher) fixed level when the activity level increases outside that range (and so on).

All the costs (regardless of whether they might be viewed as direct or indirect) need to be divided into variable costs and fixed costs. Semi-variable costs are divided into their fixed and variable components. There are numerical techniques for dividing them into variable and fixed elements. One of these, the 'high-low' method is studied later in this chapter. Once the total variable and fixed costs have been determined, only the variable (or marginal) costs are linked to the units of output to provide a cost per unit. This enables a 'contribution' towards the fixed costs (and ultimately profit) to be calculated either per unit, or for a specified output level.

Unit Contribution   The difference between the selling price per unit and the variable costs per unit. It is the amount that each unit sold contributes towards the fixed costs of the organisation and profit.

Total Contribution   The difference between the sales income and the variable costs of the units sold in a period. This amount is the total contribution that the sales of all the units in the period make towards the fixed costs of the organisation and profit.

Fixed costs are taken straight to the profit statement, and are deducted from the total contribution for the period to arrive at the profit for the period. You will need to be familiar with Marginal Costing, and recognise and use the formats and terminology that apply to this system.

Marginal costing has considerable advantages over absorption costing when it is used to help with making decisions. Uses of marginal costing are discussed later in this chapter.

Case Study

THE MARGINAL COMPANY: MARGINAL COSTING

The Marginal Company manufactures one product, the Marg. The following costs relate to a financial year, when 100,000 units of Marg are made:

Direct Materials	£350,000
Direct Labour	£230,000
Indirect Costs	£310,000

Investigations into the behaviour of the costs have revealed the following information:

- direct materials behave as variable costs
- direct labour behaves as a variable cost
- of the indirect costs, £270,000 behaves as a fixed cost, and the remainder as a variable cost

required

1 Calculate the cost of one unit of Marg using Marginal Costing.

2 If each unit of Marg sells for £10, and all the production of 100,000 units is sold, draft a marginal costing statement for the financial year showing the contribution (per unit and in total), and the profit for the year.

solution

1 costing a unit of Marg

Using only the variable (marginal) costs to cost one unit of Marg:

Direct Materials (£350,000 ÷ 100,000)	£3.50
Direct Labour (£230,000 ÷ 100,000)	£2.30
Variable Overheads	
(£310,000 – £270,000 = £40,000) ÷ 100,000	£0.40
Total marginal cost per unit	£6.20

2 Marginal Costing Statement for the Financial Year.

	Per unit £	For year £
Sales	10.00	1,000,000
Less Variable Costs	6.20	620,000
Contribution	3.80	380,000
Less Fixed Overheads		270,000
Profit		£110,000

Note that the fixed costs are not calculated in per unit terms, but are simply deducted in total from the total contribution.

ACTIVITY BASED COSTING (ABC)

background to ABC

Activity based costing was developed in the 1970s and 1980s as an alternative to absorption costing. Since the time when absorption costing was initially developed (at the time of the Industrial Revolution), many aspects of manufacture had changed, and it was felt that absorption costing was not providing information of sufficient quality. The points that were made by advocates of ABC were:

Overheads (indirect costs) typically now account for the major part of product costs, and should therefore be accounted for in a less arbitrary way than they would under absorption costing. For example, simply absorbing overheads based on just one basis (e.g. direct labour hours) does not acknowledge the complexity of costs that can make up overheads.

Both production methods and batch sizes can have a major impact on product costs, yet these are largely ignored by absorption costing. For example the cost involved in setting up equipment will be far greater per unit of output for small production runs than for large ones.

Modern production methods do not lend themselves to the use of absorption rates such as direct labour hours or machine hours. Integrated production systems can often operate with minimal human intervention.

cost pools and cost drivers

ABC works by identifying the indirect activities, and grouping their costs into 'cost pools', one for each major activity. For each cost pool there must be a factor that drives the costs and causes those costs to change. This 'cost driver' is identified and its rate calculated. The rate is then used to charge the output with cost, based on the output's use of the activity.

For example in a stores department (which would typically form one service cost centre under absorption costing), the activities could be determined as:

1 Receiving goods inwards, and
2 Issuing goods to production.

The costs of running the stores department would be analysed into the costs for carrying out each of these activities – the 'cost pools'. The cost drivers might be agreed as:

1 Number of Deliveries Received (for receiving goods inward), and
2 Number of Requisitions (for issuing goods).

The rate per cost driver would then be calculated by dividing the cost pool by the cost driver for that pool.

Using this technique, a product that required many different components that were delivered separately and then issued frequently to production, would be charged with a high cost from the activities in the stores department. In comparison a product that was made from components delivered together and issued to production in bulk would incur fewer costs.

Using a suitable analysis of costs and their drivers, an organisation can adapt the system to its own circumstances. Each different product will then be charged with a more accurate cost based on its use of the activities than if absorption costing had been used.

The diagram below shows how the system works. Study it and then read the two Case Studies that follow. They both illustrate the application of activity based costing, the first in a manufacturing company and the second to a college operating in the service sector.

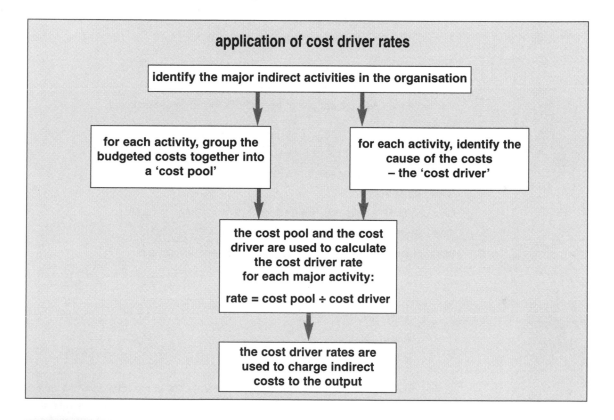

application of cost driver rates

identify the major indirect activities in the organisation

for each activity, group the budgeted costs together into a 'cost pool'

for each activity, identify the cause of the costs – the 'cost driver'

the cost pool and the cost driver are used to calculate the cost driver rate for each major activity:

rate = cost pool ÷ cost driver

the cost driver rates are used to charge indirect costs to the output

Case Study

ABC COMPANY: ACTIVITY BASED COSTING

The ABC Company has introduced activity based costing to cost its output. It makes several products on mechanised production lines, including AB, and BC. AB is a product that is usually made in large batches of 1,000 units, since it sells in large quantities. BC is a specialised product selling to a niche market, and is therefore made in small batches of 20 units.

As a part of the introduction of ABC the company has identified one major activity as 'setting up the production equipment'. The cost associated with this activity in a

financial year is budgeted at £250,000, and therefore this amount forms the cost pool for setting up production equipment.

The company has identified the cost driver of this activity as 'number of set-ups performed', since if the number increases the cost will be proportionally greater. One batch of any product requires one set-up to be performed.

The budgeted figure of £250,000 was based on an estimated 500 set-ups in the financial year.

The unit costs for AB and BC have already been calculated excluding the set-up costs, as follows:

AB	£50.00 per unit
BC	£55.00 per unit

required

Calculate the total cost per unit of AB and BC, including set-up costs.

solution

The cost driver rate for set-ups = £250,000 ÷ 500 = £500 per set-up

Charging at this rate:

One unit of AB would incur set-up cost of £500 ÷ 1,000 = £0.50

One unit of BC would incur set-up cost of £500 ÷ 20 = £25.00

Incorporating this into the previous costs gives per unit costs of:

	AB	BC
	£	£
Costs excluding set-ups	50.00	55.00
Cost of set-ups	0.50	25.00
Total Cost	50.50	80.00

In this case study set-ups account for approximately 1% of the total cost of a unit of AB, compared to 31% of the total cost of a unit of BC. These differences would not be identified using a traditional absorption costing system that treated set-ups as a part of general overheads.

Case Study

ABC COLLEGE:
ACTIVITY BASED COSTING IN THE SERVICE SECTOR

The ABC College is a small private college, providing a variety of part-time business related courses. The college has determined that there are four major activities that are undertaken, that have the following cost pools for the financial year and cost drivers.

Activity	Cost pool	Cost driver information
Teaching	£500,000	Teaching Hours (25,000 in year)
Course Preparation	£300,000	New Courses (30 in year)
Lesson Preparation	£100,000	Teaching Hours (25,000 in year)
Student Administration	£100,000	Number of Students (1,000 in year)

The costs for two separate courses are to be calculated using ABC.

The first is the Advanced Marketing Course. This course will run for 250 teaching hours, and should attract 20 students. The course has been run previously.

The second is a new course in Taxation for Exporters to Scandinavia. The course will run for 100 teaching hours, and there are 5 prospective students.

required

Calculate the cost per course and cost per student for each of the two courses.

solution

First the cost driver rates need to be established:

Teaching	£500,000 ÷ 25,000	= £20 per teaching hour
Course Preparation	£300,000 ÷ 30	= £10,000 per new course
Lesson Preparation	£100,000 ÷ 25,000	= £4 per teaching hour
Student Administration	£100,000 ÷ 1,000	= £100 per student

Secondly, these rates are applied to the courses according to their demand for the activities:

1 Advanced Marketing Course

Teaching	£20 x 250 =	£5,000
Course Preparation	(existing course)	-
Lesson Preparation	£4 x 250 =	£1,000
Student Administration	£100 x 20 =	£2,000
Cost for course		£8,000
Cost per student	£8,000 ÷ 20 =	£400

2 Taxation for Exporters to Scandinavia

Teaching	£20 x 100 =	£2,000
Course Preparation	£10,000 x 1 =	£10,000
Lesson Preparation	£4 x 100 =	£400
Student Administration	£100 x 5 =	£500
Cost for course		£12,900
Cost per student	£12,900 ÷ 5 =	£2,580

Although the two Case Studies were for very different organisations, the same logic applies to the absorption of overheads in each situation. In the first Case Study it can be clearly seen that the short production runs for the 'BC' product resulted in much greater set up costs being incurred for each unit produced. Similarly, in the second Case Study the 'course preparation' cost is mainly responsible for the much higher cost per student attending the 'taxation for exporters to Scandinavia' course.

In both these Case Studies, if activity based costing had not been used then all overhead costs (including set-ups etc) would have been absorbed on the same basis to all the outputs. This would mean that some products would absorb too little cost, while others would absorb an unfairly large amount.

COSTING SYSTEMS AND RECORDED PROFIT

variations in inventory valuation

One of the reasons that organisations use a costing system is so that the value of the inventory (stock) of finished goods (and work in progress) can be calculated and incorporated into profit statements. Since the different approaches to costing that we have examined give different costs per unit, they will result in different valuations of inventory, and this will in turn affect the profit calculation when inventory levels change. A marginal costing system will value inventory at just the variable costs, but a system that absorbs fixed costs into the inventory valuation can result in fixed costs being charged to a period other than the one in which they were incurred.

the effect of inventory valuation on profit

The costs incurred in producing goods in a period, together with the cost of the opening inventory must equal the cost of sales for the period, added to the cost of the closing inventory.

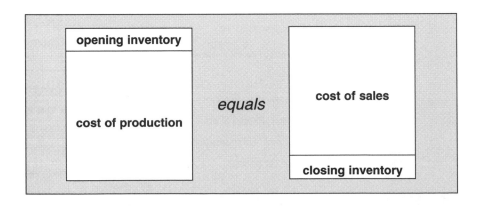

The valuation of the closing inventory will therefore affect the cost of sales, and therefore recorded profit.

The following Case Study uses the same data under different costing systems to illustrate the situation.

THE ALTERNATIVE COMPANY:
COSTING METHODS AND PROFIT

The Alternative Company manufactures a single product, and produces monthly management accounts.

In each of Month 1 and Month 2, 10,000 units were produced, and the following costs were incurred:

Direct Material	£100,000
Direct Labour	£150,000
Fixed Overheads	£250,000
Total Costs	£500,000

Both the costs and the volume of output were in line with the budget.

Units were sold for £70 each, and in Month 1 the whole production of 10,000 units were sold, whereas in month 2 only 8,000 units were sold. There was no inventory at the start of Month 1.

Direct Material and Direct Labour are both variable costs.

required

1 Calculate the cost per unit using:
   (a) absorption costing using units as an absorption base
   (b) marginal costing

2 Draft management accounts for each month using:
   (a) absorption costing
   (b) marginal costing

3 Reconcile and comment on the reasons for any difference in profits.

solution

1 Calculation of cost per unit

   (a)   Absorption Costing (using all costs)
           £500,000 ÷ 10,000 = £50 per unit

   (b)   Marginal Costing (using variable costs only)
           £250,000 ÷ 10,000 = £25 per unit

2 Draft management accounts

(a)   Absorption Costing

	Month 1 £		Month 2 £	
Sales		700,000		560,000
Less cost of sales:				
opening inventory	–		–	
cost of production				
(10,000 x £50)	500,000		500,000	
less closing inventory	–			
(2,000 x £50)			100,000	
		500,000		400,000
Profit		200,000		160,000

(b)   Marginal Costing

	Month 1 £		Month 2 £	
Sales		700,000		560,000
Less variable cost of sales:				
opening inventory	–		–	
Variable cost of production				
(10,000 x £25)	250,000		250,000	
less closing inventory	–			
(2,000 x £25)			50,000	
		250,000		200,000
Contribution		450,000		360,000
Less fixed costs		250,000		250,000
Profit		200,000		110,000

3 Reconcile and comment on the reasons for differences in profit

	Month 1 £	Month 2 £
Profit under absorption costing	200,000	160,000
Less:		
Fixed costs absorbed into closing inventory	-	(50,000)
Profit under marginal costing	200,000	110,000

The profits are identical when there is no change in inventory level, as in Month 1, when both opening and closing inventories are zero. However when the inventory

level changes between the start and end of the period (as in Month 2) the inventory valuation has an impact on profit.

The additional reported profit of £50,000 (£160,000 compared with £110,000) by using the absorption system is due to £50,000 of the fixed costs being absorbed into the closing inventory and effectively carried into the next period. If the inventory again fell to nil in Month 3 the profit difference would be reversed.

The differences in reported profits are only timing differences – the differences in profit are just reported in different periods.

conclusion

■ Where inventory levels increase, absorption costing will record a higher profit than marginal costing, as more of the cost incurred is pushed into the next period.

■ Where inventory levels decrease, absorption costing will record a lower profit than marginal costing as more of the costs from the previous period are set against income.

■ Where inventory levels are constant, then, providing there has been no change in unit costs, there will be no difference in recorded profit under either system.

You can therefore see that if an organisation uses absorption costing, significantly building up (or reducing) inventory levels can distort profits.

COMPARISON OF ABSORPTION AND MARGINAL COSTING

In the last section we learned how absorption and marginal costing systems can produce different results when used for reporting profits. We will now examine each of these costing systems so that we can establish their strengths and weaknesses. We can then understand why one approach may be better in some circumstances than another.

absorption costing

A clear benefit of using absorption costing is that the product cost developed is a 'full' cost – it includes an element of all the costs of production. The main problem is that the calculation of this full cost relies on two key issues:

■ Arbitrary decisions that have been made regarding the apportionment and absorption of indirect costs (overheads). Although each decision may be logical (for example apportioning heating costs by using floor area), different costs would be arrived at if other decisions had been made (for example, apportioning heating costs using building volume). There are many examples of such decisions in the calculation of absorption costs, including the choice of absorption base (for example, direct labour hours or machine hours), all of which have an impact on the product cost.

■ The expected volume of output (or activity level) will have been calculated in advance to arrive at an absorption rate. Any variation between the actual volume produced and this planned volume will mean that the product costs are inaccurate. This is also one of the main reasons that overheads can be either under absorbed or over absorbed. These terms relate to overheads that should (in an ideal world) be part of the product costs. Instead they are charged (debited) to the income statement if there is under absorption, or credited if there is over absorption. In both cases it results in inaccurate product costs.

The first issue can be addressed by the use of activity based costing, which can provide a more considered approach to the apportionment and absorption of overheads into product costs.

The problems in the use of absorption costing mean that it is most effective when:

■ the decisions made about apportionment and absorption are logical and consistent and do not distort the product cost unduly, and

■ the volume (or activity level) can be predicted with a reasonable level of accuracy.

If we consider the main uses of management accounting of:

■ planning

■ monitoring and control, and

■ decision making,

then we can see that absorption costing may be useful for planning, monitoring and control, provided the above issues are considered. This is because all costs are taken into account (which is important for planning), and monitoring and control can use a system that compares actual and expected figures on a like for like basis. One monitoring and control system is 'standard costing' which we will be examining in great detail later in this book, and which often uses absorption costing.

Absorption costing is likely to be of very limited use in decision making, since expected volumes are often uncertain and many decisions need an awareness of cost behaviour which is not part of absorption costing.

In spite of the problems of sometimes distorting profit (as we saw in the last section), the valuation of inventory for financial accounting purposes needs to include an element of indirect costs to comply with accounting standards, and absorption costing fulfils this requirement. In particular, the standard dealing with inventory valuation (IAS 2) requires a valuation that includes fixed and variable manufacturing overheads as part of the 'costs of conversion'.

One other use for calculating product costs is to provide a starting point for establishing a selling price. Provided the expected production and sales volume can be predicted fairly accurately, then the absorbed cost can be used to help with normal pricing by adding to it a suitable amount to cover non-factory overheads and profit. This is known as 'full cost plus pricing', and works by adding a profit mark-up to the full cost which has been arrived at through absorption costing. This is a popular method of pricing in many industries.

MARGINAL COSTING

Marginal costing, as we have already learned, uses knowledge of cost behaviour to analyse costs into variable costs and fixed costs. The product cost is then made up only of variable costs, and fixed costs are treated as relating to a period of time and charged directly to the Income Statement.

Marginal costing does not provide a 'full' product cost – since no fixed costs are included. A benefit of this approach is that the marginal product cost does not depend on volumes – the variable cost per unit will be the same no matter how many are produced or sold. This leads to some important techniques that can only be used with marginal costing, which are particularly useful for decision making. You will be familiar with some of these techniques already, and the following provides a summary of the main ones.

■ **Minimum price-setting**

The marginal cost of a product or service can be used as the absolute minimum that could be charged. While not applicable to normal price-setting, it can be useful to help calculate the price to be charged for additional orders if all the fixed costs have already been covered by normal sales. For example, it can be used by hotels to set discounted prices that are used to fill otherwise empty rooms.

■ **Break-even analysis**

This enables the calculation of the number of items (or sales value) that will result in zero profit. This provides a baseline against which expected volumes can be compared, in the knowledge that higher volumes will result in higher profits.

■ **Margin of safety**

This follows from break-even analysis and shows how far away (often in percentage terms) the planned volume level is from the break-even volume.

■ **Contribution analysis**

The calculation of contribution per unit (by deducting variable costs from selling price) provides a mechanism for quickly calculating profit. This is carried out by deducting the fixed costs from the total contribution which is based on the expected volume.

■ **'What-if' analysis**

Marginal costing is an important tool in testing the outcomes of various scenarios. In addition to break-even analysis and margin of safety noted above, these situations could include (for example):

- make or buy decisions
- limiting factor decision-making
- closure of a business segment
- mechanisation

Later in the book we will examine these situations in detail, and explain how to tackle them.

■ **Long term decision making**

The use of discounted cash flow (DCF) techniques often relies on the concept of marginal costing. We will be outlining DCF techniques later in this chapter, and later in the book learning how to apply these techniques in various situations.

COST BEHAVIOUR

You will be familiar with the main categories of cost behaviour, as shown below.

fixed costs

A cost is described as fixed if the total cost does not change when the level of activity changes. Note that we are not saying that fixed costs never change – just that they do not change because of a change in the activity level.

step fixed costs

A cost is described as a step fixed (or step) cost if its total changes in steps at certain levels of activity, remaining unchanged in-between. It relates to a cost (for example relating to a person or machine) that can deal with up to a certain level of activity, beyond which further costs are incurred (and so on).

variable costs

A cost is described as variable if the total cost varies in direct proportion to the level of activity. The cost per unit of activity (eg per unit produced) will be constant.

semi-variable costs

A cost is described as semi-variable if it is made up of a fixed part and a variable part. The total cost will rise if the activity level rises, but less steeply than if the whole cost were variable.

calculating fixed and variable costs – the high-low method

A useful technique that can provide the cost data for marginal costing is the 'high-low' method. This can be used where costs are behaving as semi-variable in total, and the amount of the fixed and variable elements are required.

The high-low method can be used where the total of a semi-variable cost is known for at least two different activity levels. If the total is known for more than two levels, then the highest and lowest are chosen for the calculation.

The Case Study that follows illustrates the high-low method.

Case Study

HILO PRODUCTS: THE HIGH-LOW METHOD

Hilo Products makes ladders. We are given the total of a semi-variable cost at four different levels of activity, as follows

Level of activity (units)	400	650	800	900
Total cost (£)	6,200	6,950	7,400	7,700

First we identify the lowest and highest totals, which are:

£6,200 for 400 units and £7,700 for 900 units.

To calculate the variable cost per unit, we use the fact that the extra cost has been caused by the variable cost of the extra units. That is:

	Cost	Units		
High	£7,700	900		
Low	£6,200	400		
Difference	£1,500	÷ 500	= £3 per unit	

Using £3 per unit, we then calculate the variable part of the cost for 400 units:

£3 x 400 = £1,200

But the total cost for 400 units is £6,200

Therefore the fixed part (which is the same for any number of units)

= £6,200 − £1,200 = £5,000

We can now check the solution by calculating the total cost for 900 units, using our answers:

Total cost = Fixed cost + (variable cost per unit x number of units)

= £5,000 + (£3 x 900)

= £5,000 + £2,700

= £7,700 which agrees with the original data.

The following graph illustrates the behaviour of the total cost in this Case Study. The variable cost per unit determines the gradient (slope) of the line, and the fixed cost is shown where the line cuts the vertical axis. The total costs for 650 units and 800 units lie exactly on the line, but in some cases the points between the high and low may not fit exactly. The high-low method still gives useful information provided that the cost behaviour is approximately semi-variable – that is provided that all the points are approximately in a straight line.

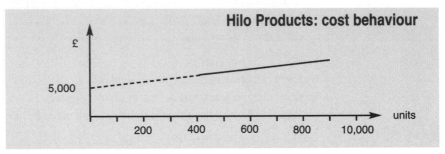

Now check your understanding of this subject by reading through the summary below:

---

high-low method summary

1   identify the highest and lowest cost totals and their levels of activity
2   calculate the difference between the two cost totals
3   calculate the difference in units between the two levels of activity
4   divide the difference in cost by the difference in units: this gives the variable cost per unit
5   use the variable cost per unit to calculate the variable part of one of the cost totals
6   deduct the variable part from the cost total to obtain the fixed part
7   check the answers by using them to calculate the other cost total, which should agree with the given data

---

the high-low method incorporating stepped fixed costs

As well as using the high-low method as explained above, we can also use this method when the fixed costs incorporate a step. This means that the fixed costs are not the same at all levels of output, but rise (in a step) at a certain output level, and then remain fixed at the higher level.

Provided we have sufficient information about the way that the costs behave we can still use the high-low method to work out the fixed and variable cost elements.

In addition to the total costs and two different output levels we will also need to know one of the following pieces of data:

■   the fixed cost below the step
■   the fixed cost above the step
■   the increase in fixed costs at the step
■   the variable cost per unit

This may sound more difficult than it is. The process is quite logical and simply uses the normal high-low method plus the extra information provided. In this example we are told the increase in fixed costs (ie the size of the step in fixed costs).

example

The costs for a product have been calculated as follows based on two possible production levels:

Volume of production	20,000 units	28,000 units
Total cost	£500,000	£680,000

It has been established that the fixed cost element contains a step of £20,000 when volume exceeds 25,000 units. Other costs are variable.

Using the high-low method, estimate the total stepped fixed costs at each production level and the variable costs per unit.

solution

The difference in total cost of £680,000 − £500,000 = £180,000 is due to:

- the step in fixed costs of £20,000
- the variable costs for 28,000 − 20,000 = 8,000 units

Variable cost per unit is therefore: (£180,000 − £20,000) / 8,000 = £20.00 per unit.

Fixed costs account for the difference between the variable costs and the total costs.

At 20,000 units:

Total costs	£500,000
Variable costs (20,000 x £20)	£400,000
Therefore fixed costs are	£100,000

At 28,000 units:

Total costs	£680,000
Variable costs (28,000 x £20)	£560,000
Therefore fixed costs are	£120,000

This also agrees with the step in the fixed cost of £20,000; the fixed costs rise from £100,000 to £120,000.

Activities 1.7 and 1.8 at the end of this chapter can be used to practise this technique.

the high-low method incorporating quantity discounts to variable costs

We can also use the high-low method when the variable costs change at a certain level – for example because a quantity discount is available. This discount would reduce the cost per unit for all units, provided the number of units produced exceeds a certain number.

There are two ways that we could be given information about the discount, and each requires a slightly different approach, as follows:

- A discount of a known amount in £ per unit, or
- A discount of a percentage off the usual variable cost

We will illustrate each approach with an example.

example – known discount amount in £ per unit

The costs for a product have been calculated based on two different production levels:

Volume of production	1,000 units	4,000 units
Total cost	£20,000	£42,000

It has been established that a quantity discount of £2 per unit applies to all units when production exceeds 2,000 units, and this has been taken account of in the total cost figures. The fixed costs do not incorporate any steps in cost.

Use the high-low method, estimate the total fixed costs, and the variable costs per unit that apply at different production levels.

solution

The key to this calculation is to realise that the quantity discount applies at the 4,000 unit level, but not at the 1,000 unit level.

The simplest approach is to first adjust the total cost at 4,000 units so that the quantity discount is ignored. This will enable us to use a consistent variable cost to calculate the fixed cost element. We can then adjust the variable cost afterwards.

The total cost at 4,000 units if we ignore the discount would be increased by 4,000 units x £2 per unit, giving a notional total cost of £42,000 + £8,000 = £50,000.

We can then use the high-low method as normal:

	Cost (ignoring discount)		Units	
High	£50,000		4,000	
Low	£20,000		1,000	
Difference	£30,000	÷	3,000	= £10 per unit

The variable cost that applies after the discount must be £10 – £2 = £8.

We can then either use the variable cost of £10 per unit to work out the fixed cost at 1,000 units, or use the variable cost of £8 per unit to calculate the fixed cost at 4,000 units. Remember if using the discounted variable cost to also use the actual total cost that applies at 4,000 units.

Both calculations should give the same answer (since there is no step).

Using 1,000 units: Fixed cost = £20,000 – (£10 x 1,000 units)   = £10,000

Using 4,000 units: Fixed cost = £42,000 – (£8 x 4,000 units)   = £10,000

example – discount as % of variable cost

The costs for a product have been calculated based on two different production levels:

Volume of production	3,000 units	6,000 units
Total cost	£24,000	£36,000

It has been established that a quantity discount of 25% of the variable cost applies to all units when production exceeds 7,000 units. The fixed costs do not incorporate any steps in cost.

■ Use the high-low method, estimate the total fixed costs, and the variable costs per unit that apply at different production levels.

■ Estimate the total costs at a production level of 7,500 units, assuming that the fixed costs remain unchanged

solution

The following technique can be used provided the figures used to apply the 'high-low' method do not cross the point at which the discount comes into effect. This means that both production levels must be either above or below the discount point. If you are provided with total cost at more than two levels, you will need to choose carefully the figures to use.

We firstly use the normal high-low method to establish the variable cost. In this example it will not incorporate the discount as both figures used are below 7,000 units. We can then apply the percentage discount to production levels where it applies.

	Cost		**Units**	
High	£36,000		6,000	
Low	£24,000		3,000	
Difference	£12,000	÷	3,000	= £4 per unit

This provides the variable cost before any discount, and either figure can be used to establish the fixed cost, as normal:

Using 6,000 units: Fixed cost = £36,000 – (£4 x 6,000 units)   = £12,000

The discount that applies to production levels over 7,000 units of 25% would give a variable cost of £3 per unit.

The costs at 7,500 units would therefore be:

Variable Cost:	7,500 x £3	=	£22,500
Fixed Costs			£12,000
Total Costs			£34,500

In this example, the total costs of producing 7,500 units are less than the total costs of producing 6,000 units, due to the discount.

practical limitations of cost behaviour

A problem that can arise when analysing costs based on their behaviour is that they may not always follow the (rather simplistic) categories of variable or fixed costs. For example, production costs which are often considered as fixed such as maintenance, cleaning, depreciation and insurance may in fact increase slightly as the activity level increases.

Unit costs which are normally categorised as variable (for example materials), may reduce due to bulk discounts or increase due to problems with availability as volumes increase. Costs which do not behave quite as variable costs are sometimes said to have 'non-linear behaviour' based on the way that the unit cost would appear on a graph when plotted against volume – ie not a straight line.

ADD-VANTAGE LIMITED: CHOICE OF COSTING SYSTEM

situation

Add-vantage Limited is an accountancy training company. You have been asked to trial some learning material that is to be used to help the trainees understand the advantages and disadvantages of absorption and marginal costing.

required

Sort the following statements, based on whether they apply to absorption costing or marginal costing, and use the statements to complete the table.

Statements

1   This system relies on analysing costs based on their behaviour.
2   The unit cost produced under this system can be used to help establish normal selling price.
3   When inventory levels increase this system records a lower profit than the alternative system.
4   The accuracy of unit costs calculated under this system relies heavily on activity levels being as expected.
5   This system relies on some decisions about apportionment and absorption that may be arbitrary.
6   This system can be used to establish break-even levels and margins of safety.
7   Absolute minimum selling prices can be calculated with this system, and these can be used to help price 'extra' sales.
8   A practical problem with the analysis used for this system is how to deal with non-linear costs.
9   The unit costs calculated using this system can be used to value inventory for financial accounting purposes, since the method complies with accounting standards.
10 The high-low method can be used to help analyse costs so that they can be used in this costing system.

Absorption Costing	Marginal Costing

solution

Absorption Costing	Marginal Costing
The unit cost produced under this system can be used to help establish normal selling price.	This system relies on analysing costs based on their behaviour.
The accuracy of unit costs calculated under this system relies heavily on activity levels being as expected.	When inventory levels increase this system records a lower profit than the alternative system.
This system relies on some decisions about apportionment and absorption that may be arbitrary.	This system can be used to establish break-even levels and margins of safety.
The unit costs calculated using this system can be used to value inventory for financial accounting purposes, since the method complies with accounting standards.	Absolute minimum selling prices can be calculated with this system, and these can be used to help price 'extra' sales.
	A practical problem with the analysis used for this system is how to deal with non-linear costs.
	The high-low method can be used to help analyse costs so that they can be used in this costing system.

FUNCTIONAL ORGANISATION AND REPORTING

Organisations are managed as a group of different functions – for example 'Production' (for a manufacturing organisation), 'Sales and Distribution', 'Administration', and 'Finance'. This structure is illustrated in the sample organisation chart shown on the next page. These functions can also be sub-divided into areas of control according to the needs of the organisation.

As well as each of these functions being controlled by individual managers, the accounting systems (both financial and management) will have been developed to operate with the same structure. As an important part of the management accounting system, management control systems will use the functional structure, and reporting carried out to the functional managers.

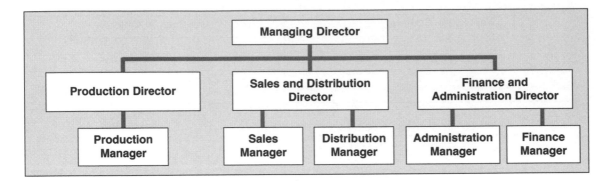

RESPONSIBILITY CENTRES

As already mentioned, an important area of management accounting is the monitoring and control of costs. This is usually carried out by making certain managers responsible for each of the various aspects of the organisation and the costs that are incurred there. This concept is known as responsibility accounting. Standard costing, which will be examined in detail in the next few chapters usually makes good use of the idea of responsibility accounting.

Responsibility accounting often divides the organisation into 'responsibility centres' of three main types.

cost centres

These are responsibility centres where costs are charged and can be monitored and controlled. They are parts of the organisation that incur costs but do not have any direct income, and therefore the manager responsible for a cost centre could only be held accountable for the costs incurred there. We have already seen the role that cost centres can play in absorption costing where costs are allocated or apportioned to cost centres before being absorbed into product costs.

profit centres

Profit centres are parts of the organisation where costs are incurred, but income is generated as well. This means that profit can be calculated, and the manager responsible would be accountable for the amount of profit based on both the income and the expenditure in that responsibility centre. The profit would be measured in monetary amount, and also as a percentage of sales income.

investment centres

Investment centres are responsibility centres where the manager is responsible for income and expenditure (as in a profit centre), but also for the level of investment. The investment could be in the form of non-current (fixed) assets, and also could include elements of working capital such as inventory (stock), receivables (debtors), and payables (creditors) and maybe also cash. An investment centre is in effect a mini business within the main organisation. Monitoring would be carried out by comparing the profit with the investment, often by measures such as return on net assets or return on capital employed.

TECHNIQUES USING DISCOUNTED CASH FLOW (DCF)

You are probably familiar with the use of discounted cash flow techniques from your earlier studies. This section will act as revision of the main principles, which will then be applied later in this book.

DCF is used to help with long term decision making, by taking account of the 'time-value' of money when comparing cash flows. It works by using factors to multiply by the actual future cash flows to convert them into 'present value' cash flows. Once all future cash flows have been converted into their equivalent present values, they can be added or subtracted from each other since they are all now comparable.

The logic of DCF is that future incoming cash flows have less value than current ones because we have to wait to receive the money. If we had received it immediately then it could have been invested to grow in value. For example, £751 invested now at 10% interest per year would grow to £1,000 after 3 years. This calculation is based on compound interest – check the figures yourself. In the language of DCF we would say that £1,000 in 3 years' time has a 'present value' of £751.

The further into the future the cash flow occurs (and the greater the assumed interest rate) the greater the difference between the actual future cash flow and its present value. We would be provided with 'discount factors' to convert the cash flows into present values. For example the discount factor for three years based on 10% is 0.751, and for five years at the same rate is 0.621. The interest rate used for discount factors is often the cost of capital to the organisation.

We use the term 'net present value' to describe the net result of comparing the present values of all the relevant future cash flows – deducting negative flows from positive ones. If the result is positive this shows that even after taking account of the 'time-value' of the cash flows, the incoming flows are greater than the outgoing flows. This usually means that the situation or project that the figures are based on is worthwhile.

The term 'internal rate of return' (IRR) is used to describe the interest rate that when applied to the cash flows from a project results in a net present value of zero. For example, if a project shows a positive net present value based on 10%, but a negative net present value when using an interest rate of 20%, we would know that the internal rate of return must be somewhere in-between these figures. We could calculate roughly what the IRR is by trial and error, and provided it is greater than the organisation's cost of capital then the project may be worthwhile.

Later in the book we will look at various applications of this technique, but for now we will use a fairly simple Case Study to remind us of how DCF works.

Case Study

SOLAR SAVINGS:
CALCULATING NET PRESENT VALUE

situation

A company is considering installing solar panels on the roof of a block of flats that it is building to provide hot water for all the tenants. The solar panels will cost £30,000 to purchase and install, and have an expected useful life of 6 years. The total received from tenants would increase from the normal rental income of £45,000 per year to £52,400 per year if they were to be supplied with solar powered hot water. The company's cost of capital is 10%, and this rate is to be used for the DCF calculation.

required

Using the following discount factors, calculate whether the installation of solar panels is likely to be worthwhile.

Year	Discount factor
1	0.909
2	0.826
3	0.751
4	0.683
5	0.621
6	0.564

solution

Year	Detail	Cash flow £	Discount factor	Present value £
0	Purchase and installation	(30,000)	1.000	(30,000)
1	Increased	7,400	0.909	6,727
2	receipts from	7,400	0.826	6,112
3	tenants	7,400	0.751	5,557
4		7,400	0.683	5,054
5		7,400	0.621	4,595
6		7,400	0.564	4,174
Net Present Value				2,219

The net present value of £2,219 is positive, so the installation of solar panels appears worthwhile based on these figures.

- Management Accounting is guided by its usefulness to managers, and has no external rules or formats that must be followed.

- Management Accounts are based around the organisation's costing system, which can be derived from Absorption Costing, Marginal Costing, or Activity Based Costing. Each system uses different terminology and different ways of calculating the cost of an organisation's output or activities. The different ways that inventory can be valued in management accounts affects the amount of profit that is recorded in each period when inventory levels change.

- There are strengths and weaknesses of absorption and marginal costing, and each may be better in certain circumstances. Absorption costing can often be successfully used for planning, monitoring and control. Marginal costing is usually best for decision making.

- Cost behaviour (based on what happens to costs when the activity level changes) is an important tool for management accounting.

- Responsibility accounting often uses cost centres, profit centres and investment centres to divide up an organisation into manageable and accountable sections.

- Discounted cash flow techniques need to be understood and applied.

financial accounting	the branch of accounting that is concerned with reporting performance to those outside the organisation
management accounting	the branch of accounting that is concerned with providing useful information to managers within the organisation. This book is concerned with some of the main aspects of Management Accounting
absorption costing	this is a system that attempts to determine a 'full' production cost for each unit of output. It therefore includes both direct and indirect costs, and uses the mechanisms of allocation, apportionment and absorption to incorporate the indirect production costs
marginal costing	this costing system categorises costs according to their cost behaviour, and divides them into variable and fixed costs. This system uses a cost for each unit of output based purely on the variable (or 'marginal') costs. All fixed costs are regarded as time based and are therefore linked to accounting periods rather than units of output

activity based costing	this is a development of absorption costing, and uses a more sophisticated system to deal with the indirect costs. This involves examining indirect costs to determine what causes them, and using this information to charge the costs to the units of output in an appropriate manner
fixed costs	costs which do not change in total due to changes in activity levels
step fixed costs	costs which change in total (in steps) at various activity levels, remaining unchanged in-between
variable costs	costs which change in total in proportion to the activity level
high-low method	a method used to analyse semi-variable costs into their variable and fixed components so that costs can be predicted at various output levels
responsibility accounting	management accounting based on departments, activities or functions, each of which is the area of responsibility of an individual
discounted cash flow	a technique that takes account of the 'time-value' of money by discounting future cash flows to their present value

Activities

1.1 The System Company manufactures one product, the Tem. Budgeted production is 4,000 Tems per week. During each of the first two weeks of this year it had costs as follows, exactly as budgeted:

Direct Materials	£5,000
Direct Labour	£9,000
Fixed Overheads	£6,000

The company had no finished goods in inventory at the start of week 1. In both weeks it produced 4,000 units. Sales in week 1 were 3,000 units, and in week 2 were 5,000 units, all at £8 per Tem.

Both Direct Materials and Direct Labour behave as Variable Costs.

(a) Produce profit statements for each of the two weeks, using:

1 Absorption costing, absorbing fixed overheads on a per unit basis.
2 Marginal Costing.

(b) Reconcile the difference between recorded profits for each week under the alternative costing systems.

1.2 A company manufactures a single product and uses the units of output method for absorption of fixed production overheads. The budgeted fixed overheads for the period were £126,500 and the budgeted output was 55,000 units.

The actual fixed overheads were £129,000 and 56,000 units were actually produced.

Required:

Calculate the following:
- The fixed overhead absorption rate.
- The amount of fixed overheads that were absorbed during the period.
- The amount of under or over absorption of fixed overheads during the period.

1.3 A company manufactures a single product and uses the units of output method for absorption of fixed production overheads. The budgeted fixed overheads for the period were £282,600 and the budgeted output was 36,000 units.

The actual fixed overheads were £279,500 and 34,500 units were actually produced.

Required:

Calculate the following:
- The fixed overhead absorption rate.
- The amount of fixed overheads that were absorbed during the period.
- The amount of under or over absorption of fixed overheads during the period.

1.4 The following table shows examples of situations where different costing systems may be appropriate. Select the costing system that is most appropriate for each situation by ticking the relevant column.

Situation	Absorption costing	Marginal costing	Activity based costing
(a) A company that has restricted capacity and needs to choose which products should be given priority			
(b) A hotel that wishes to sell some rooms on a 'last minute' basis at the minimum price without incurring losses			
(c) A company that makes a wide range of different products using advanced manufacturing technology. Design costs are significant. In the competitive market place it is important that unit costs are as accurate as possible.			
(d) A company that builds large commercial premises that take a considerable time to complete. Most costs can be attributed to specific buildings.			
(e) A company that makes an established range of products where volumes can be accurately predicted. All products are made in similar size batches.			

1.5   A specific semi-variable cost totals £6,200 when output is 900 units. The variable cost per unit is £5 per unit.

Calculate the total cost when output is 1,050 units.

1.6   A specific semi-variable cost totals £9,650 when output is 1,450 units. The fixed cost element is £5,590.

Calculate the total cost when output is 1,200 units.

1.7   The costs for a product have been calculated as follows based on two possible production levels:

Volume of production	30,000 units	36,000 units
Total cost	£380,000	£466,000

It has been established that the fixed cost element contains a step when volume exceeds 31,000 units. Below this level fixed costs are £200,000. Other costs are variable.

Using the high-low method, estimate the total stepped fixed costs at each production level and the variable cost per unit.

1.8   The costs for a product have been calculated as follows based on two possible production levels:

Volume of production	12,000 units	17,000 units
Total cost	£136,000	£186,000

It has been established that the variable cost element is £3 per unit, and that the fixed costs increase when the production volume exceeds 14,000 units.

Using the high-low method, estimate the total stepped fixed costs at each production level.

1.9   A company is considering purchasing machinery that will result in savings in labour costs. The machinery will cost £60,000 and last for 3 years with no residual value. The labour savings if the machine is acquired are expected to be £25,000 per year. The company's cost of capital is 10%. Savings can be considered as being generated at the end of each year.

Complete the following table to calculate the net present value of the proposal to purchase the machinery:

	Year 0	Year 1	Year 2	Year 3
Net cash flows £				
Discount factor	1.000	0.909	0.826	0.751
Present values £				
Net present value £				

1.10 A company is considering purchasing machinery that will result in savings in labour costs. The machinery will cost £70,000, plus installation costs of £4,500, and last for three years with scrap value of £1,000. The running costs of the machinery will be £1,500 per year, payable at the end of each year. In addition, the machinery will need to be serviced at the end of year 2, costing £8,000. The labour savings if the machine is acquired are expected to be £38,500 per year. The company's cost of capital is 10%. Savings can be considered as being generated at the end of each year.

Complete the following table to calculate the net present value of the proposal to purchase the machinery:

	Year 0	Year 1	Year 2	Year 3
Cash inflows £				
Cash outflows £				
Net cash flows £				
Discount factor	1.000	0.909	0.826	0.751
Present values £				
Net present value £				

1.11 The costs for a product have been calculated based on two different production levels:

Volume of production	4,500 units	7,500 units
Total cost	£48,500	£61,250

It has been established that a quantity discount of £1.50 per unit applies to all units when production exceeds 6,000 units, and this has been taken account of in the total cost figures. The fixed costs do not incorporate any steps in cost.

Use the high-low method, estimate the total fixed costs, and the variable costs per unit that apply at different production levels.

1.12 The following data is available about total costs at various production levels:

Volume of production	2,000 units	5,000 units	8,000 units
Total cost	£58,000	£108,000	£162,000

It has been established that:

- A discount of 10% of the variable cost applies to all units when production is 4,000 units or more, and
- Fixed costs remain constant throughout the range of production levels shown

Required:

- Estimate the variable costs (before and after discount), and the fixed costs
- Estimate the total costs for production of 3,000 units

2 Standard costing – direct costs

this chapter covers...

In this chapter we will start to examine one of the major topics of this learning area – standard costing. This chapter concentrates on using standard costing in conjunction with direct costs – we will examine overheads in Chapter 3.

The chapter commences with an overview of the background to standard costing and how it can be useful. It then goes on to see how standard costs are built up and what information is available to those in the organisation who set the standards.

A large part of the chapter is devoted to the calculation of variances relating to direct costs. These are the differences between standard and actual costs that are related to specific components of the cost. It is vital that you understand fully how the variances are derived so that you can carry out a variety of calculations if required.

The main variances covered in this chapter are:

- *total direct material variance*
- *direct material price variance*
- *direct material usage variance*
- *total direct labour variance*
- *direct labour rate variance*
- *direct labour efficiency variance*

We will also discover how to use variances to reconcile standard and actual costs, and the chapter is rounded off with a summary of the main underlying causes of direct cost variances.

STANDARD COSTING SYSTEMS

Different organisations will have developed individual systems to control their revenue and costs which depend on their managers' needs. These control systems often simply use existing accounting information to monitor performance. Where this performance is measured against budgets that have been prepared in advance this is known as a budgetary control system. A budgetary control system involves agreeing financial plans for all areas of the organisation that coordinate activities. These budgets are then used to compare with actual performance so that appropriate action can be taken if things don't go quite according to plan. Budgetary control is covered in detail in the Osborne Books text 'Management Accounting: Budgeting'.

Many manufacturing organisations which produce standardised ranges of products may choose to go beyond just using budgetary control systems, and develop their own standard costing system. A standard costing system is a formal method for calculating the expected costs of products. The system can then be used for monitoring and controlling performance by comparing actual costs with standard costs.

It differs from general budget setting (which is normally concerned with the costs of sections of the organisation), because it focuses on the cost of what the organisation produces (the 'cost units'). It is often used in conjunction with budgets, so that they work together consistently.

Standard costing establishes in detail the standard cost of each component of a product, so that a total cost can be calculated for that product.

Standard costing is ideal for situations where components are identical and manufacturing operations are repetitive.

advantages of standard costing

The main advantages of operating with a standard costing system in place are that the standard costs can be used:

- to help with decision making, for example as a basis for pricing decisions
- to assist in **planning**, for example to plan the quantity and cost of the resources needed for future production
- as a mechanism for **monitoring and controlling** costs: the standard costs for the actual production can be compared with the actual costs incurred, and the differences (called 'variances') calculated. This is so that appropriate action can be taken

Advantages of using standard costing to assist with monitoring and control of costs include:

■ Standard costs include details of both price and quantity of inputs. This will provide much better information than simple cost variances. The use of responsibility accounting in which managers are held accountable for performance of specific parts of the organisation fits in with this approach and enables the managers to control the costs armed with good information.

■ Because the data will be input on an ongoing basis as part of the clerical process, an effective standard costing system will be able to provide cheap and accurate information in almost real time. This enables action to be taken quickly if necessary. Contrast this with the calculation of budgeting variances that are normally produced after the period end.

■ Information can be provided in the form of operating statements that reconcile the actual costs with the standard costs of the output through the various standard cost variances that we will examine shortly. This will provide a very clear analysis of the differences between actual and expected costs – all the way to profit differences if required. We will look in more detail at such operating statements and the information that they can provide later in this chapter.

In addition there may be other benefits to setting up and using a standard costing system:

■ The preliminary examination of current production techniques and resources may reveal hidden inefficiencies and unnecessary expenditure.

■ The fact that costs are to be monitored may increase the cost consciousness of the workforce (and the management).

■ The system lends itself to exception reporting. This is a technique where results are only reported when they are outside a predetermined range so that action can be taken. For example, a company may decide that only when costs are more than 2% away from the standard should the variances be reported.

There are therefore a variety of arguments for developing and using a standard costing system. The main uses that a particular organisation intends to make of the system will determine how it goes about setting standards.

SETTING STANDARDS

We will now examine in more detail how standards may be set, and how this can have an impact on our interpretation of variances.

types of standard

There are three main types of standard that may be set:

1 **Ideal Standard** makes no allowances for inefficiency or wastage of labour or materials, and therefore assumes perfect conditions.

2 **Attainable Standard** allows for a small amount of normal wastage and inefficiency, but is set at a level that is considered to be a challenging target based on current operating conditions.

3 **Basic Standard** is an historical (and therefore effectively out-of-date) standard that allows comparisons to be carried out over long periods of time.

You may also come across the terms 'current', 'normal' and 'target' applied to standards. These are effectively variations on the idea of attainable standards, and are fairly self-explanatory. Current standards are based on current operating conditions. Normal standards are set at the expected level under normal conditions, whereas target standards are at the level that the organisation wishes to achieve under current conditions. Target standards may also be linked to the idea of target costing that will be examined later in this book.

ideal and attainable standards and actual results

The link between ideal and attainable standards and the actual results is reflected in the difference between strategic and operational management.

Strategic management is concerned with long-term planning and decision making.

Operational management centres around the day-to-day activities taking place within an organisation. The way in which these types of management may rely on different standards can be illustrated by the diagram below:

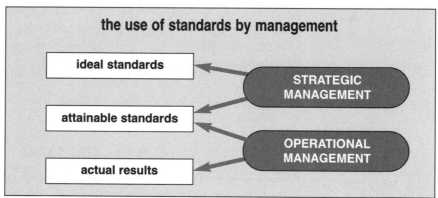

Strategic management can examine ways of moving what is attainable closer to the ideal over the longer term, whilst operational management is more concerned with moving the actual results closer to what is attainable in the short term. Total Quality Management (see pages 244-247) is one technique that can be used to bring the actual results closer to the ideal level.

IDEAL STANDARDS AND THEIR IMPLICATIONS

the tendency for dual standards

When an organisation implements a standard costing system, the way that the standard is set will affect the interpretation of the variances. If an ideal standard is used, with no allowances for wastage or inefficiency then the variances for material usage and labour efficiency will tend to be adverse. This in turn will mean that managers will come to expect adverse variances, and that action will only be taken when the variances are outside what they consider to be a reasonable tolerance level. If the use of an ideal is extended to setting material cost and labour rate standards by using the cheapest prices and the lowest labour rates then the managers will become used to finding that all the variances recorded are adverse. They will tend to ignore the adverse variances that are reasonably small, and concentrate their attention on the larger variances. In this way they will have started to operate a system of informal **dual standards**, whereby the standard that is set is not the one that it is expected will be achieved.

This has important implications when standard costing is used to help a business with its planning. Where standards set at an ideal level are used for planning purposes then the result will always be inaccurate. For example when using ideal standards to specify the amount of materials or labour time that will be required, the resources will tend to be under-estimated. This could result in lower production being achieved than was planned, or that additional resources are needed to complete the required production. This is because the ideal standards do not incorporate any allowance for the wastage or inefficient working that will always occur to some extent. Managers may get around this problem informally by adding an additional amount into their resource requirements. They are then effectively using their own version of a standard. The same situation will occur with material prices and labour costs, so that unless an amount is added to the standard when the anticipated production is costed, the result will almost invariably be under costing.

the dangers of informal standards

It could be argued that making such adjustments as described above is just a logical extension of the setting and use of standards. But problems could arise if different managers had different ideas of what tolerance levels were acceptable. The use of **exception reporting** whereby results are only reported if they are outside an agreed range is universally recognised as a useful management tool, and can form part of the wider technique of **management by exception**. This is where management time is concentrated on situations in which the actual results vary from the plans. Both these techniques can only work effectively if there is genuine agreement about the level at which results should be reported and acted upon instead of ignored. A situation could develop where not just informal dual standards were in operation, but a range of standards was in use by different managers for different purposes.

practical example

Consider the following situation:

The Production Scheduler may add an allowance of say 10% to the standard usage of materials when planning the amount to be bought for a production run and requisitioning the goods. The production supervisor may consider that a usage variance of up to 8% from standard is reasonable. The Production Manager views a tolerance level of 5% as being within an acceptable range.

If the variance is reported at 6% then the Production Supervisor may feel that he/she has performed well, whereas the production manager is expecting answers from him/her as to why the usage is so high. Meanwhile the excess purchases of raw material are sitting in the stores!

This situation would not be a good demonstration of how to use standard costing and variance analysis as a form of responsibility accounting. In order to make different managers responsible for different variances they must be clear as to exactly what standards they are expected to achieve. This can be difficult enough with the impact of the interdependence (interrelationship) of variances, without the additional confusion created by having different informal versions of the standards in existence.

ideal standards and motivation

A further area that is influenced by the way that standards are set is that of **motivation**. As discussed earlier, variances resulting from a system where standards are set at an ideal level will generally be adverse. Whether linked to a reward system or not, targets will only tend to work well if they are considered fair and achievable. It cannot be easy to motivate staff at any level to perform well if all you can measure is by how far they have fallen short of the standard on each occasion. The natural human reaction may be to feel that since the standards cannot be achieved there is no point in even attempting to work efficiently. The standards may be felt to be irrelevant by the staff – hardly the atmosphere of cost-consciousness that most businesses would like to develop!

The use of ideal standards will also effectively prevent businesses from setting up a traditional labour bonus system based on paying a percentage of time saved compared with the standard time. It will be clear that if the standards are set at an ideal level, then there will never be any time saved, and therefore no bonus is likely to be payable.

ATTAINABLE STANDARDS AND THEIR IMPLICATIONS

Setting standards at an attainable level should avoid most of the problems identified with setting ideal standards, and most businesses using standard costing opt for some version of attainable standards. Where the standards are carefully set, the resultant variances should typically be a mixture of adverse and favourable, as the organisation will tend to sometimes exceed the standard and sometimes not quite achieve it.

Not everybody considers what is 'attainable' as being the same thing, and there will be no standard that will be considered fair by everyone. It could be thought of as a range rather than a single point. If standards are set following consultation within the organisation there will always need to be some compromise as different managers and employee groups argue from their own perspectives. There are common problems arising from encouraging participation in the setting of both standards and budgets. While standards which are set by making use of the expertise of a range of participants will tend to be more easily accepted and 'owned', the conflicting needs and desires of the personnel involved can make the standard setting process long and difficult.

BASIC STANDARDS AND THEIR IMPLICATIONS

Maintaining standards at a 'basic' level will tend to have several disadvantages. Since the standard was set some time ago its relevance may be questionable, and large variances will tend to become normal. This will mean that comparison is most useful if it is based on the **trend** in variances and this procedure will enable managers to identify with ease the way in which costs have changed over a long period.

A clear disadvantage of using basic standards is that the standards themselves may not be comparable with current conditions, and the individual variances may be virtually meaningless. The impact of inflation and changes in working practices will mean that the standard cannot be used as either a target or an estimate of expected cost levels. For these reasons basic standards are rarely used as the only standard by an organisation, but may be used alongside variance analysis which is based on more current data to obtain a longer term view of changes which have occurred.

INTERPRETING VARIANCES

The interpretation of variances, and the taking of appropriate action will be influenced by the way in which the standard was set. We will now examine some of the other issues that need to be considered in interpreting variances and taking appropriate action. The steps involved can be seen illustrated in the diagram on page 45, which is then discussed further.

is the variance significant? – control limits

The first issue to consider is whether the variance is significant enough for any action at all to be worthwhile. The idea of tolerance levels was mentioned earlier, and it is important to establish how large a variance should be in order to justify an investigation into its cause followed by appropriate action. Since any investigation or action will have a cost implication (at least in terms of management time), it would not make sense to do this unless there was an expected benefit that would justify it. **Control limits** within which a variance is acceptable may therefore be set by the organisation (*see the diagram below*). These limits will quickly identify the variances which need investigating.

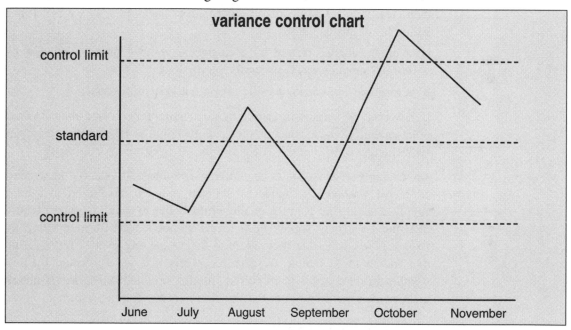

Variances are recorded chronologically from left to right on the chart, either individually or cumulatively. The control levels are agreed in advance. If a variance moves beyond these limits then investigation will be needed and appropriate action can be taken. In the chart shown here the control limit is exceeded in October.

The cumulative effects of variances must also be taken into account. The **trends** in variances that individually are small and may be considered immaterial may point to a situation that requires action. If, for example, efficiency levels amongst the direct labour force are very slowly decreasing then some action (perhaps retraining) will be needed to avoid excess costs occurring over a long period.

modifying standards

An important question to ask is:

'Is the variance due entirely to the way the standard was set, or is there a current situation that needs investigating?'

If a poorly set standard is creating a variance out of an otherwise acceptable situation, the most logical approach will be to amend the standard at the next opportunity. Resetting the standard will also be the most appropriate action if there is a long-term change to costs, otherwise 'false' variances will arise in future.

short-term changes

The cause of the variance will dictate whether or not action is required. If the variance is caused by a temporary change that will automatically right itself then clearly no action is needed other than to check later to see that it has. Examples of this could be:

- a price variance caused by a change to another supplier because the normal supplier was temporarily out of stock
- a machine breakdown causing excess wastage of material

If, however, the variance is caused by some temporary change that may recur often enough to cause concern, then action should be taken either to prevent such changes or to alter the standard if the changes are uncontrollable.

An example of this could be individual batches of material that cause excessive wastage. A change of supplier may be a solution, but if all suppliers are having a similar quality problem due to some common situation then the issue may simply need to be acknowledged by monitoring the variances to ensure that they return to their expected level in future. If the material in this example were coffee beans that were affected by poor weather in the world's main coffee growing regions then it would clearly make some sense to monitor the situation over the coming seasons.

long-term changes

Sometimes variances are the result of situations that are potentially long-term. Perhaps there has been a change in working practices or wage rates resulting in different costs, and if the managers consider the situation is acceptable then it would be logical to reset the standards. The same would apply to a general price change that is seen as reasonably permanent and uncontrollable. If, however, a price rise could be avoided by changing suppliers, then there would be no need to alter the standards, provided that managers considered that this was the best solution.

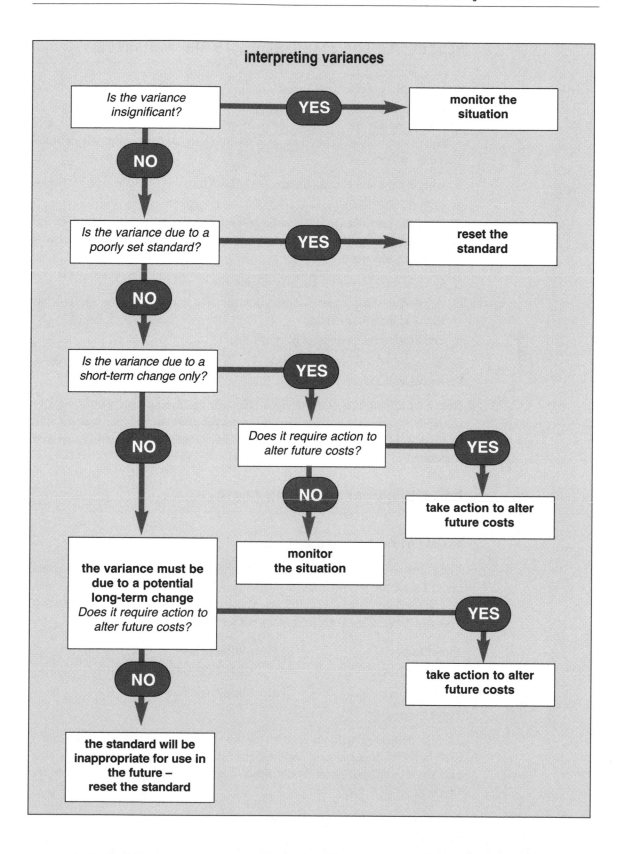

ACCOUNTING FOR STANDARD COSTS AND VARIANCES

If standard costing is used by an organisation, the double-entry accounting system must also reflect the use of standard costing. The aim of the system will be to reflect the standard costs in the various cost accounts, with the variances eventually debited or credited to the statement of profit or loss. This can be achieved by

- entering the actual cost figures (as debits) into the relevant cost accounts as normal, and then

- enter the variances into the same cost accounts, with a double entry to the statement of profit or loss (or operating statement), probably via a variance account.

If, for example, a cost variance is favourable it will be

- **debited** to the cost account (so that the cost account will be brought up to the standard cost), and

- **credited** to the statement of profit or loss.

In this way all favourable variances will increase profit, and all adverse variances will reduce profit.

Note that although a computerised standard costing system would usually calculate variances automatically, it is vital for your studies that you are able to accurately calculate them manually. This process will be explained and illustrated in detail.

COMPOSITION OF STANDARD COSTS

elements of standard costs

The composition of standard costs – whether you are calculating the standard cost of a rubber washer, an aeroplane, or a hip replacement operation – can be analysed into common elements. These are the same elements of cost that you will be familiar with from your earlier studies:

Direct Costs	**Indirect Costs**
Direct Materials	Variable Overheads
Direct Labour	Fixed Overheads
Direct Expenses	

In this chapter we will concentrate on the standards and variances for direct materials and direct labour, and in the next chapter we will examine variable and fixed overheads. You do not need to study direct expense variances for this unit.

absorption costing and marginal costing models

The breakdown of costs (shown on the previous page) into direct and indirect costs is based on the **absorption costing** model, where a suitable portion of all production costs (indirect as well as direct) is absorbed into the product's cost. A great many standard costing systems use this approach.

You should also be familiar with the **marginal costing** model. Here costs are analysed on the basis of the way they behave in relation to activity levels, and split into variable costs and fixed costs. This then gives the following alternative production cost breakdown:

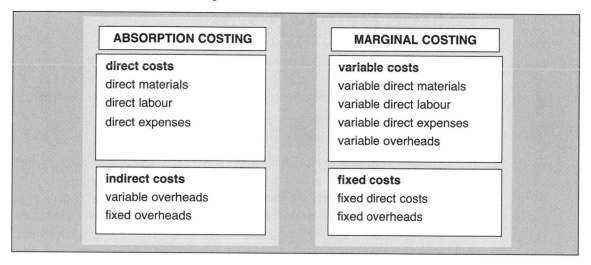

ABSORPTION COSTING	**MARGINAL COSTING**
direct costs	**variable costs**
direct materials	variable direct materials
direct labour	variable direct labour
direct expenses	variable direct expenses
	variable overheads
indirect costs	**fixed costs**
variable overheads	fixed direct costs
fixed overheads	fixed overheads

Any category of direct or indirect costs could behave as either variable or fixed costs, but once the cost behaviour is established, standard marginal costing is very straightforward to use. The standard costs for direct materials and labour under absorption costing are developed in the same way as variable direct materials and labour under marginal costing.

standard direct material costs

You can assume when developing a standard direct material cost (and calculating variances) that this cost behaves as a variable cost. For example, it is reasonable to expect that the material cost for 2,000 items will be twice the cost of 1,000 of the same item. This assumption allows us to work out the standard cost for individual units, so that we can then multiply it by the quantity produced. It also explains why the absorption and marginal versions of these standards are effectively the same.

The standard direct material cost for a product comprises two elements:

- the amount of the material, and
- the cost of the material.

For example, a batch of 1,000 rubber washers may require 3 kilos of rubber, which costs £1.00 per kilo. If this data were accepted as the standard figures, then the standard direct material cost for each batch of washers would clearly be 3 kilos x £1.00 = £3.00.

The fact that the data needed to calculate a standard direct material cost is based on two elements determines:

■ where the information will come from, and

■ how the variances can be calculated.

standard direct labour costs

The composition of the standard direct labour cost for a cost unit is very similar to the material cost. It is also based on the implied assumption that this type of cost is variable, and so twice as many products will cost about twice as much. The standard direct labour cost for a product also consists of two elements:

■ the amount of labour time to be used, and

■ the labour cost per unit of time (the labour rate).

Using our example of a batch of rubber washers, if the standard direct labour time needed to manufacture them was 2 hours, and the standard labour cost was £12 per hour, then the standard direct labour cost would obviously be £24 per batch. Assuming there were no other direct costs, the total standard direct cost would be:

	£
Materials	3.00
Labour	24.00
	27.00 for one batch of washers

You will be familiar with this idea, and probably find the concept quite elementary, but it is a vital foundation for further understanding.

variable and fixed overheads

We will look in detail at how overheads can be dealt with in the next chapter. Variable overheads can be calculated by using an amount per unit. At this point we will show how fixed overheads could be incorporated into standard costs quite simply, by dividing the total fixed overheads by the expected number of units to be produced. The following Case Study shows how a 'standard cost card' could be completed using data for direct materials, direct labour and overheads to arrive at the total standard cost for one unit of output.

Case Study

STANDARD LIMITED:
COMPLETING A STANDARD COST CARD

The following information has been calculated for the production of one unit of a product called 'Alpha'.

• Each unit will require 8 kilograms of direct material at a cost of £6.80 per kilogram.

• Each unit will require 3 hours of direct labour at a total cost of £33.

• Each unit will incur variable overheads of £5.

• Fixed overheads total £225,000, and the estimated output will be 7,500 units of Alpha.

required

Complete the standard cost card shown below. Note that the column headed 'cost per unit' refers to units of input (e.g. for materials it refers to cost per kilogram).

1 Unit of Alpha	Quantity	Cost per unit *(£)*	Total Cost *(£)*
Direct material			
Direct labour			
Variable overheads			
Fixed overheads			
Total			

solution

1 Unit of Alpha	Quantity	Cost per unit *(£)*	Total Cost *(£)*
Direct material	8	6.80	54.40
Direct labour	3	11.00	33.00
Variable overheads	1	5.00	5.00
Fixed overheads	1	30.00	30.00
Total			122.40

Note that:

• The hourly rate for direct labour is calculated by dividing the total labour cost by the number of hours.

• The fixed overhead per unit of Alpha is calculated by dividing the total overheads by the estimated output in units of Alpha.

SOURCES OF INFORMATION FOR STANDARD SETTING

Now we are familiar with the elements that make up a direct cost standard, we can go on to look at the information sources for each of those elements. The way an organisation chooses to set standards will have an impact on how reliable and accurate they are, and for how long they can remain useful. There will be a range of values that could be used for each figure, and the organisation should have a policy that will guide managers in setting standards, and this will also determine how any variances are ultimately interpreted.

The following examples of sources of information should not be learnt as lists. You are advised to think about each one so that you can see how it could be useful. In this way you can then suggest suitable information sources for a situation in a given Case Study.

the amount of material

The main information sources could be:

- product specifications (the 'recipe' for the product being made)
- technical data from the material supplier (eg recommended usage)
- historical data on quantities used in the past
- observation of manufacture

Standard setting may also need to take into account:

- estimates of wastage
- quality of material
- production equipment and machinery available, and its performance

the cost of material

The information sources could include:

- data from suppliers
- records of previous prices paid
- anticipated cost inflation (measured by general or specific price indices)
- anticipated demand for scarce supplies
- production schedules and bulk buying policy (in conjunction with availability of bulk discounts)
- seasonality of prices
- anticipated currency exchange rates

the amount of labour time

Here information sources could include:

- data on previous output and efficiency levels
- results of formal observations (work study, or 'time & motion' study)

- anticipated changes in working practices or productivity levels
- the level of training of employees to be used

the labour cost per unit of labour time

Possible sources of data include:

- current pay rates
- anticipated pay rises
- the expected effects of bonus schemes

To establish an appropriate rate it may also be necessary to take into account:

- equivalent pay rates of other employers in the locality
- changes in legislation (eg minimum wage rates)
- general or industry-specific wage cost indices
- grade of labour (or sub contractors) to be used

THE CALCULATION OF DIRECT COST VARIANCES

One of the most important uses of standard costing is the calculation and interpretation of the differences between the standard costs of the actual production and the actual costs incurred. These differences are called 'variances', and are described as adverse (abbreviated to 'A') when the actual position is worse than expected, or favourable (abbreviated to 'F') when the actual position is better than expected.

There are four direct cost sub-variances that we need to be able to calculate; two relating to materials and two to labour, as well as a total material variance and a total labour variance.

We will examine the direct cost variances in this chapter, and the fixed overhead variances in Chapter 3.

DIRECT MATERIAL VARIANCES

Direct material variances consist of a total direct material variance that can be divided into two sub-variances.

total direct material variance

The total direct material variance =

| the standard cost of materials for the actual production level | *minus* | the actual cost of materials for the actual production level |

So it is simply measuring the difference between what the materials were expected to cost for the actual production level and what the materials did cost. Notice that we are using the **actual production level** in both cases; this is quite logical and also means that we are making a valid comparison by comparing 'like with like'.

If you have studied the Unit 'Management Accounting: Budgeting' you will be familiar with flexed budgets and the calculation of variances from the flexed budgets. The total **direct material variance** is exactly the same variance that would be calculated from comparing the **flexed budget** with the **actual direct material costs**. The standard costs would have been used to calculate the flexed budget, and we are using the actual production level for both the standard and the actual costs. If you haven't studied Budgeting yet, don't worry – this topic can be studied quite independently.

What standard costing allows us to do is to analyse this variance as follows to provide additional information.

The two sub-variances that relate to the cost of materials are:

■ the direct material **price** variance
■ the direct material **usage** variance

The **price** variance measures how much of the difference between the expected and actual cost of materials is due to paying a **price** for materials that is different to the standard.

The direct material **usage** variance measures how much of the difference between the expected and actual cost of materials is due to **using a different quantity** of materials.

Together these two variances will account for the whole difference between the expected and actual cost of the materials.

direct material price variance

The direct material price variance =

the standard cost of the actual quantity of material used	*minus*	the actual cost of the actual quantity of material used

We are making a comparison between two values – the standard cost of the actual materials and the actual cost. Notice that both figures relate to the **actual materials used**, so that we are comparing two costs that both relate to the same actual quantity.

If the actual cost is less than the standard then the variance will be favourable; if it is more, the variance will be adverse.

If you carry out the calculation as outlined above, then a positive answer will be favourable and a negative one adverse.

direct material usage variance

The direct material usage variance =

the standard quantity of material for actual production at standard price	*minus*	the actual quantity of material used at standard price

With this usage variance we are also making a comparison between two values. This time the comparison is based on two quantities – the standard quantity for the actual production and the actual quantity used. These quantities are turned into values by costing them both at **standard price.**

remembering how to calculate direct variances

The key to calculating the variances accurately is remembering the basis of the formulas. One method that may help is the mnemonic 'PAUS', based on:

Price variances are based on

Actual quantities, but

Usage variances are based on

Standard prices.

One explanation why the variances are calculated in this way is that purchases are sometimes converted to standard price (and a price variance calculated) when the materials are bought. This price variance would relate to the actual materials bought. The materials in inventory (stock) would then be valued at standard price, and the usage variance would be calculated based on the amounts issued to production at standard price.

The two material sub-variances that we have looked at will account for the whole of any difference between the standard cost of the material used for the actual production level and the actual cost – the total direct material variance that was explained earlier. This provides a useful check that our calculations appear to be correct.

We will now demonstrate in a Case Study how the variances that we have looked at so far can be calculated in practice.

Case Study

THE PINE DOOR COMPANY: DIRECT MATERIAL VARIANCES

The Pine Door Company makes cottage doors from reclaimed pine. The company uses standard costing to plan and control its costs. The standard direct material cost for a door is as follows:

2.5 square metres of pine at £10.00 per square metre = £25 per door.

During the month of August, the company made 35 doors. The actual costs incurred were:

86 square metres of pine, costing £950 in total.

required

- Calculate the standard material cost of the August production of 35 doors.
- Calculate:
  - the total direct material variance
  - the direct material price variance
  - the direct material usage variance
- Check that, between them, the two sub-variances account for the total direct material variance.
- Explain what each of the variances tells us.

solution

The standard material cost of the 35 doors made in August is:

£25 per door x 35 doors = £875.

Notice that this amount is less than the actual cost of material.

The total direct material variance =

the standard cost of materials for the actual production level	minus	the actual cost of materials for the actual production level

£875 (calculated above) – £950 (from the data provided)

= £75 Adverse

This represents the difference between the standard cost of materials for 35 doors and the actual cost. It is adverse because the actual cost was greater (which is 'bad news').

The two sub-variances which will now be calculated should show how much is due to **prices** and how much is due to the **quantity** used.

The direct material price variance =

the standard cost of the actual quantity of material used	minus	the actual cost of the actual quantity of material used

86 square metres of pine were actually used, so the standard and the actual costs of this quantity of material can be compared as follows:

(86 sq metres x £10 per sq metre) – £950

£860 – £950 = £90 Adverse

The variance is adverse because the actual cost was more than the expected (standard) cost. This is confirmed by a negative numerical answer.

The direct material usage variance =

the standard quantity of material for actual production at standard price	minus	the actual quantity of material used at standard price

It was expected that 2.5 square metres of pine would be used for each of the 35 doors that were made. This gives a standard quantity of 87.5 sq metres for production. This standard quantity of 87.5 sq metres and the actual quantity of 86 square metres at the standard price of £10 per square metre are compared to calculate the variance.

(87.5 sq metres x £10) – (86 sq metres x £10)

£875 – £860 = £15 Favourable

Here the variance is favourable because less material was used than the standard quantity. This is confirmed by the fact that the numerical answer works out to a positive figure.

The calculation above could also be shown as:

£10 x (87.5 sq metres – 86 sq metres)

checking the overall position

Material price variance	£90 Adverse
Material usage variance	£15 Favourable
Total material cost variance	£75 Adverse

This is a useful check – although it is not a guarantee that the calculations are correct.

We can also use the sub variances to reconcile the standard cost of the actual production (the flexed budget) with the actual cost, as follows:

Standard cost of direct materials for actual production		£875
Add adverse material price variance	£90	
Less favourable material usage variance	£15	
		£75
Actual cost of direct materials		£950

what the variances tell us

The material price variance shows that a higher price than standard was paid for the pine that was used, and this cost £90 more than expected. Against that cost can be set the fact that slightly less pine was used than allowed for, and this saved £15. Overall, the material for the 35 doors that we made cost £75 more than planned.

DIRECT LABOUR VARIANCES

The approach for calculating direct labour variances is very similar to direct material variances.

Direct labour variances consist of a total direct labour variance that can be divided into sub-variances.

total direct labour variance

The total direct labour variance =

the standard cost of labour for the actual production level	*minus*	the actual cost of labour for the actual production level

It is measuring the difference between what labour was expected to cost for the actual production level and what labour actually cost. Notice that again we are using the **actual production level** in both cases.

The **total direct labour variance** is the same variance that would be calculated by comparing the direct labour costs in the **flexed budget** (which is developed from standard costs) with the **actual costs**. This works because we are using the actual production level for our comparisons. Flexed budgets will be familiar if you have studied the 'Management Accounting: Budgeting' unit.

The two most important sub-variances that relate to the cost of labour are:

■ the **direct labour rate variance**
■ the **direct labour efficiency variance**

The direct labour rate variance measures the labour cost difference due to the rate paid, and the direct labour efficiency variance measures the cost difference due to the amount of labour time used. The concept of labour 'rate' is similar to material 'price', and labour 'efficiency' is similar to material 'usage', as explained below. This makes remembering the calculation method and interpreting the variances much easier.

direct labour rate variance

The direct labour rate variance =

the standard cost of the actual labour hours used	*minus*	the actual cost of the actual labour hours used

We are again making a comparison between two values – the standard cost of the actual labour hours and the actual cost. Just like the material price variance, the labour rate variance is comparing two figures that both relate to an actual quantity – here the actual quantity is the **actual number of labour hours**.

direct labour efficiency variance

The direct labour efficiency variance =

standard labour hours for actual production at standard rate	*minus*	actual labour hours used at standard rate

This also has a strong resemblance to the material usage variance; we are simply considering the quantity of labour hours instead of the quantity of material.

Just like the material usage variance, we are using a standard figure to value these two quantities – this time it is the standard labour rate that is used. Although this variance is all about comparison of two amounts of time, we must remember to convert the answer into an amount of money by valuing the hours at the standard rate.

Provided we can remember the similarity of the labour variances to the material ones, there is probably no need to use any other memory aid. The direct labour variances must add up to the total difference in labour cost between standard and actual – the total direct labour variance.

Case Study

THE PINE DOOR COMPANY: DIRECT LABOUR VARIANCES

The Pine Door Company (see page 53) makes cottage doors from reclaimed pine. The company uses standard costing to plan and control its costs. The standard direct labour cost for a door is as follows:

6 hours direct labour at £14.00 per hour = £84 per door.

During the month of August, the company made 35 doors. The actual costs incurred were:

200 hours direct labour costing £2,860 in total.

required

- Calculate the standard labour cost for the August production of 35 doors.
- Calculate
  - the total direct labour variance
  - the direct labour rate variance
  - the direct labour efficiency variance
- Check that, between them, the two sub-variances account for the total direct labour variance.
- Explain what each of the variances tells us.

solution

The standard labour cost of the 35 doors made in August is:

£84 per door x 35 doors = £2,940

Notice that this amount is more than the actual cost of labour given as £2,860.

total direct labour variance =

the standard cost of labour for the actual production level	minus	the actual cost of labour for the actual production level

£2,940 (calculated above) − £2,860 (from the data provided)

= £80 Favourable

The two sub-variances which will now be calculated should show how much is due to **rate** and how much is due to the **amount of time** used.

direct labour rate variance =

the standard cost of the actual labour hours used	*minus*	the actual cost of the actual labour hours used

200 direct labour hours were actually used in August, so this is the basis of our comparison of costs for this variance.

(200 direct labour hours x £14) – £2,860 =

£2,800 – £2,860 = £60 Adverse

The numerical answer is negative because the actual cost of the direct labour hours used is greater than the standard cost of the same number of hours. This means that the hourly rate paid is greater than the standard hourly rate. This variance is therefore adverse.

direct labour efficiency variance =

standard labour hours for actual production at standard rate	*minus*	the actual labour hours used at standard rate

The standard labour time to make each of the 35 doors is 6 hours. This gives standard labour time of 210 hours for production.

We will value both the standard hours and the actual 200 hours used at the standard rate of £14 per hour to calculate the variance.

(210 hours x £14) – (200 hours x £14)

£2,940 – £2,800 = £140 Favourable

Here the variance is favourable because we actually spent less time making the doors than the standard time – the labour force have been efficient. This is confirmed by the fact that the numerical answer works out to a positive figure.

The calculation above could also be shown as:

£14 x (210 hours – 200 hours)

checking the overall position

Labour rate variance	£60 Adverse
Labour efficiency variance	£140 Favourable
Total labour variance	£80 Favourable

As before, we can also use the sub variances to reconcile the standard cost of the actual production (the flexed budget) with the actual cost, as follows:

Standard cost of direct labour for actual production		£2,940
Add adverse labour rate variance	£60	
Less favourable labour efficiency variance	£140	
		£80
Actual cost of direct labour		£2,860

what each variance tells us

The labour rate variance shows that (on average) a little more was spent than the standard labour rate, and this cost an extra £60. However £140 was saved because the work was carried out more quickly than the standard time. Overall the labour cost for the 35 doors that were made was £80 less than planned.

idle time variance

We have seen that the total direct labour variance can be divided into two sub-variances – the direct labour rate variance and the direct labour efficiency variance. The direct labour efficiency variance values (at standard rate) the difference in time taken for the production between standard and actual.

In some circumstances this measurement of 'efficiency' may be considered misleading if it includes time where the labour force was 'idle' – being paid but not actually working on production. This could arise for a variety of reasons, for example a machine breakdown, and may not be within the control of the employees.

If this is the situation, and the amount of idle time is known, the original direct labour efficiency variance can be divided into two further sub-variances. These are the variance related to the idle time, and the remainder of the direct labour efficiency variance, which can now be considered as the efficiency variance.

The direct labour variance relating to idle time is (not surprisingly) known as the **direct labour idle time variance**.

The direct labour idle time variance =

actual **productive** labour hours used at standard rate	*minus*	**total** actual labour hours used at standard rate

The difference between 'productive' labour hours and total labour hours is equal to idle time, so a simpler way of expressing the idle time variance is:

actual idle time at standard rate

This variance will always be adverse (or zero), since the total actual hours will never be less than the productive hours. If the productive hours are the same as the total actual hours then there is no idle time and the idle time variance will be zero.

Where there is an idle time variance calculated, the efficiency variance normally excludes the part caused by the idle time. This efficiency variance is based on comparing the standard time for the output with the actual productive time, as follows:

Where there is an idle time variance, the efficiency variance =

standard labour hours for actual production at standard rate	*minus*	actual **productive** labour hours used at standard rate

This efficiency variance, plus the idle time variance will equal what the efficiency variance would have been calculated at if there had been no idle time.

We can use the Case Study on pages 53-55 and 57-59 to demonstrate how this variance can be calculated.

Case Study

THE PINE DOOR COMPANY: IDLE TIME VARIANCE

The Pine Door Company (see pages 53 and 57) makes cottage doors from reclaimed pine. The company uses standard costing to plan and control its costs. The standard labour cost for a door is as follows:

6 hours direct labour at £14.00 per hour = £84 per door.

During the month of August the company made 35 doors. The actual labour costs incurred were:

200 hours direct labour costing £2,860 in total.

The original direct labour efficiency variance has already been calculated as £140 favourable.

Information just obtained reveals that in August there were 8 labour hours when the labour force were idle waiting for more material, leaving 192 productive hours.

required

- Calculate the direct labour idle time variance.
- Calculate the revised direct labour efficiency variance.

solution

- Calculation of variances

direct labour idle time variance =

actual **productive** labour hours used at standard rate	*minus*	**total** actual labour hours used at standard rate

(192 hours x £14.00) − (200 hours x £14.00) =

£2,688 − £2,800 = £112 Adverse

This is the same as:

> actual idle time
> at standard rate

8 hours x £14.00 = £112 Adverse

revised direct labour efficiency variance =

| standard labour hours for actual production at standard rate | *minus* | actual **productive** labour hours used at standard rate |

(35 doors x 6 hours x £14.00) – (192 hours x £14.00)

£2,940 - £2,688 = £252 favourable.

Note that the idle time variance of £112 adverse together with the revised efficiency variance of £252 favourable equal the £140 favourable efficiency variance that was originally calculated before the idle time was identified.

MATERIAL PRICE VARIANCES USING BOUGHT QUANTITIES

In our studies so far we have calculated the material price variance based on the actual quantity of material used to make the units. This is quite logical, and means that the cost reconciliation will always agree.

An alternative approach is to calculate a material price variance as soon as the materials are purchased – when they are brought into the stores. Using this method the material price variance would be calculated using the quantity of materials bought. This may not be the same quantity that is subsequently used.

The calculation of the material price variance using this approach is no more difficult than the calculation that was learnt earlier. Instead of the quantity of materials used, we insert the quantity of materials bought.

The direct material price variance becomes:

| the standard cost of the actual quantity of materials **bought** | *minus* | the actual cost of the actual quantity of materials **bought** |

If this approach is used it means that materials can be converted to standard price when they are purchased (and the variance calculated at that point). The materials will then be held in inventory and issued to production at standard price. This means that the only material variance that is based on the production level is the direct material usage variance. Some businesses prefer to organise their systems in this way.

This approach does, however, have some important implications (unless the quantities purchased and used were identical):

■ a total direct material variance would not normally be calculated since the actual cost of materials used would not be available, and

■ a full cost reconciliation would not normally be produced

Any task should make it clear which approach is to be taken. However if the quantities purchased are the same as those used then either approach will, of course, produce the same result.

THE PINE DOOR COMPANY:
ALTERNATIVE MATERIAL PRICE VARIANCE

The Pine Door Company (see earlier pages) uses standard costing. The manager is interested to see how changing to a system where the material price variance was calculated based on the materials bought would impact on the material price variance calculation.

The standard direct material cost for one door is as follows:

2.5 square metres of pine at £10 per square metre = £25 per door

During the month of August, the company made 35 doors.

There was no pine held in inventory at the start of August. The company then purchased 110 square metres of pine, costing £1,200 in total, and used 86 square metres of this to manufacture the 35 doors.

required

• Calculate the direct material price variance, based on the pine that was purchased.

• Explain how the pine that was issued to production would be valued under this system, and how the pine that remains in inventory at the end of August would be valued.

solution

The direct material price variance (based on purchases) =

the standard cost of the actual quantity of materials **bought**	*minus*	the actual cost of the actual quantity of materials **bought**

110 square metres x £10 – £1,200

£1,100 – £1,200   = £100 Adverse

Note that this is a different calculation to the one carried out earlier in the chapter.

The pine issued to the production area would be valued at the standard cost of £10 per square metre. This would value the 86 square metres used in manufacture at £860. This value would then be used to calculate the direct material usage (as it was in the earlier Case Study).

The pine remaining in inventory at the end of August would also be valued at the standard cost of £10 per square metre. The pine inventory of 110 − 86 = 24 square metres would be valued at 24 x £10 = £240.

OTHER CALCULATIONS USING VARIANCES

Sometimes you may be asked to work 'backwards' through variance calculations to calculate an unknown figure. This is so that you can demonstrate that you fully understand variance calculations (and can carry out appropriate arithmetic). Although it's impossible to list all the possible ways that this sort of task could be set, the following examples should give you a good idea of what you could be faced with.

For example, if we know the direct material price variance, we could calculate either

■ the standard price, or

■ the actual price, or

■ the actual quantity of material.

Let's work through an example:

example

We are given the following information: direct material price variance £55 adverse; standard price of material £12.50 per kilo; actual quantity of material 45 kilos. We are asked to calculate the actual price paid for the material.

We can easily work out the standard price of the actual material – it is £12.50 x 45 kilos = £562.50.

Because the direct material price variance is adverse the actual price must be more than the standard price – by £55.

The actual price of the material must therefore be £562.50 + £55.00 = £617.50.

We could check our answer by working back through the variance calculation to make sure it comes to the answer that we already know:

The direct material price variance is:

the standard cost of the actual quantity of material used	*minus*	the actual cost of the actual quantity of material used

£12.50 x 45 kilos − £617.50

= £55 Adverse (as we expected!)

The standard price or the actual quantity could alternatively be calculated in a similar way, provided only one piece of information was unknown.

We could also use other direct variances to find missing pieces of information.

We will use a further example to demonstrate using labour variances.

---

example

We are given the following information: direct labour efficiency variance £675 favourable; standard hours for actual production 1,070; actual hours 1,020.

We are asked to calculate the standard labour rate per hour.

The efficiency variance is based on the difference in hours, valued at the standard rate. We can see that the difference in hours is 50 (1,070 − 1,020), and can confirm that the variance is favourable because the actual hours are fewer than standard hours for actual production. The variance of £675 is therefore 50 multiplied by the standard labour rate per hour, so we can calculate the standard labour rate by dividing £675 by 50 = £13.50 per hour.

What we've done is used an algebraic technique:

If we call the standard rate per hour 'S', then

'S' x 50 hours = £675

We can rearrange this to show that:

'S' = £675 / 50 = £13.50

If you practise a few examples (there are some at the end of this chapter) then you should find this technique quite straightforward.

USING VARIANCES TO RECONCILE ACTUAL WITH STANDARD COSTS

reconciliation statements

It is important that we can show how variances account for all the cost differences between the standard cost of the production and the actual cost. We can do this by using a reconciliation statement. This is sometimes known as an 'operating statement'. Note that we must compare like with like and use the data for the standard cost of the actual production to compare with the actual cost. The actual cost will of course also relate to the actual production. The reconciliation statement can start with either the standard or the actual cost, and will arrive, via the variances at the other figure. We are accounting for the differences, in the same way that a bank reconciliation statement accounts for the differences between the cash book balance and the bank account balance.

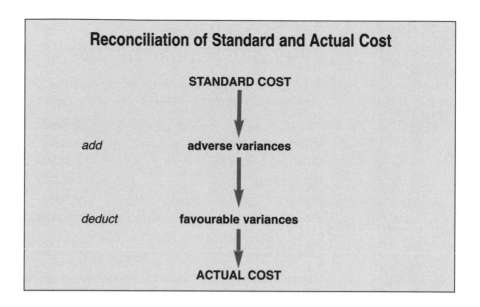

If we start the statement with the standard cost of the production, then each adverse variance will be added to this amount, since the actual cost we are working towards will be higher. Any favourable variances will be deducted since this accounts for a lower actual amount. Since a reconciliation only takes a short time to prepare, it is often worth producing since it will show if any variances are inaccurate.

Where summary variances and sub-variances have been calculated (for example total direct material variance and direct material price and usage variances), do not add the summary variance as well as the others into the statement. If you did you would be counting its value twice.

Remember that, like agreement of a trial balance, a satisfactory variance reconciliation is not a guarantee that the variances are correct!

In this chapter we are only examining direct cost variances, so our reconciliation will be just based on that part of the cost. We will see later how indirect costs can be incorporated into a full reconciliation.

Although standard costing can be applied to revenue as well as costs, sales variances are not required for your studies in this unit. A reconciliation that includes sales variances to arrive at a profit figure will therefore not be examined.

The following Case Study demonstrates how to prepare a statement that reconciles the standard direct cost of production with the actual cost. It also illustrates how standard cost information (for one unit of output) can be derived from budget information based on a specific output level. This is a useful technique which is frequently tested.

Case Study

DIRECT VARIANCES: ORME PRODUCTION COMPANY

The Orme Production Company has the following direct cost results for its production of the Orme for the month of September:

	Budget	Actual
Production Level (Ormes)	1,500	1,800
Material Quantity (kilos)	6,000	7,100
Material Cost	£45,000	£54,770
Direct Labour Hours	2,250	2,850
Labour Cost	£31,500	£38,800

required

Calculate the two direct material sub-variances and the two direct labour sub-variances for the September production of 1,800 Ormes. Produce a statement reconciling the standard direct cost of production with the actual direct cost of production.

solution

1. Direct Material Variances

The first stage is to work out the standards for one Orme. We will do this by using the budget data, since the budget would originally have been built up using standard data.

Standard Material Quantity per Orme 6,000 kilos ÷ 1,500 Ormes	=	4 kilos
Standard Price of Material per Kilo £45,000 ÷ 6,000 kilos	=	£7.50

We can then work out the standards for the actual production level. Note that we do not use the budgeted production level for calculating direct variances – they are always calculated using the actual production level.

We will first work out some standard data that we will find useful later on:

Standard Material Quantity for actual production level	4 kilos x 1,800 Ormes	= 7,200 kilos
Standard Material Cost for actual production level	7,200 kilos x £7.50	= £54,000

The variances can now be calculated:

direct material price variance =

the standard cost of the actual quantity of material used	*minus*	the actual cost of the actual quantity of material used

(7,100 kilos x £7.50) – £54,770

£53,250 – £54,770 = £1,520 Adverse

direct material usage variance =

the standard quantity of material for actual production at standard price	*minus*	the actual quantity of material used at standard price

(7,200 kilos x £7.50 per kilo) – (7,100 kilos x £7.50 per kilo)

£54,000 – £53,250 = £750 Favourable

Notice that the two material variances that we have calculated – the material price variance of £1,520 (adverse) and the material usage variance of £750 (favourable) equal £770 adverse. This accounts for the difference between the standard material cost of £54,000 and the actual cost of £54,770 (the total direct material variance).

A reconciliation statement could be used to demonstrate this as follows:

Budgeted / Standard cost of materials for actual production			£54,000
Variances	**Favourable**	**Adverse**	
Direct material price		£1,520	
Direct material usage	£750		
Total variance		£770	£770
Actual cost of materials for actual production			£54,770

2. Direct Labour Variances

The approach here will be almost identical to the calculation of the material variances as carried out earlier. The following calculations are therefore shown with little comment. Make sure that you can see the similarity to the earlier workings, and check that you can see where the figures come from and why they are used.

Standard Labour Hours per Orme	2,250 hours ÷ 1,500 Ormes	= 1.5 hours
Standard Labour Rate per hour	£31,500 ÷ 2,250 hours	= £14.00
Standard Labour Hours for Actual Production Level	1.5 hours x 1,800 Ormes	= 2,700 hours
Standard Labour Cost for Actual Production Level	2,700 hours x £14.00	= £37,800

direct labour rate variance =

| the standard cost of the actual labour hours used | *minus* | the actual cost of the actual labour hours used |

(2,850 hours @ £14.00) – £38,800

£39,900 – £38,800 = £1,100 Favourable

direct labour efficiency variance =

| standard labour hours for actual production at standard rate | *minus* | the actual labour hours used at standard rate |

(2,700 hours x £14) – (2,850 hours x £14)

£37,800 – £39,900 = £2,100 Adverse

Again we can see that the two labour variances that we have calculated (£1,100 favourable and £2,100 adverse) account for the difference between the standard labour cost of £37,800 and the actual cost of £38,800 (the total direct labour variance).

Again, we could produce a reconciliation statement for just a part of the direct costs – this time the labour costs, as follows:

Budgeted / Standard cost of labour for actual production			£37,800
Variances	**Favourable**	**Adverse**	
Direct labour rate	£1,100		
Direct labour efficiency		£2,100	
Total variance		£1,000	£1,000
Actual cost of labour for actual production			£38,800

The full reconciliation of the direct costs can now be prepared.

Direct Cost Reconciliation Statement for September:

Production of 1,800 Ormes

	£
Standard Direct Cost of Production (£54,000 + £37,800)	91,800
Add adverse direct material price variance	1,520
Less favourable direct material usage variance	(750)
Less favourable direct labour rate variance	(1,100)
Add adverse direct labour efficiency variance	2,100
Actual Cost of Production (£54,770 + £38,800)	93,570

THE MAIN CAUSES OF VARIANCES

It is important that we can not only calculate variances accurately, but also understand what has caused the individual variances.

This interpretation of variances is carried out by:

■ identifying the possible range of causes for each variance, and then

■ investigating the situation to establish the cause in the particular circumstances.

We will now look at the possible causes of the variances that we have studied so far.

If you are familiar with the sources of data for creating variances, and what each variance means, it should not be necessary to learn lists of possible causes of variances. Instead it should be possible to logically think your way through each situation to see its impact on variances. You may be given a scenario and asked to suggest the possible causes of variances. It is far better to use the facts given to you about the situation to develop a reasoned commentary, than to remember an 'all purpose' list of causes and simply regurgitate it.

Some situations may give rise to more than one variance. For example, purchasing cheaper material of lower quality could cause a favourable price variance but an adverse usage variance if there was higher wastage. This is often referred to as the interdependence of variances. It can result in unfair praise or blame if different managers are responsible for each variance.

Unfair comparisons may also arise from the use of an unrealistic or out of date standard.

The table on the next page gives examples of possible causes of variances. Read it carefully, and ensure that you can appreciate the logic of including each item, and its effect.

There may be situations where you can envisage the cause creating further variances, since the table is not intended to be exhaustive.

'A' or 'F' refers to whether adverse or favourable variances may result.

DIRECT VARIANCE: Possible Cause	Material Price	Material Usage	Labour Rate	Labour Efficiency
Poorly set standard	A or F	A or F	A or F	A or F
Different material supplier	A or F			
Different material quality	A or F	A or F		A or F
Different currency exchange rate	A or F			
Poor training		A		A
Higher grade staff		F	A	F
Unexpected pay increase			A	
High general inflation	A		A	
Improved production machinery		F		F
Unexpected bulk discounts	F			
Low bonus payments			F	A
Machine breakdowns		A		A

INTERPRETING SPECIFIC DIRECT VARIANCES

At this stage it is worth looking back at the direct variances that we have examined, and making sure that we can link possible causes with each variance. We will now discuss each variance in turn. The total variances are not examined here, since the causes of these will be based on the causes of the appropriate sub-variances.

direct material price variance

The key to interpreting any variance is to remember what it is measuring. Here (as the variance title clearly tells us), the variance is concerned with the **price** of materials. We can therefore ignore any issues that are not related to price. Some of the reasons for price variances include:

- world-wide price changes (due to specific supply / demand issues or general inflation or deflation)
- change of supplier
- change of quality of material (better quality usually, but not always, costing more)

■ changes in quantity purchased (obtaining better or worse quantity discounts)

Some of these reasons could also affect other variances. As noted earlier, these situations are sometimes referred to as the 'interdependence of variances'. The example often quoted is higher priced, better quality material creating an adverse material price variance, but also generating less wastage and therefore contributing to favourable material usage variances. Possibly even favourable labour efficiency variances could also arise if the material is easier to use.

direct material usage variance

Usage of material is concerned with how much material is used compared with the standard quantity that would be expected. Perhaps the most obvious example is the amount of wastage being higher or lower than expected. This could also be linked to material quality, or to skill level of labour or to poor machine maintenance.

However, the general assumption that a favourable variance is always 'good news' and that an adverse variance is always bad does not always apply for usage variances.

Sometimes any usage variance could be an indicator of a problem. For example, if making concrete products a favourable usage variance for cement may mean that the mix is too weak and the final products will not be strong enough.

Another situation where a favourable variance could be an indicator of a problem is if the final product is undersize or underweight. This could occur in both manual operations and automated ones. For example, tins of paint may be only 95% filled by a machine that is poorly calibrated. The system would record a favourable usage variance, but legal action could result from the quantity of paint not being as described on the tin.

Sometimes usage variances are due to a deliberate decision made in response to the available material. For example, additional sugar may need to be added to a fruit drink mixture if the fruit used was less sweet than usual.

As with other variances, it is always important to examine the circumstances and any additional information provided before making a judgement.

direct labour rate variance

The labour rate variance is concerned with how much the rate of pay costs the organisation. Here the background splits into two main situations:

■ using the planned labour force, but paying a different rate, and

- using a different labour force than planned, often causing a different rate to be paid.

When using the planned labour force, the cost of labour could be different to standard for any of the following reasons:

- a pay rate change (usually a rise) that was either not built into the standard, or is more or less than the expected pay rate change
- bonuses paid at more or less than the expected amount; if bonuses are included in the standard rate the amount will be based on an expected average level
- more or less overtime being paid than expected; this depends on whether the overtime premium is charged to direct costs or overheads – if it is charged to overheads it would not be reflected here
- a change in costs of employment – for example national costs like employers' national insurance contributions, which are normally incorporated in labour costs

Sometimes the labour rate variance will be linked to a change in the labour force being used, for example:

- a higher or lower grade of labour being used than planned, or trainees being used instead of fully trained operatives; this could also link to other variances including labour efficiency and material usage
- contractors or agency staff being used instead of the normal employees; these are often more flexible in terms of contracts, but usually cost a higher rate (including a charge to the agency where appropriate)

direct labour efficiency variance

This variance focuses on the time spent by the labour force in producing the output. More or less time spent could relate to how long individuals spend on the work, or to more or less people being used.

The amount of idle time that may have occurred will impact on the efficiency variance. This could be because no idle time is incorporated into the standard time (but some actually occurs), or because the actual idle time is more or less than expected. An idle time variance could be used to calculate the impact of idle time.

Although efficiency often appears to be entirely in the control of the labour force and their managers, there are also outside influences that can result in variances. The range of causes for labour efficiency variances include:

- level of training of staff
- the learning effect – individuals gradually become more efficient as they become more familiar with the work
- quality of materials

- availability of materials or components (for example awaiting a delivery)
- efficiency of machinery including breakdowns (ranging from hand held tools to production lines)
- working conditions (for example excessive heat or cold)

looking beyond the obvious

We saw that some causes can link to more than one variance – for example a cheap, poor quality material causing a favourable price variance but an adverse usage variance. However quality is not always in line with the price. A cheap material may be of better quality than more expensive material, or the opposite may be true. You should also consider carefully comments made by managers who may be trying to avoid the blame for poor performance. A production manager could try to justify poor usage by blaming the quality of cheap materials (and therefore the Purchasing Manager's fault) whereas the problem may really be something else. You should therefore consider all possibilities.

Case Study

DRINK-COCOA LIMITED
CALCULATING AND INTERPRETING VARIANCES

Drink-Cocoa Limited manufactures and distributes cocoa. One of its main products is Chocco-Smooth, a cocoa blended from Foro and Trino beans. Chocco-Smooth is sold in 1 kilogram packs. Budgeted production is 10,000 one kilogram packs.

You work as an Accounting Technician reporting to the Finance Director.

The company operates an integrated standard cost system in which:

- purchases of materials are recorded at standard cost
- direct material costs are variable
- production overheads are fixed and absorbed on a unit basis
- production costs include labour costs for maintenance and setting up of the machines

The actual results for November are as follows:

		Actual
Production (1 kilogram packs)		9,500
Direct materials (Foro beans)	4,000 kilograms	£12,800
Direct materials (Trino beans)	6,000 kilograms	£8,400
Direct packaging materials (foil)	110 square metres	£550
Fixed production overheads		£7,500
Total cost		£29,250

The standard cost card for production of 1 kilogram of Chocco-Smooth cocoa is:

	Quantity	Unit price	Total cost
Product: 1 kilogram of Chocco-Smooth			£
Direct materials (Foro beans)	500 grams	£3 per kilogram	1.50
Direct materials (Trino beans)	500 grams	£1.50 per kilogram	0.75
Direct packaging materials (foil)	0.01 square metres	£10 per square metre	0.10
Fixed production overheads			0.65
Standard cost			3.00

required – part one

(a) Calculate the following variances for November:

(1) direct material (Foro) price variance

(2) direct material (Foro) usage variance

(3) direct material (Trino) price variance

(4) direct material (Trino) usage variance

(5) direct packaging material (foil) price variance

(6) direct packaging material (foil) usage variance

(b) Prepare an operating statement reconciling the actual material cost of producing 9,500 one kilogram packs of Chocco-Smooth with the standard material cost of producing 9,500 one kilogram packs.

solution – part one

(a)

(1) Direct material (Foro) price variance

Actual cost of £12,800 compared with standard cost of actual quantity purchased (4,000 x £3) = £800 adverse

(2) Direct material (Foro) usage variance

Standard cost per kg of Foro = £3
Total number of kgs used = 4,000
Total number of kgs which should have been used = 9,500 x 0.5 = 4,750
therefore variance = (4,750 – 4,000) x £3 = £2,250 favourable

(3) Direct material (Trino) price variance

Actual cost of £8,400 compared with standard cost of actual quantity purchased (6,000 x £1.50) = £600 favourable

(4) Direct material (Trino) usage variance

Standard cost per kg of Trino = £1.50
Total number of kgs used = 6,000
Total number of kgs which should have been used = 9,500 x 0.5 = 4,750
therefore variance = (4,750 – 6,000) x £1.50 = £1,875 adverse

(5) Direct packaging material (foil) price variance

Actual cost of £550 compared with standard cost of actual quantity purchased (110 x £10) = £550 favourable

(6) Direct packaging material (foil) usage variance
Standard cost per metre of foil = £10
Total number of square metres used = 110
Total number of square metres which should have been used = 9,500 x 0.01 = 95
therefore variance = (95 -110) x £10 = £150 adverse

(b)

Actual total direct material cost			£21,750
Variances	Favourable	Adverse	
Direct materials (Foro) price		£800	
Direct materials (Foro) usage	£2,250		
Direct materials (Trino) price	£600		
Direct materials (Trino) usage		£1,875	
Direct materials (foil) price	£550		
Direct materials (foil) usage		£150	
Total variance	£3,400	£2,825	£575
Standard total direct material cost of actual production *(working 1)*			£22,325

Working 1

(£1.50 + £0.75 + £0.10) x 9,500 = £22,325

Additional data

You have been given the following information about Foro and Trino cocoa beans:

• Foro beans are a higher quality and provide a richer flavour whereas Trino beans are considered lower quality and tend to be bitter in taste. The cost of Foro beans is set by the market and recently the price has risen sharply due to a poor harvest. The purchaser has to take the price quoted on the market. The quality of the beans was as expected.

• An automated mixing machine broke down which led to more Trino beans being added to the mix. The breakdown has been blamed on the loss of maintenance personnel due to a lower than market pay rise.

• The price of Trino beans is set by the market and the price has recently fallen due to a good harvest. The purchaser has to take the price quoted on the market. The quality of the beans was as expected.

• In order to maintain the quality of the cocoa blend, the percentage of Foro beans should not fall below 45% of the weight of the blend.

required – part two

Using this information, prepare a report to the Production Director stating:

- Possible reasons for the Foro and Trino variances you calculated in part one.
- Whether the company could have taken any action and if so what action could have been taken.
- How the direct materials usage variances for Foro beans and Trino beans are linked.

solution – part two

To:	Production Director	From:	AAT student
Subject:	Reason for variances		

Direct material (Foro) price variance

The price variance for Foro beans is £800 adverse.

This is due to the market price of beans increasing due to the poor harvest, meaning there is lower supply therefore the price increases.

The company could not have taken any action as the market sets the price.

Direct material (Foro) usage variance

The usage variance for Foro beans is £2,250 favourable.

This has been caused by the mixing process making an error and adding a greater amount of Trino beans to the mix. The result is that the company has saved money on the purchase of the beans, but the mix is outside of the range recommended to produce an acceptable quality blend. Therefore the customers may be unhappy. The company could have secured the maintenance personnel by paying a market rate, or outsourcing the maintenance.

Direct material (Trino) price variance

The price variance for Trino beans is £600 favourable.

This is due to the market price of beans decreasing due to a good harvest meaning there is a larger supply, therefore the price reduces. The company could not have taken any action as the market sets the price.

Direct material (Trino) usage variance

The usage variance is £1,875 adverse because the company used more beans than expected. This was because of the automated mixing machine breaking down. The company could have ensured that maintenance was undertaken to prevent the machine breaking down. The Foro usage variance (2,250 favourable) is favourable which offsets the adverse Trino usage variance (1,875 adverse). In financial terms the overall position is a gain of £375. However the quality of the mix may be a problem as the percentage of Foro beans is below 45%. The company may therefore lose customers or have returned goods.

<table>
<tr><td>

Chapter Summary

</td><td>

■ Standard costing was developed in the manufacturing industry as a method of predicting the cost of products. When comparing actual costs with the expected (standard) costs, it enables variances to be calculated that help explain differences in the costs. There are various other benefits from setting up and using a standard costing system.

■ Standards can be set at an Ideal, Attainable, or Basic level. There are also variations in attainable standards, called 'normal' standards and 'target' standards.

■ The level at which a standard is set has implications for interpretation of variances, and the behaviour of employees.

■ Actions to be taken resulting from variances will depend on materiality, whether the causes are short or long term, and how controllable they are.

■ Actions to be taken can be divided into those that will change future costs or those that will require adjustment of the future standard.

■ Standard costs can be used based on a traditional absorption costing system, or on a marginal costing system. The main difference arises in the treatment of fixed overhead variances: direct cost variances are calculated in the same way under both types of costing. The direct cost variances for materials and labour can be divided into variances based on the cost per unit of the resource (Price or Rate variances) and the quantity of resource used (Usage and Efficiency variances).

■ Information for setting standards can be derived from inside and outside the organisation. This information includes formal and informal historical data and technical specifications, and can be general or specific.

■ Direct cost variances are calculated according to rules that help ensure uniformity. The variances can be used to reconcile the standard cost for the production with the actual costs.

■ There can be many causes of variances, some influencing just one variance, while others affect several. The accurate calculation of a variance does not provide information on the cause itself, but the causes can often be deduced by examining the factors surrounding the situation.

</td></tr>
</table>

Key Terms	**standard costing**	a formal method for predetermining the cost of cost units or products
	variance analysis	the comparison of actual costs with standard costs and the calculation of variances which account for differences in the costs
	marginal costing	a technique that values cost units based on variable costs only. Fixed costs are considered to relate only to the reporting period of time
	absorption costing	a technique that values cost units based on a suitable part of all the costs of production, whether fixed or variable in behaviour
	responsibility accounting	management accounting based on departments, activities or functions, each of which is the area of responsibility of an individual
	ideal standard	a standard set at a level that makes no allowance for losses, and which can only be attainable under the most favourable conditions
	attainable standard	a standard set at a level that assumes efficient levels of operation, but includes allowances for normal loss, waste, and machine downtime
	basic standard	a standard set some time ago which can be used to identify trends or develop other standards
	tolerance level	the range around the standard within which performance is considered acceptable and action does not need to be taken
	exception reporting	the practice of reporting only the information which is significant. In terms of variances it could involve only reporting variances outside the agreed tolerance level (control limits)

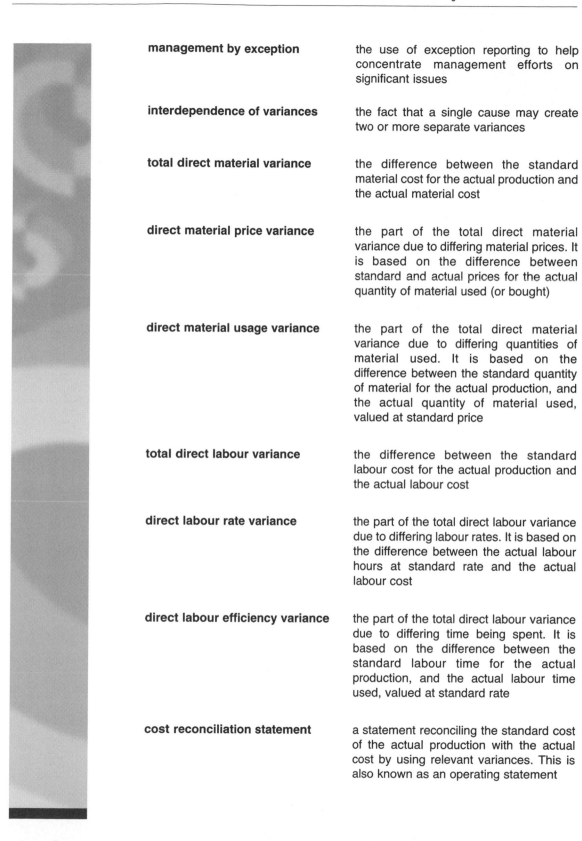

management by exception	the use of exception reporting to help concentrate management efforts on significant issues
interdependence of variances	the fact that a single cause may create two or more separate variances
total direct material variance	the difference between the standard material cost for the actual production and the actual material cost
direct material price variance	the part of the total direct material variance due to differing material prices. It is based on the difference between standard and actual prices for the actual quantity of material used (or bought)
direct material usage variance	the part of the total direct material variance due to differing quantities of material used. It is based on the difference between the standard quantity of material for the actual production, and the actual quantity of material used, valued at standard price
total direct labour variance	the difference between the standard labour cost for the actual production and the actual labour cost
direct labour rate variance	the part of the total direct labour variance due to differing labour rates. It is based on the difference between the actual labour hours at standard rate and the actual labour cost
direct labour efficiency variance	the part of the total direct labour variance due to differing time being spent. It is based on the difference between the standard labour time for the actual production, and the actual labour time used, valued at standard rate
cost reconciliation statement	a statement reconciling the standard cost of the actual production with the actual cost by using relevant variances. This is also known as an operating statement

Activities

2.1 The following statements were compiled by a trainee accountant. State whether each of these statements is true or false.

		True	False
(a)	All variances should always be thoroughly investigated.		
(b)	Using standards set at a basic level may help to identify long-term trends in costs.		
(c)	In order to motivate staff, standards should generally be challenging yet achievable.		
(d)	One advantage of setting up a standard costing system is that an atmosphere of cost-consciousness is generated.		
(e)	Responsibility accounting means that the accountant is responsible for calculating all the necessary variances.		
(f)	If a variance has been caused by a short-term change that will naturally right itself then there is probably no need to adjust the standards.		
(g)	Interpretation problems arising through the interdependence of variances would not exist if variances were calculated accurately.		

2.2   The following comments were made by an inexperienced trainee accounting technician. Indicate which of the comments are valid, and which are false.

		Valid	False
(a)	The likelihood of obtaining bulk discounts cannot be relevant when setting direct material price standards.		
(b)	Work study is often used to assist in setting times for direct labour standards.		
(c)	The interdependence of variances should be considered when examining the causes for variances.		
(d)	Material price standards must always be amended when a different supplier is used.		
(e)	Future production schedules can be used to assist in setting material price standards by helping to gauge the availability of quantity discounts.		
(f)	Two of the main reasons for using standard costing are to improve planning and control.		
(g)	Standard costing can be used in conjunction with responsibility accounting. Using this technique each manager would be expected to control the variances occurring in his/her area of responsibility.		
(h)	Interpretation of variances can help point to the reasons that costs are not in line with the plans.		
(i)	The inclusion of overtime premium rates when setting direct labour rate standards would depend on the company policy, since many organisations consider that such costs are indirect.		
(j)	Proposed bonus schemes should be taken into account when setting labour rate standards.		
(k)	Reconciling standard cost with actual cost is difficult because when variances are a mixture of adverse and favourable the statement may not agree.		
(l)	If a reconciliation of standard cost for the actual production level with the actual cost agrees this guarantees that all the variances are correct.		

2.3   A company manufactures a single product X, with the following direct inputs:

- 0.75kg direct materials which cost £10 per kg
- 12 minutes of direct labour, paid at a rate of £13 per hour

Fixed overheads totalling £140,000 are recovered on a unit basis. The estimated output is 20,000 units.

Required:

(a)   Complete the standard cost card shown below:

One Unit of X	Quantity	Cost per unit of input £	Total cost £
Direct Materials			
Direct Labour			
Fixed Overheads			
Total			

(b)   Calculate the total standard cost of 20,000 units.

2.4   Grimley Limited has the following budgeted and actual direct cost and production data for the month of August.

	Budget	**Budget**	**Actual**	**Actual**
Production Units		20,000		19,000
		£		£
Direct Materials	40,000 kg	300,000	37,000 kg	278,000
Direct Labour	10,000 hrs	60,000	9,800 hrs	58,600
Total Costs		360,000		336,600

Required:

- Calculate the data for a standard cost card based on one unit.
- Calculate the relevant direct cost variances and use them to reconcile the standard cost for the actual production level with the actual costs.

2.5   The glazing department of the Complete Window Company uses standard costs to monitor and control its output. The standard data for glazing one window are:

- 2 square metres glass at £25 per square metre
- 0.5 hours labour at £8.00 per hour

During one week in May, the department glazed 300 windows, with actual costs as follows:

- 610 square metres of glass, costing £15,400
- 145 labour hours, costing £1,220

Required:

Calculate the following variances for the glazing department:

(a)   Direct material price variance.

(b)   Direct material usage variance.

(c)   Direct labour rate variance.

(d)   Direct labour efficiency variance.

2.6   Marge Products Ltd uses marginal costing and has the following budgeted and actual variable cost and production data for the month of August.

	Budget	Budget	Actual	Actual
Production Units		30,000		32,000
		£		£
Variable Materials	3,000 kg	75,000	3,100 kg	81,000
Variable Labour	15,000 hrs	150,000	15,900 hrs	155,000
Total Variable Costs		225,000		236,000

Required:

- Calculate the standard cost data for one unit of production.
- Calculate the relevant variable cost variances and use them to reconcile the standard marginal cost for the actual production level with the actual marginal costs.

2.7   Quango Limited has set its direct standard costs for one unit of its product, the quango as follows:

Direct Materials: 96 kg @ £9.45 per kilo.
Direct Labour: 5 hours 6 minutes @ £6.30 per hour.
During week 13 the company produced 700 units of quango, and incurred direct costs as follows:
Direct Materials: 71.5 tonnes were used, costing a total of £678,700
Direct Labour: 3,850 hours were worked, costing a total of £24,220
Note: there are 1,000 kilos in a tonne.

Required:

Calculate the relevant direct cost variances and use them to reconcile the standard cost for the actual production level with the actual costs.

2.8   A company purchases 5,000 kilograms of material at a cost of £53,000. The standard cost of material per kilogram is £10.

The material price variance is:

(a)	£0.60 A	
(b)	£3,000 F	
(c)	£3,000 A	
(d)	£6.00 A	

2.9   A company used 6,000 kilograms of material to produce 10,000 units. The budgeted production was 12,000 units, and the standard material for this output level was 6,600 kilograms at £2 per kilogram.

(a)   The material usage variance is:

(a)	500 kilograms	
(b)	£1,200	
(c)	600 kilograms	
(d)	£1,000	

(b)   State whether the variance is adverse or favourable.

2.10 A company plans to produce 20,000 units, using 15,000 direct labour hours. The actual production is 18,000 units. The standard cost of labour is £11.00 per hour.

The standard cost of labour for the actual production is:

(a) £148,500	
(b) £165,000	
(c) £264,000	
(d) £183,333	

2.11 The direct material price variance has been correctly calculated as £168 favourable. The standard price per kilo of material is £12, and the actual cost of the material used is £900.

Calculate the actual quantity of material for the actual production.

2.12 The direct labour rate variance has been correctly calculated as £536 adverse. The actual cost of labour was £12,560 and took 668 hours.

Calculate the standard rate of labour per hour.

2.13 The following direct cost operating statement has been accurately calculated and submitted to the Production Manager.

Standard Direct Cost of Production			£351,000
Variances	**Favourable**	**Adverse**	
Direct Material Price	£2,960		
Direct Material Usage		£5,350	
Direct Labour Rate		£9,260	
Direct Labour Efficiency		£5,150	
Total Direct Variances			£16,800
Actual Direct Cost of Production			£367,800

The following facts have been established:

- The actual production level was 15% greater than that originally envisaged in the budget.
- An anticipated labour pay rate increase was incorporated into the standard costs, but has not yet been paid.
- A machine worked slowly and caused excessive wastage, finally breaking down, and this led to unanticipated idle time, with overtime working needed once the machine was repaired.
- A new contract was agreed with the material supplier in which additional quantities were purchased in return for a discounted price.

Required:

Write an email to the Production Manager which outlines likely reasons for each of the variances.

2.14 The standard labour time to make one unit is 45 minutes. The standard labour rate is £10 per hour. Production was 5,000 units. Total labour time was 4,000 hours, of which 150 hours was idle time.

Required

Calculate the

- Labour efficiency variance (excluding the idle time)
- Labour idle time variance

2.15 The standard labour rate is £15.00 per hour. Each unit has a standard time of 6 minutes. The week 18 production of 6,950 units used 700 hours of productive labour plus 20 hours relating to idle time. The total labour cost for week 18 was £10,764.

Calculate the following variances and insert into the table.

	£	Adverse / Favourable
Labour rate variance		
Labour efficiency variance (excluding idle time)		
Idle time variance		

2.16 The standard labour time to make one unit is 3 hours. The standard labour rate is £11.00 per hour. Production during February was 5,800 units. The direct labour force were paid for 17,690 hours, costing £198,128 (an average of £11.20 per hour). Of the paid hours, 90 hours were classed as idle time.

The following figures (some of which are accurate variances) have been calculated by a trainee relating to the activities:

£3,538 Adverse	£6,728 Adverse	£1,008 Adverse
£3,190 Adverse	£2,240 Adverse	£990 Adverse
£2,200 Adverse	£3,480 Adverse	

Required:

Select the appropriate variances from those produced by the trainee, and incorporate them into the following reconciliation of standard and actual direct labour costs.

Standard labour cost of 5,800 units			£191,400
Direct labour rate variance		£	
Direct labour idle time variance	£		
Direct labour efficiency variance	£		
Direct labour idle time + efficiency variances		£	
Total direct labour variance			£
Actual labour cost of 5,800 units			£198,128

3 Standard costing – variable and fixed overheads

this chapter covers...

In this chapter we will continue with our examination of standard costing, and look in detail at overheads.

We will start by looking at variable overheads and learn that their calculation is similar to the direct cost variances already studied.

We will then discuss why fixed overheads and their variances need a different approach to direct costs. The approach that is taken also depends on whether we are going to use marginal costing (and treat fixed costs as relating to a period of time), or use absorption costing (and treat fixed overheads as part of the product cost).

We will then learn how to calculate fixed overhead variances and to understand how they are derived. The fixed overhead variances that we will examine are:

- *expenditure variance*
- *volume variance*

Finally we will see how we can interpret the variances that we have calculated and examine possible causes.

OVERHEAD VARIANCES

In the last chapter we examined direct cost variances and learned how they were calculated. In this chapter we will look at the variances for overheads (indirect costs). The two types of overhead that we need to deal with are variable overheads and fixed overheads. This distinction is based on the way that the overhead costs behave when the level of output changes.

The calculation of variances for variable and fixed overheads is entirely different, so we must be careful to use the correct methods. We will first examine variable overhead variances, before looking at the more complex calculations involved in fixed overhead variances.

VARIABLE OVERHEADS

Variable overheads are made up of indirect costs that tend to vary in total in proportion to activity levels. Variable overheads could include

■ indirect materials (for example cleaning materials)

■ indirect labour (for example a supervisor's production-based bonus)

■ indirect expenses (for example the cost of power to run machinery)

Variable overheads are often calculated at a standard rate per direct labour hour or per machine hour. It is assumed that the total cost of variable overheads will be in proportion to these hours. You will be familiar with the use of hourly rates as it is also commonly used as a basis for fixed overhead absorption.

The total standard variable overhead for a particular production level will be calculated as the standard hourly rate multiplied by the number of standard hours that the production should take.

The calculation of variable overhead variances is very similar to the calculation of direct labour variances. This is because:

■ both direct labour costs and variable overheads use an hourly rate, and

■ both direct labour costs and variable overheads are treated as variable costs

The total variable overhead variance is made up of two variances that we need to be able to calculate:

■ the variable overhead expenditure variance

■ the variable overhead efficiency variance

variable overhead expenditure variance

The variable overhead expenditure variance =

the standard variable overhead cost for the actual hours used	minus	the actual variable overhead cost incurred

This calculation can be used whether the hours refer to direct labour hours or machine hours.

The variance is calculated in a similar way to the direct labour rate variance. Here we are measuring how much of the total variable overhead variance is due to the hourly expenditure being different to the standard hourly rate.

Notice that (just like in the direct labour rate variance) we are using the actual hours to make our comparison.

variable overhead efficiency variance

The variable overhead efficiency variance =

standard hours for actual production at standard variable overhead rate	minus	actual hours used at standard variable overhead rate

This calculation can also be used whether the hours refer to direct labour hours or machine hours.

The variance is the equivalent of the direct labour efficiency variance. In fact if the variable overheads are charged using direct labour hours then this variance will be showing the impact of the labour efficiency on the variable overheads.

Notice that (just like in the direct labour efficiency variance) we are using a standard rate to value the difference between two amounts of time.

We will now illustrate the calculation of these variances by using the Case Study from the previous chapter with some additional information.

Case Study

THE PINE DOOR COMPANY: VARIABLE OVERHEAD VARIANCES

The Pine Door Company makes cottage doors from reclaimed pine. The company uses standard costing to plan and control its costs. The company uses direct labour hours to charge the variable overheads. The standard variable overhead cost for a door is as follows:

6 direct labour hours at £2.00 per hour = £12 per door.

During the month of August, the company made 35 doors. The actual variable overhead costs incurred were £412 in total. 200 direct labour hours were worked during the month.

required

Calculate:

- The variable overhead expenditure variance.

- The variable overhead efficiency variance.

solution

The variable overhead expenditure variance =

the standard variable overhead cost for the actual hours used	*minus*	the actual variable overhead cost incurred
(200 direct labour hours x £2)	–	£412
£400	–	£412

= £12 Adverse

The variable overhead efficiency variance =

standard hours for actual production at standard variable overhead rate	*minus*	actual hours used at standard variable overhead rate
(6 hours per door x 35 doors x £2)	–	(200 hours x £2)
£420	–	£400

= £20 Favourable

Notice that because direct labour hours are being used to charge variable overheads this calculation is very similar to the direct labour efficiency variance shown on page 56, and both result in favourable variances. The only difference is that here we have used the standard variable overhead rate of £2 per hour. To calculate the direct labour efficiency variance the direct labour rate of £7 per hour was used.

FIXED OVERHEADS

We will now turn our attention to dealing with fixed overheads and the related variances. The way fixed overheads are tackled depends on whether absorption costing or marginal costing is being used, so we will start with a reminder of how these systems operate.

fixed costs: absorption or marginal costing?

When fixed costs are involved in costing products there are two traditional schools of thought about how they should be dealt with.

Absorption costing attempts to incorporate fixed costs into the cost of the product by absorbing a suitable part of the expected fixed cost into each unit produced.

Marginal costing views fixed costs as time-based rather than product based, and therefore does not attempt to incorporate these costs into each unit produced. Instead it costs each unit based on only the variable costs, and deals with the fixed costs in the statement of profit or loss for the appropriate reporting period.

using absorption costing for fixed costs

One advantage that standard absorption costing can claim is that the standard cost for a product will be a 'full' cost, and incorporate a portion of all the costs of production. Therefore, provided the actual production level is close to the projected level, and all cost estimates are reasonably accurate, the standard cost of the product will be close to the actual full cost. However, the standard will give an inaccurate forecast of product cost:

- if the costs are not as expected, and/or
- if the production volume is not in line with expectations

For this reason the fixed overhead variances produced under standard absorption costing need to take account of:

- overhead costs
- production volumes

using marginal costing for fixed costs

With marginal costing, by contrast, the volume of production will not affect the standard marginal cost of a product, because the only costs contained in the standard are variable costs – fixed costs are excluded. As fixed costs are dealt with by comparing the expected fixed cost for the period with the actual fixed cost, the only fixed overhead variance that needs to be calculated under marginal standard costing is simply the difference between these two figures.

We will now look in detail at the treatment of fixed overhead variances using marginal costing.

FIXED OVERHEAD VARIANCES – MARGINAL COSTING

fixed overhead expenditure variance

Under standard marginal costing the only fixed overhead variance is usually called the **fixed overhead expenditure variance**. It is very simple to calculate, as follows:

Budgeted Fixed Overhead for period	minus	Actual Fixed Overhead for period

The variance would therefore be calculated for the week, month, quarter or other reporting period, and the number of items produced would not form part of the calculation.

If the actual cost was **lower** than the budgeted amount the variance would be **favourable**, and if it was **higher**, it would be considered **adverse**. The variance could be used as part of a reconciliation between actual and standard costs for the production in a period of time.

Note: throughout this and later Case Studies in this chapter, 'A' and 'F' have been used to denote Adverse and Favourable variances respectively.

Case Study

WENSHAM WHEELBARROWS: FIXED OVERHEAD VARIANCES – MARGINAL COSTING

Wensham Wheelbarrows manufactures a single product – the 'Wensham' wheelbarrow. The company had the following results for their third quarter. The company used standard marginal costing. Both direct materials and direct labour are considered to behave as variable costs. There are no variable overheads.

	Budgeted	Actual
Number of Units	10,000	12,000
Direct Materials	£ 50,000	£ 65,000
Direct Labour	£ 80,000	£ 94,000
Fixed Overheads	£ 75,000	£ 81,000
Total Costs	£205,000	£240,000

The direct variances have already been calculated (based on information not shown) as follows:

Direct material price variance	£6,000 A
Direct material usage variance	£1,000 F
Direct labour rate variance	£4,000 F
Direct labour efficiency variance	£2,000 A

required

1 Calculate the fixed overhead expenditure variance.
2 Calculate the standard cost of the actual production.
3 Reconcile the standard cost of the actual production with the actual cost of the production.

solution

Step 1
Fixed overhead expenditure variance

= Budgeted Fixed Overhead for period – Actual Fixed Overhead for period

= £75,000 – £81,000

= £6,000 A

This variance can logically be confirmed as adverse since the fixed overheads actually cost more than the amount that was budgeted.

Step 2

At first glance the direct variances that have been given in the Case Study do not seem to fit in with the rest of the data. This is because the budgeted production level is different to the actual level. To see how the direct variances would reconcile we must acknowledge that the standard variable cost must be based on the actual production level, as follows:

Standard Variable Cost of Actual Production:

Direct Materials (£50,000 ÷ 10,000) x 12,000	£ 60,000
Direct Labour (£80,000 ÷ 10,000) x 12,000	£ 96,000
Total	£156,000

Step 3
We can then reconcile the figures as follows:
Note that the format of this reconciliation (also called an 'operating statement') is specific to marginal costing.

	Favourable	Adverse	
Budgeted / Standard variable cost for actual production			£156,000
Budgeted fixed costs			£ 75,000
Variances	**Favourable**	**Adverse**	
Direct materials price		£6,000	
Direct materials usage	£1,000		
Direct labour rate	£4,000		
Direct labour efficiency		£2,000	
Fixed overhead expenditure		£6,000	
Total variance		£9,000	£9,000
Actual cost of actual production			£240,000

FIXED OVERHEAD VARIANCES – ABSORPTION COSTING

The fixed overhead variances under standard absorption costing are more complicated than under marginal costing. As mentioned earlier they attempt to take account of:

■ differences arising due to cost

■ differences resulting from the volume of production.

The variances analyse the differences between the amount of fixed overhead absorbed by a standard absorption costing system, and the actual cost of the fixed overheads.

total fixed overhead variances and expenditure and volume variances

The absorption rate is agreed before the period starts, and is arranged so that the planned level of output will cause enough overhead absorption to exactly match the expected overheads. If the absorption base is units, then the output will be measured in units, but if the absorption base is labour hours or machine hours, then we must also measure the output in standard labour or machine hours.

If everything goes to plan there will be no under-absorption or over-absorption, and no fixed overhead variances! The plan could be illustrated as shown on the next page.

This diagram is based on the planned figures and so they will always agree. It would not make sense to plan for any other situation!

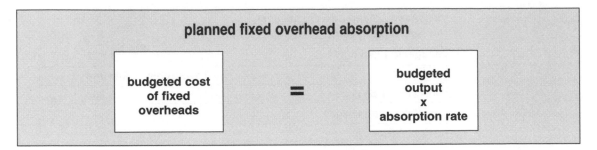

will the plan work? – possible imbalances

When actual figures are used there may be an imbalance – ie they may not always agree. This could be due to either:

■ the fixed overheads not costing what was expected, or

■ the output not turning out to be as planned, or (as usually happens)

■ a combination of the two.

Since the absorption rate is worked out in advance and used throughout, the rate itself will not be a source of any imbalance.

Once the results for the period are known, then the **planned** figures on the diagram shown above can be replaced by the **actual** figures in the diagram below.

The following diagram represents the actual figures. The total of the two boxes may not agree because of the possible differences explained on the previous page. The difference between the amounts in the two boxes will form the **total fixed overhead variance** – the amount by which the fixed overheads are either under-absorbed or over-absorbed.

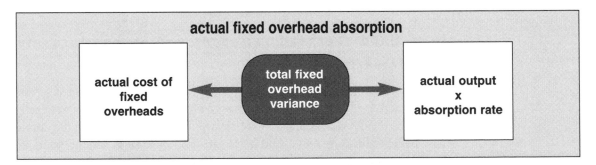

Total **fixed overhead variance** therefore equals:

Fixed Overhead Absorbed – Actual Cost of Fixed Overhead

If the actual cost of fixed overheads is more than the actual output multiplied by the absorption rate then not enough cost has been absorbed by the output – we have **under absorption**. This will give an **adverse** total fixed overhead variance.

fixed overhead expenditure and volume variances

The difference shown in the diagram on the previous page measures the **total fixed overhead variance** – this is due to the difference between the plan and what actually happens. There are two reasons why the actual results could be different from the plan, and these two reasons combine together to result in the total fixed overhead variance. They are:

1   The actual amount **spent** on fixed overheads may not be the same as the planned (or budgeted) fixed overheads. In the diagram, the left-hand box – the actual cost – will be different from the planned figure. This difference is measured by the **fixed overhead expenditure variance**.

2   The actual **volume of output** may not be the same as the planned level of output. This will cause a different amount of fixed overhead to be absorbed than was expected. In the diagrams the figures in the right-hand box will differ. This difference is measured by the **fixed overhead volume variance**.

The actual figures to be used in the diagram on the opposite page are likely to be different from the plan because of changes in expenditure and output volume levels. It is the **combination** of these two differences/variances which will result in an overall **total fixed overhead variance**.

The main variances can be summarised when we bring the two diagrams together like this:

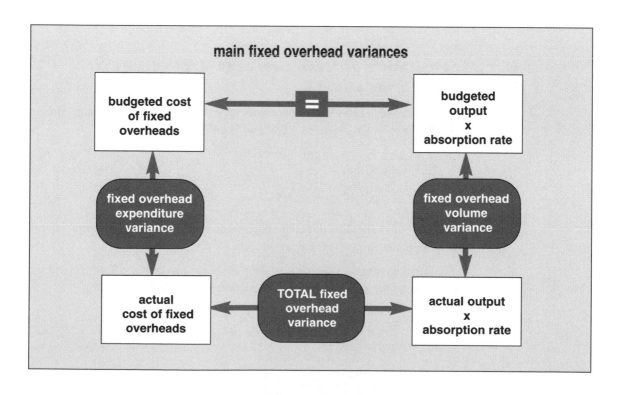

the absorption base

Remember that the amount of fixed overhead absorbed will be based on the actual output multiplied by the absorption rate. The way that the output is measured here will depend on the way that absorption is to take place (the absorption base). If the absorption base is production units, then the output needs to be measured in that form.

If the absorption base is direct labour hours, then the output must be measured in standard labour hours (ie the standard direct labour hours for the actual output). This is often a source of confusion. Remember that what we are measuring is the output; the standard hours for that output is sometimes a convenient way of expressing it.

The same principle will apply if the absorption base is machine hours. The actual output would then need to be expressed in standard machine hours.

Where standard hours are used as an absorption base it is vital to appreciate that absorption will normally take place based on the standard hours for the actual production level, not the actual time taken.

This is so that every identical item produced will absorb the same amount of fixed overhead – even if it took a bit more or less time to make. This will give us a uniform standard amount of overhead that will be absorbed for each identical product, that can be added to the standard material, labour and variable overhead costs to provide the standard absorption cost of that product.

calculation of fixed overhead expenditure and volume variances

The **fixed overhead expenditure variance** is shown on the left-hand side of the diagram on the previous page, and is calculated as follows:

Budgeted Cost of Fixed Overheads	*minus*	Actual Cost of Fixed Overheads

If the actual cost is less than the budgeted cost the variance is favourable, and if it is greater the variance is adverse.

The **fixed overhead volume variance** is shown on the right-hand side of the diagram on the previous page, and is calculated as follows:

Actual Output x Absorption Rate	*minus*	Budgeted Output x Absorption Rate

If the actual output is greater than the budgeted output, the calculation will result in a favourable variance. This is because producing more than planned will reduce costs per unit – which is a good thing.

As mentioned above in relation to the total fixed overhead variance, the form in which the output needs to be expressed will depend on the form of the absorption rate. If the absorption rate is expressed in an amount per unit, then the output should also be in units. If the absorption base is some form of standard hours, then the output must be expressed in standard hours, and the volume variance can be written as:

Standard Hours for Actual Output x Absorption Rate	*minus*	Standard Hours for Budgeted Output x Absorption Rate

The volume variance is therefore a straight comparison of the overheads that would be absorbed by the two output levels (actual and planned).

Some form of standard hours is often used to help measure output because:

- it can be used to convert different kinds of output into a common form – eg a carpenter who produces both tables and chairs, and,

- it enables further analysis of costs – eg by dividing the fixed overhead volume variance, which is not required in this unit.

If an organisation makes a single product then the fixed overhead variances discussed so far will be identical whichever absorption base is used, as illustrated in the Case Study that follows.

Case Study

NODGE LIMITED: FIXED OVERHEAD VARIANCES

Nodge Limited manufactures a single product – the 'nodge'. The company had the following budgeted and actual data for the first year of production. Each unit was budgeted to take four direct labour hours to produce, two of which would be using manned machines.

	Budget	Actual
Production Units	20,000	23,000
Standard Direct Labour Hours	80,000	
Standard Machine Hours	40,000	
Fixed Overheads	£ 200,000	£ 195,000

required

Calculate the total fixed overhead variance, and the breakdown into expenditure and volume, assuming the overhead absorption base is:

1   Units
2   Standard direct labour hours
3   Standard machine hours

solution

1   Absorption base of Units

The absorption rate would be £200,000 ÷ 20,000 units = £10 per unit

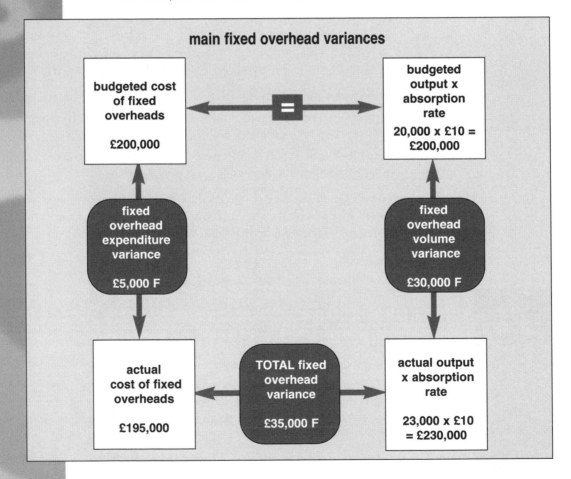

Here the combination of the higher volume achieved and lower actual cost of overheads has resulted in over-absorption and a favourable total fixed overhead variance.

2 Absorption base of Standard Direct Labour Hours

The absorption rate would be £200,000 ÷ 80,000 = £2.50

The standard direct labour hours for the actual production would be:

23,000 units x 4 hours = 92,000.

The total fixed overhead variance equals:

Fixed Overhead Absorbed – Actual Cost of Fixed Overhead

(£2.50 x 92,000) – £195,000 = £35,000 F

The volume variance equals:

Absorption Rate x (Actual Output – Budgeted Output)

Since we are measuring outputs in standard direct labour hours, we will insert the following figures:

Actual Output (in standard direct labour hours) is 92,000 (as calculated above)

Budgeted Output (in standard direct labour hours) is 80,000 (the figure given in the Case Study)

The volume variance therefore equals:

£2.50 x (92,000 – 80,000) = £30,000 F

This is the same result that is achieved when we use units as an absorption base.

The expenditure variance is also unchanged at £5,000 F.

3 Absorption base of Standard Machine Hours

The absorption rate would be £200,000 ÷ 40,000 = £5.00

The standard machine hours for the actual production would be:

23,000 units x 2 hours = 46,000

The total fixed overhead variance equals:

Fixed Overhead Absorbed – Actual Cost of Fixed Overhead

(£5.00 x 46,000) – £195,000 = £35,000 F

The volume variance equals:

Absorption Rate x (Actual Output – Budgeted Output)

Since we are measuring outputs in standard machine hours, we will insert the following figures:

Actual Output (in standard machine hours) is 46,000 (as calculated above)

Budgeted Output (in standard machine hours) is 40,000 (the figure given in the Case Study)

The volume variance therefore equals

$$£5.00 \times (46,000 - 40,000) = £30,000 \text{ F}$$

This is again the same result that is achieved when we use units as an absorption base.

The expenditure variance is again unchanged at £5,000 F.

The fixed overhead variances that we have calculated can be shown in the form of a reconciliation statement (similar to the ones that we used in the last chapter for direct costs). This statement reconciles budgeted fixed overheads for actual production with actual fixed overheads. It uses the same information as the boxes in the diagram used earlier in this Case Study.

Budgeted / Standard fixed cost for actual production			£230,000*
Variances	**Favourable**	**Adverse**	
Fixed overhead expenditure	£5,000		
Fixed overhead volume	£30,000		
Total variance	£35,000		–£35,000
Actual fixed cost for actual production			£195,000

Working
Actual output x absorption rate per unit (as calculated in 1 above)
    23,000 units x £10 per unit = £230,000
Calculation on other absorption bases gives same result.

Case Study

WALMER LIMITED:
OVERHEAD VARIANCES AND SUB-VARIANCES

The Finance Department of Walmer Limited has recorded the following data:

- The budgeted production level is 5,000 standard hours. This will enable the absorption rate of £3.00 per hour to absorb the budgeted fixed overheads of £15,000
- Actual fixed overheads amount to £13,000
- Actual output is 5,800 standard hours

required

Calculate the Total Fixed Overhead Variance, and analyse it into the Expenditure Variance and the Volume Variance.

solution

We can either use the diagram to help with the calculation, or use the formulae.

using the diagram

Using the diagram on page 98, and inserting first the known figures – and then the variances as differences – gives this result:

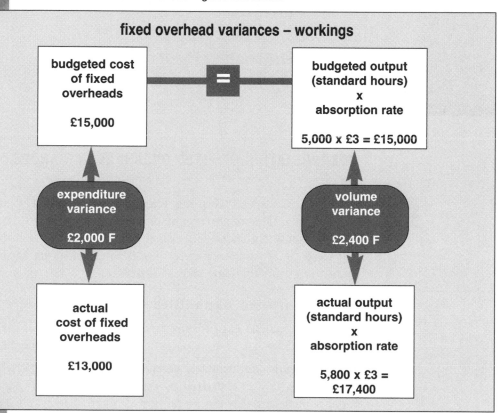

fixed overhead variances – workings

| budgeted cost of fixed overheads £15,000 | = | budgeted output (standard hours) x absorption rate 5,000 x £3 = £15,000 |

expenditure variance £2,000 F | volume variance £2,400 F

actual cost of fixed overheads £13,000 | actual output (standard hours) x absorption rate 5,800 x £3 = £17,400

Using the formulas

Using the formulas we can confirm the results shown in the diagram.

The Expenditure Variance equals:

Budgeted Cost of Fixed Overheads – Actual Cost of Fixed Overheads.

£15,000 – £13,000 = £2,000 F

The Volume Variance equals:

Absorption Rate x (Standard Hours for Actual Output – Standard Hours for Budgeted Output)

£3 x (5,800 – 5,000) = £2,400 F

Note that the volume and expenditure variances must add up to the total fixed overhead variance.

The Total Fixed Overhead Variance equals:

Fixed Overhead Absorbed – Actual Cost of Fixed Overhead

(£3 x 5,800) – £13,000 = £4,400 F

A summary of the overhead variances reads:

Fixed Overhead Expenditure Variance	£2,000 F
Fixed Overhead Volume Variance	£2,400 F
Total Fixed Overhead Variance	£4,400 F

INTERPRETATION OF FIXED OVERHEAD VARIANCES

Once we understand what the fixed overhead variances are trying to measure, their interpretation becomes quite straightforward. There may be a variety of different underlying causes for these variances in the same way that there are for direct variances, but the individual variances are always trying to measure the same kind of differences.

fixed overhead expenditure variance

The **fixed overhead expenditure variance** shows whether actual spending on fixed overheads was more or less than the budgeted amount.

The fixed overhead expenditure variance is measuring the difference between the budgeted cost of the fixed overheads and the actual cost. An adverse variance indicates that the actual cost is more than was expected, and a favourable variance that the actual cost is less. The reasons for the variances could include poor budgeting, or the fact that actual costs are different due to unforeseen price changes. The cost of these overheads are not expected to change because of differing output levels since they are defined as 'fixed' costs so any difference in output is irrelevant in the interpretation of this variance.

fixed overhead volume variance

The **fixed overhead volume variance** shows the difference between the overheads that would be absorbed by the planned volume of output and the amount absorbed by the actual volume of output.

The fixed overhead volume variance is measuring how much more or less fixed overheads have been absorbed compared to the planned amount of absorption. As the variance name indicates, this is entirely concerned with how the actual volume of output compares with the planned volume. The reason for this is because the system attempts to cost a set amount of overhead onto each unit of output. When the actual output is different to that which was planned, a volume variance will arise.

The effect of lower actual output than was planned would be an amount of overhead that has been left over and not accounted for as part of the output cost. This would mean that ideally (if adjustments could have been made in time) a larger amount of overhead should have been added to each unit. As this is not possible after the event there is an amount of unabsorbed overhead, which needs to be written off in the accounts. This is why low output causes an adverse variance that results in a further cost to be written off (debited) in the accounts.

output volume differs from budgeted volume?

If the actual output is greater than expected, the volume variance will be favourable, representing an amount which can be credited to the accounts to compensate for more overhead being absorbed than was planned.

The reasons behind a volume variance will be concerned with either:

■ the setting of the budgeted level of output (eg unrealistically high output or output set at too conservative a level), or

■ something which caused the actual output to differ from the budget, eg more or less resources (eg labour) used, or resources used more or less efficiently than expected.

Case Study

WALMER LIMITED (continued):
INTERPRETATION OF FIXED OVERHEAD VARIANCES

solution

Using the data in the Case Study on page 100, the following interpretation could be put on the numerical results.

• The fixed overheads actually cost less than the budgeted amount by £2,000. This was demonstrated in the expenditure variance. We do not have any evidence as to whether this was caused by poor estimation of costs, or by changes in the overhead cost structure that occurred after the budget was prepared.

• The actual volume of output achieved was greater than was budgeted, and this caused £2,400 more fixed overhead to be absorbed than was planned.

• In all, through the combination of lower cost and greater output a total of £4,400 more fixed overhead was absorbed than the fixed overheads actually cost. This over-absorption is represented by the total favourable variance, which will be credited to the accounts.

In Chapter 2 we examined direct cost variances, and we have now seen how both fixed and variable overhead variances can be calculated. The following Case Study illustrates how all these calculations can be carried out and reconciled.

DELTA PRODUCTS LIMITED: VARIANCE ANALYSIS

Delta Products Limited manufactures a single product, and uses standard absorption costing for planning and monitoring costs. The standard cost of each unit produced is as follows, based on the budgeted production level of 5,000 units per month.

Direct Materials	150 litres @ £1.25 per litre
Direct Labour	5 hours @ £8.00 per hour
Variable Overheads	5 hours @ £2.00 per hour
Fixed Overheads	5 hours @ £8.50 per hour

The variable and fixed overheads are absorbed based on the standard direct labour hours for the production level achieved.

In September the following data is available on actual production level and costs incurred:

Production Level	5,500 units produced
Direct Materials	820,000 litres were used, costing £1,020,000 in total
Direct Labour	26,000 hours were taken, costing £208,000 in total
Variable Overheads	Total expenditure on variable overheads was £53,500
Fixed Overheads	Total expenditure on fixed overheads was £222,800

required

1   Calculate the standard cost of the actual production of 5,500 units.

2   Calculate the following variances, and use them to reconcile the actual costs incurred with the standard cost of the actual production.

- Direct Material Price Variance
- Direct Material Usage Variance
- Direct Labour Rate Variance
- Direct Labour Efficiency Variance
- Variable Overhead Expenditure Variance
- Variable Overhead Efficiency Variance
- Fixed Overhead Expenditure Variance
- Fixed Overhead Volume Variance

solution

1   Standard cost of one unit

Direct Materials	150 litres @ £1.25 per litre =	£187.50
Direct Labour	5 hours @ £8.00 per hour =	£40.00
Variable Overheads	5 hours @ £2.00 per hour =	£10.00
Fixed Overheads	5 hours @ £8.50 per hour =	£42.50
		£280.00

Standard cost of 5,500 units £280.00 x 5,500 units = £1,540,000.

2   The cost variances can be calculated as follows:

- Direct Material Price Variance

   (820,000 litres x £1.25) – £1,020,000   =   £5,000 FAV

- Direct Material Usage Variance

   £1.25 x ([150 litres x 5,500 units] – 820,000 litres) =   £6,250 FAV

- Direct Labour Rate Variance

   (26,000 hours x £8.00) – £208,000   =   £0

- Direct Labour Efficiency Variance

   £8.00 x ([5 hours x 5,500 units] – 26,000 hours)   =   £12,000 FAV

- Variable Overhead Expenditure Variance

   (26,000 hours x £2.00) – £53,500   =   £1,500 ADV

- Variable Overhead Efficiency Variance

   £2.00 x ([5 hours x 5,500 units] – 26,000 hours)   =   £3,000 FAV

Using the format explained earlier to calculate the fixed overhead variances, the diagram appears as shown on the next page:

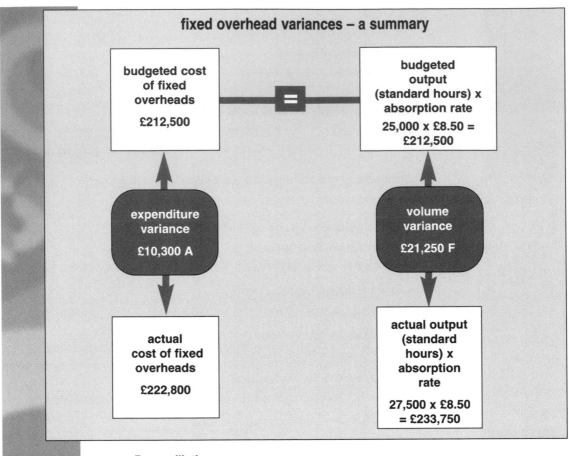

fixed overhead variances – a summary

budgeted cost of fixed overheads £212,500	**=**	budgeted output (standard hours) x absorption rate 25,000 x £8.50 = £212,500

expenditure variance £10,300 A

volume variance £21,250 F

actual cost of fixed overheads £222,800

actual output (standard hours) x absorption rate 27,500 x £8.50 = £233,750

Reconciliation

	£	£	£
Standard cost of production of 5,500 units			1,540,000
Direct Variances:			
Direct Material Price Variance		(5,000) F	
Direct Material Usage Variance		(6,250) F	
Direct Labour Rate Variance		0	
Direct Labour Efficiency Variance		(12,000) F	
			(23,250)
Variable Overhead Variances:			
Expenditure Variance		1,500 A	
Efficiency Variance		(3,000) F	
			(1,500)
Fixed Overhead Variances:			
Expenditure Variance		10,300 A	
Volume Variance		(21,250) F	
			(10,950)
Actual Cost of Production (£1,020,000 + £208,000 + £53,500 + £222,800)			£1,504,300

Chapter Summary

- Variable overhead variances are calculated in a similar way to direct cost variances. Two main variable overhead variances can be calculated – the variable overhead expenditure variance and the variable overhead efficiency variance.

- Fixed overhead variances differ from other variances due to the way that fixed costs behave and the way the chosen costing system deals with them.

- When marginal costing is used, fixed costs are considered time-based, and are not absorbed by the output. The fixed overhead variance under this system is a simple measurement of more or less expenditure than planned and is passed through the accounts.

- When absorption costing is used, fixed overheads are absorbed into the output based on a predetermined rate. The total fixed overhead variance is the amount by which the amount of overhead absorbed differs from the overhead actually incurred. This can be due to the expenditure on overhead being different to what was planned, or the volume of output being different, or both.

- Fixed overhead variances can be calculated either using a diagram or learning traditional formulas. Whatever method is used care must be taken to avoid errors.

Key Terms

variable overheads	indirect costs which vary in proportion to the volume of production or other output
variable overhead expenditure variance	measures how much of the variable overhead variance is caused by the hourly cost differing from the standard hourly rate
variable overhead efficiency variance	measures how much of the variable overhead variance is caused by the amount of hours (labour or machine) used differing from standard
fixed overheads	indirect costs which do not vary in proportion to the volume of production or other output
marginal costing	a technique that values cost units based on variable costs only. Fixed costs are considered to relate only to the reporting period of time

fixed overhead expenditure variance (marginal costing)	the only fixed overhead variance generated using marginal costing. It measures the difference between the budgeted expenditure and the actual expenditure on fixed overheads in a reporting period
absorption costing	a technique that values cost units based on a suitable part of all the costs of production, whether fixed or variable in behaviour
absorption base	the mechanism by which absorption costing absorbs indirect costs into cost units. It may be simply per cost unit, or (for example) per standard labour or machine hour
total fixed overhead variance (absorption costing)	the difference between the actual expenditure on fixed overheads, and the amount of fixed overhead absorbed by the actual output. The expenditure and volume variances will combine in this total variance
fixed overhead expenditure variance (absorption costing)	the difference between the budgeted expenditure and the actual expenditure on fixed overheads in a reporting period
fixed overhead volume variance (absorption costing)	the difference between the fixed overhead which would have been absorbed by the budgeted output and the fixed overhead which was absorbed by the actual output.

Activities

3.1 A company uses direct labour hours to charge variable overheads. The standard labour hours per unit produced is 5 hours, and the standard hourly charge is £1.50. During the month 500 units were produced, using 2,420 direct labour hours. The actual variable overheads for the month were £3,910.

Required:

Calculate:

(a) The variable overhead expenditure variance.

(b) The variable overhead efficiency variance.

3.2 A company uses machine hours to charge variable overheads. The standard machine hours per unit produced is 1.5 hours, and the total standard variable overhead cost per unit is £30.

During the month 1,250 units were produced, using 1,900 machine hours. The actual variable overheads for the month were £38,600.

Required:

Calculate:

(a) The variable overhead expenditure variance.

(b) The variable overhead efficiency variance.

3.3 You have been provided with the following information:

· Budgeted fixed overheads are £500,000

· Budgeted output is 25,000 units

· Actual output is 30,000 units

· Actual fixed overheads are £480,000

Required:

Calculate:

(a) The fixed overhead volume variance.

(b) The fixed overhead expenditure variance.

3.4   You have been provided with the following information:

- Budgeted fixed overheads are £60,000
- Budgeted output is 5,000 units and 500 labour hours
- Actual output is 3,500 units and 430 labour hours
- Actual fixed overheads are £58,000

Required:

Calculate:

(a)   The fixed overhead expenditure variance.

(b)   The fixed overhead volume variance.

3.5   Sofa-so-Good Limited manufactures sofas and sells them to furniture shops. The company uses standard absorption costing, with an absorption rate of £200 per sofa for fixed overheads.

The budget for the year was to manufacture 2,200 sofas and incur £440,000 of fixed overheads.

The actual production for the year was 2,150 sofas, and the actual fixed overheads incurred amounted to £428,000.

Required:

(a)   Calculate the following variances:

- Fixed overhead expenditure variance
- Fixed overhead volume variance

(b)   Explain one disadvantage that Sofa-so-Good Limited may experience by absorbing overheads on a per-sofa basis.

(c)   Complete the following reconciliation between budgeted fixed overheads for actual production and actual fixed overheads.

Budgeted / Standard fixed cost for actual production			
Variances	**Favourable**	**Adverse**	
Fixed overhead expenditure			
Fixed overhead volume			
Total variance			
Actual fixed cost for actual production			

3.6   Zorbant Ltd absorbs fixed overheads based on the budgeted fixed overheads of £94,600, and the budgeted number of standard direct labour hours to be worked of 2,200.

The actual output for the period turned out to be 2,500 standard hours. The actual fixed overheads for the period were £99,000.

Required:

(a)   Calculate the fixed overhead absorption rate.

(b)   Calculate the fixed overhead variances.

(c)   State which of the following comments are valid, based on the above data:

1   The expenditure variance is adverse due to the increased volume of output which has been produced.

2   The expenditure variance is favourable since the actual fixed overheads are less than were budgeted for.

3   The expenditure variance is adverse since the actual fixed overheads are more than were budgeted for.

4   The favourable volume variance reflects the fact that more output was achieved than was budgeted for.

5   The favourable volume variance is due to the overheads being less than anticipated.

6   The adverse volume variance is due to more output being achieved than was budgeted for.

3.7   G Loop Manufacturing Limited makes a single product, the Gloop, and absorbs fixed overheads on the basis of standard labour hours.

For the year it had budgeted to make 2,000 Gloops, and take 14,000 standard labour hours to do so. It budgeted that its fixed overheads would amount to £448,000.

During the year the company actually made 1,800 Gloops, taking a total of 12,000 actual labour hours.

The fixed overheads for the year actually amounted to £455,000.

Required:

(a)   Calculate the budgeted absorption rate per standard hour.

(b)   Calculate the standard hours to make one Gloop.

(c)   Calculate the standard hours to make the actual output of 1,800 Gloops.

(d)   Calculate:

The fixed overhead expenditure (or price) variance, and

The fixed overhead volume variance:

(e)   Reconcile the overhead absorbed by the standard hours for the actual production of 1,800 Gloops, with the actual fixed overheads using the above variances.

3.8 The Maxima Office Furniture Company manufactures a range of desks and chairs and sells them to furniture shops.

The company uses standard absorption costing, using standard direct labour hours as an absorption base.

Each desk takes 5 standard hours to produce, and each chair takes 2 standard hours.

The budget for the year was to utilise 40,000 direct labour hours by making 5,000 desks and 7,500 chairs.

The budget for fixed overheads for the year was £600,000.

The actual production for the year was 5,100 desks and 7,000 chairs. The actual fixed overheads incurred amounted to £603,500.

Required:

(a) Calculate the standard direct labour hours for the actual production.

(b) Calculate the fixed overhead absorption rate per standard direct labour hour.

(c) Calculate the following variances:

  • Fixed overhead expenditure variance

  • Fixed overhead volume variance

  • Total fixed overhead variance

3.9 Heatit Ltd manufactures domestic radiators. You work as an accounting technician reporting to the Finance Director.

Heatit Ltd operates a standard marginal costing system in which:

  • direct material and direct labour costs are variable

  • production overheads are fixed

The budgeted activity and actual results for the month of April are as follows:

	Budget		Actual	
Production units (radiators)		5,000		5,200
Direct materials (steel)	20,000 sq mt	£30,000	21,320 sq mt	£30,914
Direct materials (paint)	500 litres	£2,500	505 litres	£2,600
Direct labour	2,500 hours	£27,500	2,650 hours	£31,800
Fixed overheads		£60,000		£58,500
Total cost		£120,000		£123,814

Required:

(a)   Calculate the following variances for April:

　　　1　　　Direct material (steel) usage variance.

　　　2　　　Direct labour rate variance.

　　　3　　　Direct labour efficiency variance.

(b)   Complete the following sentence by selecting from the phrases shown below.

　　　'An adverse variance is [　　　　　　] the statement of profit or loss (income statement),

　　　and a favourable variance is [　　　　　　] the statement of profit or loss (income

　　　statement).'

　　　Phrases:　　　a debit to

　　　　　　　　　　a credit to

　　　　　　　　　　not shown in

(c)   Complete the marginal costing operating statement below.

Budgeted / Standard variable cost for actual production			
Budgeted fixed costs			
Variances	Favourable	Adverse	
Direct materials (steel) price	£1,066		
Direct materials (steel) usage			
Direct materials (paint) price		£75	
Direct materials (paint) usage	£75		
Direct labour rate			
Direct labour efficiency			
Fixed overhead expenditure			
Total variance			
Actual cost of actual production			

3.10 The following budgetary control report has been provided for a liquid soap manufacturer.

	Budget		Actual	
Production units (bottles)		5,000		5,500
Direct materials (liquid soap)	1,250 litres	£7,500	1,400 litres	£7,700
Direct materials (plastic bottles)	5,000 units	£1,000	5,650 units	£1,017
Direct labour	150 hours	£1,650	175 hours	£1,663
Fixed overheads		£3,500		£3,750
Total cost		£13,650		£14,130

The following variances have been calculated:

Fixed overhead expenditure	£250
Direct materials (liquid soap) price	£700 F
Direct materials (bottles) price	£113 F
Direct materials (liquid soap) usage	£150 A
Direct materials (bottles) usage	£30
Direct labour rate	£262
Direct labour efficiency	£110 A
Fixed overhead volume	£350 F

Required:

Calculate the standard (budgeted) cost of the 5,500 units produced, and complete the operating statement on the next page.

Standard cost for actual production			£
Variances	Favourable	Adverse	
Total variance			£
Actual cost of actual production			£

3.11 The following table shows various unrelated situations that may contribute to adverse or favourable fixed overhead variances. Place ticks in the appropriate columns to show which variances are likely to be affected or if there is no impact on these variances.

Situation	Fixed Overhead Expenditure Variance			Fixed Overhead Volume Variance		
	Adverse	Favourable	No impact	Adverse	Favourable	No impact
Production manager awarded a pay increase						
Unplanned additional day's holiday shut down						
Additional direct labour staff used to increase production						
Unplanned pay rise given to direct labour staff						
New maintenance contract implemented with reduced costs						
Additional shift working (including supervisors) used to increase production						

4 Statistical techniques

this chapter covers...

In this chapter we will explain how to calculate key statistical indicators which will help us to analyse past data and help us forecast what may happen in the future.

We will start by examining time series – strings of data that occur over time. We will see how a formula can be used to represent a straight line on a graph (regression analysis), and how this can be used to predict data at various points.

Next we will see how some data moves in regular cycles over time, and how this, together with the underlying trend can be used to develop forecasts. We will show how averaging techniques can be used to detect the trend in given data.

The third section concerns the use of index numbers. These can be used to compare numerical data over time – for example prices of commodities or general price inflation. We will see how to carry out various calculations using index numbers that can be useful.

Finally we will briefly see how index numbers can be used to analyse standard costing variances so that we can determine performance more accurately.

TIME SERIES ANALYSIS

Time series analysis involves analysing numerical trends over a time period. It is often used to examine past and present trends so that future trends can be forecast. The term 'trend analysis' is used to describe the technique that we will now examine. At its simplest the concept is based on the assumption that data will continue to move in the same direction in the future as it has in the past.

Using the sales of a shoe shop as an example we will now look at a range of techniques for dealing with trends.

an identical annual change

A shoe shop 'Comfy Feet' has sold the following numbers of pairs of shoes annually over the last few years:

20-1	10,000
20-2	11,000
20-3	12,000
20-4	13,000
20-5	14,000
20-6	15,000
20-7	16,000

It does not require a great deal of arithmetic to calculate that if the trend continues at the previous rate – an increase of 1,000 pairs a year – then shoe sales could be forecast at 17,000 pairs in 20-8 and 18,000 pairs in 20-9. Of course this is a very simple example, and life is rarely this straightforward. For example, for how long can this rate of increase be sustained?

average annual change

A slightly more complex technique could have been used to arrive at the same answer for the shoe shop. If we compare the number of sales in 20-7 with the number in 20-1, we can see that it has risen by 6,000 pairs. By dividing that figure by the number of times the year changed in our data we can arrive at an average change per year. The number of times that the year changes is 6, which is the same as the number of 'spaces' between the years (or alternatively the total number of years minus 1).

Shown as an equation this becomes:

Average Annual Sales Change =

$$\frac{(Sales\ in\ Last\ Year - Sales\ in\ First\ Year)}{(Number\ of\ Years - 1)} = \frac{(16{,}000 - 10{,}000)}{(7 - 1)}$$

=   + 1,000, which is what we would expect.

The + 1,000 would then be added to the sales data in 20-7 of 16,000 (the last actual data) to arrive at a forecast of 17,000.

This technique is useful when all the increases are not quite identical, yet we want to use the average increase to forecast the trend. A negative answer would show that the average change is a reduction, not an increase. We will use this technique when estimating the trend movement in more complicated situations.

This is not the only way that we can estimate the direction that data is moving over time, and it does depend on the data (including especially the first and last points) falling roughly into a straight line. We will note alternative methods that can be used later in this section.

constructing a graph

The same result can be produced graphically. Using the same shoe shop example we can extend the graph based on the actual data to form a forecast line.

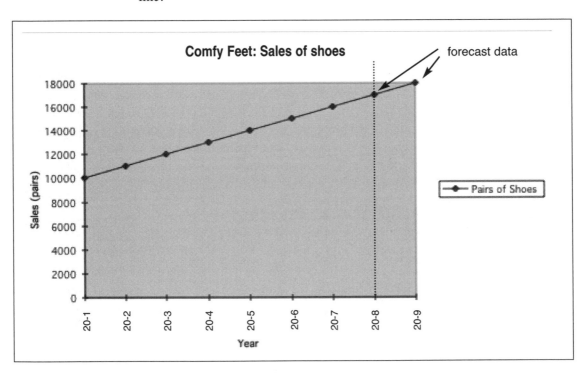

If in another situation the actual data does not produce exactly equal increases, the graph will produce the same answer as the average annual change provided the straight line runs through the first and last year's data points.

using a formula

The data in the example could have been expressed in the following formula:

$$y = mx + c$$

where

y is the forecast amount

m is 1,000 (the amount by which the data increases each year)

x is the number of years since the start year (20-1)

c is 10,000 (which is the sales figure in the start year of 20-1)

If we wanted a forecast for the year 20-9, we could calculate it as:

Forecast $\quad = \quad$ (1,000 x number of years since 20-1) + 10,000

y (the forecast) $\quad = \quad$ (1,000 x 8) + 10,000

$\quad\quad\quad\quad = \quad$ 18,000, which is what we would expect.

This formula works because the formula is based on the equation of a straight line.

using a formula for more calculations

The formula of a straight line ($y = mx + c$) that we have just used to calculate a forecast for 'y' can also be used to work out other information. The formula always has the following components:

■ a fixed value ('c' in the formula $y = mx + c$); this is the point where the straight line starts from

■ a gradient value ('m' in the formula); this determines how steep the line is, and whether it is going up (when 'm' is positive) or going down (when 'm' is negative)

The formula can be used (for example) to predict prices, costs or demand. Sometimes the formula is shown in a slightly different style (for example $y = a + bx$), but the components are still the same.

The formula of a straight line ties in with the calculations that we carried out in Chapter 1 for the 'high-low' method of calculating cost behaviour. There the fixed value represented the fixed costs, and the gradient value was the variable cost per unit. You will notice that the calculation methods that we used for analysing costs can also be used for other situations.

We will now use the formula to demonstrate how different elements can be calculated.

practical example

For example, suppose we are told that the price of a component over time is believed to increase based on the formula $Y = a + bX$, where

- Y is the price in £, and
- X is the year number

We are told that in year number 4 the price was £68, and in year number 8 the price was £76.

We would like to calculate 'a' and 'b' in the formula, and then use this information to predict the price in year 11.

We can use a calculation similar to the 'high-low' method, to determine how much the price is moving by each year:

	Price		**Year**	
	£76		8	
	£68		4	
Differences	£8	divided by	4	= £2 per year

This is the 'gradient' amount 'b', and we can use it to calculate the amount 'a' by using price information from either of the years that we know. For example, using year 4 data and putting it into the formula gives:

£68 = a + (£2 x 4 [the year number])

£68 = a + £8   So a must be £60

Now we have the full formula that we can use for any year:

Y = £60 + £2 x X

In year 11, this would give a price of:

y = £60 + (£2 x 11)   = £82

Just like in the high-low method, if you are provided with more than two pairs of data, then using the highest and the lowest will probably give the most reliable answer.

We will now use an example to illustrate the use of the formula to predict demand.

Sales of a national daily newspaper have been declining steadily for several years. The demand level is believed to follow the formula $Y = a + bX$, where Y is the demand in numbers of newspapers, and X is the year number. Calculations have already been carried out to establish the values of 'a' and 'b', which are:

- a is 200,000
- b is -2,500

Note that 'b' is a negative figure, so each year the demand decreases.

You are asked to calculate the expected sales in year 14.

If we insert the known data into the formula, we can calculate the demand for year 14 as follows:

$$Y = 200,000 - (2,500 \times 14) \quad Y = 165,000$$

linear regression

In the last section on time series analysis we saw that when some historical data moves in a consistent and regular way over time we can use it to help estimate the future trend of that data. We also saw that in these circumstances the data can be represented by

- a straight line on a graph, and / or
- an equation of the line in the form $y = mx + c$

to help us develop the trend.

Linear regression is the term used for the techniques that can be used to determine the line that best replicates that given data. You should be aware of the techniques in general terms, and be able to appreciate their usefulness. You may be given historical data or the equation of a line and asked to use it to generate a forecast.

Where data exactly matches a straight line (as with the 'Comfy Feet' data) there is no need to use any special techniques. In other situations the following could be used:

- **Average annual change**. This method was described earlier, and is useful if we are confident that the first and last points (taken chronologically since we are looking at data over time) are both representative. It will smooth out any minor fluctuations of the data in-between. We will see this method used in the 'Seasonal Company' Case Study later in this chapter.

- **Line of best fit**. Where the data falls only roughly into a straight line, but the first and last points do not appear to be very representative the average annual change method would give a distorted solution. Here a line of best fit can be drawn onto the data points on a graph that will form a better estimate of the movement of the data. The graph on the next page illustrates a situation where the line of best fit would provide a better solution than the average annual change method.

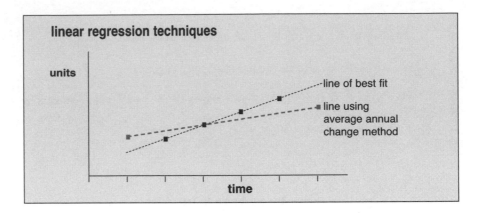

- **Least squares method**. This is a mathematical technique for developing the equation of the most appropriate line. It is more accurate than drawing a line of best fit onto a graph by eye, but the calculations involved are outside the scope of this book.

In the following example the regression line has already been calculated, and is used to forecast the cost of materials.

---

practical example

A colleague has calculated the least squares regression line (the line of best fit) as

$y = 15.75 + 1.65x$

where y is the cost per kilogram in £ and x is the period. April X5 is period 32.

You are asked to forecast the cost per kilogram for July X5.

The figures are inserted into the formula as follows (July X5 is period 35)

$y = 15.75 + (1.65 \times 35)$

Forecast cost per kilogram (y) = £73.50

All linear regression techniques assume that a straight line is an appropriate representation of the data. When looking at time series this means that we are assuming that the changes in the data that we are considering (known as the dependent variable) are in proportion to the movement of time (the independent variable). This would mean that we are expecting (for example) the sales level to continually rise over time. When we use time series analysis later in the book we must remember that sometimes data does not travel forever in a straight line, even though they may do so for a short time. For example share prices on the stock market do not continue to go up (or down) steadily, but often move in a more erratic way.

TIME SERIES ANALYSIS AND SEASONAL VARIATIONS

There are four main factors that can influence data which is generated over a period of time:

■ **The underlying trend**

This is the way that the data is generally moving in the long term. For example the volume of traffic on our roads is generally increasing as time goes on.

■ **Long term cycles**

These are slow moving variations that may be caused by economic cycles or social trends. For example, when economic prosperity generally increases this may increase the volume of traffic as more people own cars and fewer use buses. In times of economic depression there may be a decrease in car use as people cannot afford to travel as much or may not have employment which requires them to travel.

■ **Seasonal variations**

This term refers to regular, predictable cycles in the data. The cycles may or may not be seasonal in the normal use of the term (eg Spring, Summer etc). For example traffic volumes are always higher in the daytime, especially on weekdays, and lower at weekends and at night.

■ **Random variations**

All data will be affected by influences that are unpredictable. For example flooding of some roads may reduce traffic volume along that route, but increase it on alternative routes. Similarly the traffic volume may be influenced by heavy snowfall.

The type of numerical problems that you are most likely to face will tend to ignore the effects of long-term cycles (which will effectively be considered as a part of the trend) and random variations (which are impossible to forecast). We are therefore left with analysing data into underlying trends and seasonal variations, in order to create forecasts.

The technique that we will use follows the process in the diagram on the next page.

The process is as follows:

1 The historical actual data is analysed into the historical trend and the seasonal variations.

2 The historical trend is used to forecast the future trend, using the techniques examined in the last section.

3   The seasonal variations are incorporated with the forecast future trend to provide a forecast of where the actual data will be in the future.

incorporating seasonal variations into the trend

| historical actual data | | forecast of future data |

| | seasonal variations | |

| historical trend | → | forecast future trend |

forecasting using deseasonalised data

If we know (or can estimate fairly accurately) the seasonal variations, then we can use this information together with actual data to work out what the trend is. The term 'deseasonalised data' means data from which the seasonal variations have been stripped away – in other words the trend. We can then extrapolate this trend. This means forecasting how the trend will move in the future.

The seasonal variations for unit sales of a product have been calculated to be the following percentages of the underlying trend:

Quarter 1   −15%

Quarter 2   +25%

Quarter 3   +10%

Quarter 4   −20%

In year 5 the actual unit sales results are as follows:

Quarter 1   42,500

Quarter 2   75,000

Quarter 3   77,000

Quarter 4   64,000

From these figures we can calculate the 'deseasonalised' data – the trend figures. We need to be careful because the seasonal variations are calculated as percentages of the trend.

Quarter 1   The trend must be greater than 42,500 by 15% of the trend.

Therefore 42,500 must equal 85% of the trend

Trend = 42,500 x 100 / 85   = 50,000

Quarter 2   The trend must be lower than 75,000 by 25% of the trend.

Therefore 75,000 must equal 125% of the trend

Trend = 75,000 x 100 / 125   = 60,000

Using the same logic:

Quarter 3   Trend = 77,000 x 100 / 110   = 70,000

Quarter 4   Trend = 64,000 x 100 / 80   = 80,000

Having identified the trend for year 5 as 50,000, 60,000, 70,000 and 80,000 we can see that it is rising by 10,000 units per quarter. Therefore the forecast for year 6 can be worked out as follows:

Year 6	Quarter 1	Quarter 2	Quarter 3	Quarter 4
Extrapolated Trend	90,000	100,000	110,000	120,000
Seasonal Variations	−15%	+25%	+10%	−20%
Forecast	76,500	125,000	121,000	96,000

In a task the analysis of actual data may have been carried out already, or you may be asked to carry out the analysis by using 'moving averages'. If you are using moving averages it is important that:

■ your workings are laid out accurately

■ the number of pieces of data that are averaged corresponds with the number of 'seasons' in a cycle

■ where there is an even number of 'seasons' in a cycle a further averaging of each pair of averages takes place

moving averages

A moving average is the term used for a series of averages calculated from a stream of data so that:

■ every average is based on the same number of pieces of data, (eg four pieces of data in a 'four point moving average'), and

■ each subsequent average moves along that data stream by one piece of data so that compared to the previous average it

    – uses one new piece of data and

    – abandons one old piece of data.

This is easier to calculate than it sounds! For example, suppose we had a list of six pieces of data relating to the factory output over two days where a three-shift pattern was worked as follows:

Day 1	Morning Shift	14 units
	Afternoon Shift	20 units
	Night Shift	14 units
Day 2	Morning Shift	26 units
	Afternoon Shift	32 units
	Night Shift	26 units

If we thought that the shift being worked might influence the output, we could calculate a three-point moving average, the workings would be as follows:

First moving average:	$(14 + 20 + 14) \div 3$	$= 16$
Second moving average:	$(20 + 14 + 26) \div 3$	$= 20$
Third moving average:	$(14 + 26 + 32) \div 3$	$= 24$
Fourth moving average	$(26 + 32 + 26) \div 3$	$= 28$

Notice how we move along the list of data. In this simple example with six pieces of data we can't work out any more three-point averages since we have arrived at the end of the numbers after only four calculations.

Here we chose the number of pieces of data to average each time so that it corresponded with the number of points in a full cycle. By choosing a three-point moving average that corresponded with the number of shifts we always had **one** example of the output of **every** type of shift in our average. This means that any influence on the average by including a night shift (for example) is cancelled out by also including data from a morning shift and an afternoon shift.

We must be careful to always work out moving averages so that exactly one complete cycle is included in every average. The number of 'points' is chosen to suit the data.

When determining a trend line, each average relates to the data from its mid point, as the following layout of the figures just calculated demonstrates.

		Output	**Trend (Moving Average)**
Day 1	Morning Shift	14 units	
	Afternoon Shift	20 units	16 units
	Night Shift	14 units	20 units
Day 2	Morning Shift	26 units	24 units
	Afternoon Shift	32 units	28 units
	Night Shift	26 units	

This means that the first average that we calculated (16 units) can be used as the trend point of the afternoon shift on day 1, with the second point (20 units) forming the trend point of the night shift on day 1. The result is that we:

■ know exactly where the trend line is for each period of time, and

■ have a basis from which we can calculate 'seasonal variations'

Even using our limited data in this example we can see how seasonal variations can be calculated. **A seasonal variation is simply the difference between the actual data at a point and the trend at the same point**. This gives us the seasonal variations shown in the following table, using the figures already calculated.

		Output	**Trend**	**Seasonal Variation**
Day 1	Morning Shift	14 units		
	Afternoon Shift	20 units	16 units	+ 4 units
	Night Shift	14 units	20 units	- 6 units
Day 2	Morning Shift	26 units	24 units	+ 2 units
	Afternoon Shift	32 units	28 units	+ 4 units
	Night Shift	26 units		

The seasonal variation for the afternoon shift, calculated on day 1, is based on the actual output being 4 units greater than the trend at the same point (20 minus 16 units).

Case Study

THE AVERAGE COMPANY:
MOVING AVERAGES AND FORECASTS

The Average Company has sales data that follows a 3 period cycle. The sales units shown in the table below have been compiled from actual data in periods 11 to 19.

Period	Actual Data	3 Point Moving Averages (Trend)	Seasonal Variations
11	7,650		
12	7,505		
13	7,285		
14	7,590		
15	7,445		
16	7,225		
17	7,530		
18	7,385		
19	7,165		

required

(a) Using a 3 point moving average, calculate the trend figures and the seasonal variations.
(b) Extrapolate the trend to periods 20 to 25, and using the seasonal variations forecast the sales units for those periods.

solution

(a) The 3 point moving averages can be calculated for each period except the first and the last. The seasonal variations are calculated as (actual data – trend).

Period	Actual Data	3 Point Moving Averages (Trend)	Seasonal Variations
11	7,650		
12	7,505	7,480	+25
13	7,285	7,460	−175
14	7,590	7,440	+150
15	7,445	7,420	+25
16	7,225	7,400	−175
17	7,530	7,380	+150
18	7,385	7,360	+25
19	7,165		

(b) The trend calculated from 3 point moving averages can be seen to be reducing by 20 each period, and so can be easily extrapolated.

The seasonal variations operate on a 3 period repeating cycle, so can be inserted.

The forecast data is then calculated as (extrapolated trend + seasonal variations).

Period	Forecast Data	Extrapolated Trend	Seasonal Variations
20	7,470	7,320	+150
21	7,325	7,300	+25
22	7,105	7,280	-175
23	7,410	7,260	+150
24	7,265	7,240	+25
25	7,045	7,220	-175

INDEX NUMBERS

Index numbers are used to assist in the comparison of numerical data over time. A commonly used index is the Retail Price Index that gives an indication of inflation by comparing the cost of a group of expenses typically incurred by households in the UK from year-to-year. There are many other types of index numbers that have been created for specific purposes, for example:

■ the average wage rate for a particular job, or for all employment

■ the average house price either by region or throughout the UK

■ the market price of shares (eg the FTSE 100 index)

■ the quantities of specific items that are sold or used (eg litres of unleaded petrol)

■ the quantities of a group of items that are sold or used (eg litres of all motor fuel)

■ the manufactured cost of specific items or a range of items (sometimes called 'factory gate' prices)

Many government indices and other indicators are available at www.gov.uk/government/statistics. If you have the opportunity, have a look at the enormous range of data that can either be downloaded free, or can be purchased in government publications.

When using published statistics it is important to make sure that they are specific enough to be useful for your purpose. For example, data on the growth in the population of the West of England will be of limited use if you are trying to forecast the sales in a bookshop in Taunton. Of far more use would be details of proposed housing developments within the immediate area, including the numbers of new homes and the type of households that form the developers' target market.

leading and lagging indicators

Some indicators can be classified as 'leading' indicators, whilst others are known as 'lagging' indicators. This means that some indicators naturally give advance warning of changes that may take place later in other indicators. For example, an index that monitors the prices of manufactured goods ('factory gate' prices) will react to changes before they have filtered through to retail price indices. The index of 'factory gate' prices can therefore be considered to be a 'leading' indicator of retail prices, and give early warning of implications to industrial situations.

In a similar way, an index recording the volume of manufactured output from factories will lag behind an index measuring the volume of purchases of raw materials made by industrial buying departments.

weightings of indices

Those indices that are based on information from more than one item will use some form of weighting to make the results meaningful.

For example while an index measuring the retail price of premium grade unleaded petrol is based on a single product and therefore needs no weighting, this would not be true for a price index for all vehicle fuel. In this case it will require a decision about how much weight (or importance) is to be placed on each component of the index. Here the relative quantities sold of types of fuel (for example unleaded petrol and diesel) would be a logical way to weight the index. This would ensure that if petrol sales were double those for diesel, any price changes in petrol would have twice the impact on the index than a price change in diesel.

As the purchasing habits of consumers change, then the weighting and composition of complicated indices like the Retail Price Index and the Consumer Price Index are often changed to reflect this. This will include changes to the weighting of certain items, for example due to the increase in the proportion of household expenditure on holidays. It can also involve the addition or deletion of certain items entirely (for example the inclusion of certain fast foods). You may have seen news items from time to time about the revision of items contained within the RPI or CPI as consumers' tastes change.

calculations using index numbers

Whatever type of index we need to use, the principle is the same. The index numbers represent a convenient way of comparing figures.

For example, the RPI was 82.61 in January 1983, and 245.8 in January 2013. This means that average household costs had nearly tripled in the 30 years between. We could also calculate that if something that cost £5.00 in January 1983 had risen exactly in line with inflation, it would have cost £14.88 in January 2013. This calculation is carried out by:

$$historical\ price \quad \text{x} \quad \frac{index\ of\ time\ converting\ to}{index\ of\ time\ converting\ from}$$

ie £5.00   x   (245.8 ÷ 82.61)   =   £14.88

This is an increase of $\frac{(£14.88 - £5.00) \times 100}{£5.00}$ =   197.6%

You may be told that the 'base year' for a particular index is a certain point in time. This is when the particular index was 100. For example the current RPI index was 100 in January 1987.

Index numbers referring to costs or prices are the most commonly used ones referred to in the unit studied in this book. If we want to use cost index numbers to monitor past costs or forecast future ones, then it is best to use as specific an index as possible. This will then provide greater accuracy than a more general index.

For example, if we were operating in the food industry, and wanted to compare our coffee cost movements with the average that the industry had experienced, we should use an index that analyses coffee costs in the food industry. This would be much more accurate than the RPI, and also better than a general cost index for the food industry.

practical example

The following table shows the actual material costs for January for years 20-2 to 20-5, together with the relevant price index.

Period	Actual costs (£)	Cost index	Costs at January 20-2 prices
January 20-2	129,300	471	
January 20-3	131,230	482	
January 20-4	135,100	490	
January 20-5	136,250	495	

Required: Restate all the actual costs at January 20-2 prices, to the nearest £.

Solution

Period	Actual costs (£)	Cost index	Costs at January 20-2 prices
January 20-2	129,300	471	129,300
January 20-3	131,230	482	128,235
January 20-4	135,100	490	129,861
January 20-5	136,250	495	129,644

Case Study

TURNER LIMITED: ADJUSTING TO REAL TERMS

Sales revenue and Net Profit figures are given for Turner Ltd for the five years ended 31 December 20-1 to 20-5. A suitable index for Turner Ltd's industry is also given.

	20-1	20-2	20-3	20-4	20-5
Sales revenue (£000s)	435	450	464	468	475
Net Profit (£000s)	65	70	72	75	78
Industry Index	133	135	138	140	143

required

Calculate the sales revenue and profit in terms of year 20-5 values and comment on the results.

solution

To put each figure into 20-5 terms, it is divided by the index for its own year and multiplied by the index for 20-5, ie 143. For example:

Sales revenue Year 20-1 $\dfrac{435}{133}$ x 143 = 467.7

Sales revenue Year 20-2 $\dfrac{450}{135}$ x 143 = 476.7 and so on.

In year 20-5 terms:

	20-1	20-2	20-3	20-4	20-5
Sales revenue (£000s)	467.7	476.7	480.8	478.0	475.0
Net Profit (£000s)	69.9	74.1	74.6	76.6	78.0

The adjusted figures compare like with like in terms of the value of the pound, and the Net Profit still shows an increasing trend throughout, but the sales revenue decreases in the last two years.

creation of an index

You may be required to create an index from given historical data, and we will now see how this is carried out.

Suppose that you are provided with the following prices for one unit of a certain material over a period of time:

Month	Jan	Feb	March	April	May	June
Price	£29.70	£30.00	£28.30	£30.09	£31.00	£31.25

The first thing to do is to decide which point in time is to be the base point – the price at this point will be 100 in our new index. In this example we will first use January as our base point, but later we will see how another date could have been chosen.

Next, the price of another date (we'll use February) is divided by the price at the base point. The result is then multiplied by 100 to give the index at that point (ie February):

$$(£30.00 / £29.70) \times 100 = 101.01$$

Note that the index number is not an amount in £s, it is just a number used for comparison purposes. In this example we've rounded to two decimal places – and we will need to be consistent for the other figures.

If we carry out the same calculation for the March price we get the following:

$$(£28.30 / £29.70) \times 100 = 95.29$$

Notice that here the answer is less than 100, which makes sense because the price in March is lower than the price in January. Checking that each index number is the expected side of 100 (ie higher or lower) is a good idea and will help you to detect some arithmetical errors.

The full list of index numbers is as follows – make sure that you can arrive at the same figures.

Month	Jan	Feb	March	April	May	June
Price	£29.70	£30.00	£28.30	£30.09	£31.00	£31.25
Index	100.00	101.01	95.29	101.31	104.38	105.22

We could have chosen a different date to act as our base point – if we chose March, then the calculation for January would have been:

$$(£29.70 / £28.30) \times 100 = 104.95$$

Then the full list of index numbers would have been as follows:

Month	Jan	Feb	March	April	May	June
Price	£29.70	£30.00	£28.30	£30.09	£31.00	£31.25
Index	104.95	106.01	100.00	106.33	109.54	110.42

Again, make sure that you could arrive at the same figures.

Don't forget that although we have used the creation of a price index in the above example, you could also be asked to create an index from any suitable historical data. Whatever the type of data, the arithmetic required is the same.

USING INDEX NUMBERS TO ANALYSE VARIANCES

When standard costing is being used, standards for material prices will have been set based on expected costs. This will often be based on an expected level of a price index for that material (if there is one available). If the price index for the material changes significantly then we can calculate what the standard would be if it was based on the index (the 'revised' standard price). We can then see how that impacts on any price variance that has been calculated.

Once we have worked out what the 'revised' standard price would be, we can then calculate the part of a price variance explained by the index change as:

the original standard cost of the actual material	*minus*	the revised standard cost of the actual material

The remainder of the original variance would be the part not explained by the change in price index.

The following Case Study illustrates the process.

Case Study

ANALYSIS LIMITED: REVISED STANDARD PRICE

Analysis Limited operates a standard costing system and uses a raw material that is a global commodity. The standard price was set based upon a market price of £950 per kilo when the relevant price index was 315.
In April the price index was 330. The quantity of material purchased and used was 128 kilos, which cost £125,000.

required

- Calculate the material price variance, based on the original standard
- Calculate what the 'revised' standard price per kilo would be, based on the change in the index, to the nearest £
- Analyse the material price variance into the part explained by the change in the index, and the remainder.

solution

- The material price variance is

    (£950 x 128 kilos) - £125,000   = £3,400 adverse

- The 'revised' standard price per kilo would be:

    £950 x 330 / 315   = £995 to the nearest £

- The part of the price variance explained by the index change:

    (£950 x 128 kilos) – (£995 x 128 kilos)   = £5,760 adverse

The remainder of the variance is therefore:

    £3,400 adverse minus £5,760 adverse   = £2,360 favourable

In this situation the price actually paid for material is lower than would be expected from the change in the index.

Chapter Summary

- A time series is formed by data that occurs over time. If the data increases or decreases regularly (in a 'straight line') then it can be represented by a formula. The formula can then be used to predict the data at various points.

- Some data moves in regular cycles over time, and the distances that the data is from the underlying trend are known as seasonal variations. Information about the underlying trend and the seasonal variations can be used to forecast data.

- Moving averages can be used to split data into the trend and the seasonal variations.

- Index numbers can be used to compare numerical data over time. Examples of the use of index numbers are for prices of commodities or general price inflation.

- Index numbers can be used to analyse standard costing variances so that we can determine performance more accurately.

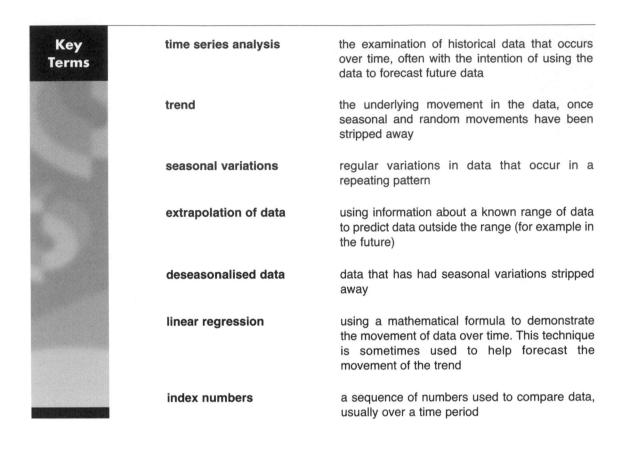

Key Terms		
	time series analysis	the examination of historical data that occurs over time, often with the intention of using the data to forecast future data
	trend	the underlying movement in the data, once seasonal and random movements have been stripped away
	seasonal variations	regular variations in data that occur in a repeating pattern
	extrapolation of data	using information about a known range of data to predict data outside the range (for example in the future)
	deseasonalised data	data that has had seasonal variations stripped away
	linear regression	using a mathematical formula to demonstrate the movement of data over time. This technique is sometimes used to help forecast the movement of the trend
	index numbers	a sequence of numbers used to compare data, usually over a time period

Activities

4.1 Sales (in units) of a product are changing at a steady rate and don't seem to be affected by any seasonal variations. Use the data given for the first three periods to forecast the sales for periods 4 and 5.

Period	1	2	3	4	5
Sales (units)	212,800	210,600	208,400		

4.2 Sales (in units) of a product are changing at a broadly steady rate and don't seem to be affected by any seasonal variations. Use the average change in the data given for the first five periods to forecast the sales for periods 6 and 7.

Period	1	2	3	4	5	6	7
Sales (units)	123,400	123,970	124,525	125,085	125,640		

4.3 The table below shows the last three months cost per kilo for material Beta, together with estimated seasonal variations:

Month	Jan	Feb	March	April	May
Actual Price £	6.80	6.40	7.00		
Seasonal Variation £	+0.40	−0.10	+0.40	−0.30	−0.40
Trend £					

- Calculate the trend figures for January to March, and extrapolate them to April and May.

- Forecast the actual prices in April and May

4.4 Computer modelling has been used to identify the regression formula for the monthly total of a specific indirect cost as

$Y = £13.20 x + £480.00$

Where   y is total monthly cost

And   x is monthly production in units

Calculate the total monthly cost when output is:

- 500 units, and

- 800 units

State whether the total cost behaves as a:

- Fixed cost, or

- Variable cost, or

- Semi-variable cost, or

- Stepped cost.

4.5 The regression formula for monthly sales of a certain product (in units) has been identified as:

$Y = 1,200 + 13X$

Where Y is total monthly sales, and X is the month number.

January 20-9 was month 30

Forecast the monthly sales in August 20-9

4.6 A company has sales data that follows a 3 period cycle. The sales units shown in the table below have been compiled from actual data in periods 30 to 36.

Period	Actual data	3 point moving averages (Trend)	Seasonal variations
30	3,500		
31	3,430		
32	3,450		
33	3,530		
34	3,460		
35	3,480		
36	3,560		
37			
38			
39			
40			

Complete the table to show your responses to the following:

(a) Using a 3 point moving average, calculate the trend figures and the seasonal variations for periods 31 to 35.

(b) Extrapolate the trend to periods 37 to 40, and using the seasonal variations forecast the sales units for those periods.

4.7 The table below shows details of 5 unrelated materials. Complete the blank parts of the table. Show all figures to two decimal places.

Material	Old price £	New price £	New price as index number with old price as base	% increase in price
A	2.13	2.16		
B	10.25	11.00		
C	3.60	3.75		
D	240.00		105.00	
E	68.00		124.00	

4.8 The table below shows details regarding purchases of a specific material. Complete the table to show the actual cost per kilo (to the nearest penny) and create an index based on the cost per kilo with January as the base, to the nearest whole number.

	January	February	March
Total cost £	20,000	24,000	25,000
Total quantity	2,000 kilos	2,200 kilos	2,140 kilos
Cost per kilo £			
Cost index			

4.9 The standard price for material M was set at £3.00 per kilo, based on a price index of 155.3. During April, 15,000 kilos of material M costing £58,500 was purchased and used. The price index in April was 179.7

Complete the following table, showing amounts to the nearest £:

	Amount £	Adverse / Favourable
Material price variance		
Part of variance explained by change in index		

5 Performance indicators

this chapter covers...

We start this chapter by examining what performance indicators can tell us and learn some of the 'ground rules' that will help. We will see how making comparisons is invaluable, and how benchmarking can play its part in making sense of the data.

Next we will start our examination of ratios by looking at those connected with profitability and how the resources of the business are used to generate profit. The last groups of ratios are those concerned with examining the statement of financial position to understand issues like liquidity and financial stability.

We will then learn how to interpret ratios, and their limitations.

We will then examine non-financial indicators which are numerical, for example number of customer complaints or number of employee-days absence. We will then go on to discuss qualitative measures that are not expressed numerically, but may refer to attitudes and opinions.

Next we will examine performance measurement in service organisations, before going on to see how managers' behaviour can be affected by the choice of indicators.

The balanced scorecard is a technique for grouping performance measurements under four categories (or 'perspectives'), and this idea is discussed and illustrated in the final section.

MEASURING THE PERFORMANCE OF ORGANISATIONS

performance indicators

It is important to be able to measure the performance of an organisation in a way which allows managers to see where improvements can be made. In Chapters 2 and 3 we have studied the analysis of cost variances. These are examples of performance measurements which can be used:

- to monitor the use of resources
- to help with control of the business
- to help with planning for the future

A list of variances for one cost centre for one period is not particularly informative. The usefulness of variances depends on being able to compare them with target levels, with the variances for other time periods or with those for other similar cost centres.

In this chapter we will consider different ways of measuring the performance of an organisation (or of a part of an organisation). For example, we can calculate profit as a percentage of sales, sales revenue per employee, the percentage of orders which are delivered late, and many other measures. An individual measurement is called a **performance indicator**. What we have seen above for variance analysis applies to any performance indicator.

A performance indicator may be used for:

- identifying problems
- controlling costs
- measuring the utilisation of resources
- measuring an individual's performance
- planning

Examples of performance indicators include:

- the direct materials usage variance, which may identify a problem relating to wastage of materials
- the administration cost as a percentage of sales, which may help with control of costs
- the number of hours of machine down time, which is relevant to how well resources are being used
- profit as a percentage of sales revenue, which may indicate how well a company has been managed
- the number of product units rejected on inspection, which may help with planning production levels

The usefulness of a performance indicator depends on:

■ comparing with standards, budgets or targets
■ comparing with other periods of time
■ comparing with other similar organisations

A range of factors can have an impact on performance indicators, and should be taken into account when evaluating performance. These include (but are not limited to) the following:

■ The learning effect – this relates to the fact that individuals (and organisations) may become more efficient as time goes on as everyone gets more used to the way things are done. However, performance will not continue to improve for ever, so the impact of the learning effect should not be over-estimated.

■ Economies of scale – where activity levels increase there may be opportunities to reduce cost due to (for example) bulk discounts or spreading fixed costs over a greater number of outputs.

■ Mechanisation – where manual operations are replaced by mechanical or computer controlled operations the performance should improve. However, the type of costs will often change, for example reduced labour costs, may be replaced by increased costs related to non-current assets.

One key area that most organisations will want to focus on is its performance in terms of productivity and efficiency. Although both these terms concentrate on the relationship between inputs and outputs, there are some important distinctions in what they are measuring.

Productivity measures the quantity of output (for example units produced) and compares this to some form of input (for example number of employees or value of non-current assets).

Efficiency takes the inputs of a process and assesses how economically they are used to produce the output. In this way, efficiency takes account of the value of the outputs in relation to the value of the inputs. Measures of efficiency therefore examine how well resources have been used to generate profits.

making comparisons – benchmarking

Comparing performance indicators with standards or targets includes **benchmarking**.

Benchmarks are standards or targets set for one or more areas of activity and should be related to what is important to the organisation.

Benchmarks may be:

■ set internally and relate to a single aspect of the work, for example: all correspondence to be answered within three working days

- set by external bodies, for example government targets relating to pollution of the environment
- set (either internally or externally) with reference to similar organisations, for example the expected level of profitability calculated as an average for the industry

A single organisation may have a number of benchmarks, including all three types described above.

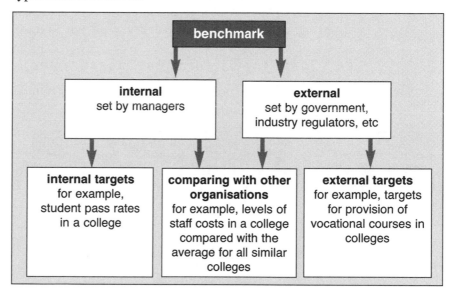

Measurement of how well an organisation (or part of an organisation) has performed in achieving these aims means that it has to record the necessary data to compare with the benchmark.

making comparisons – time series

Comparing the same indicator over a number of periods of time gives a Time Series. In Chapter 4 it has been shown how a time series may show a trend and possibly a pattern of variations around the trend. A performance indicator may show these features over a number of time periods, adding to the usefulness of the information.

For example, the number of customer complaints can be a useful performance indicator for an organisation. An overall downward trend in the number of complaints shows improvement, even if there are some fluctuations. An overall upward trend would indicate a problem to be investigated.

When items measured in money terms, such as Sales Revenue or Profit, are being compared over a number of years, it may be necessary to take out the effect of inflation. This can be done using index numbers, as shown in Chapter 4.

making comparisons – consistency

Comparisons can give very useful information. However, we must be sure that figures being compared really are 'comparable'. In other words, they must have been prepared in a **consistent** way, so that we are comparing 'like with like'.

For example, the Net Profit figures for a business over a number of years can be compared provided that the same accounting policies have been applied throughout. A change in the policy for depreciation, for example, would affect the profit figures and they would not be comparable.

data for performance measurement

The diagram below shows that there are different kinds of data that may be used for performance measurement.

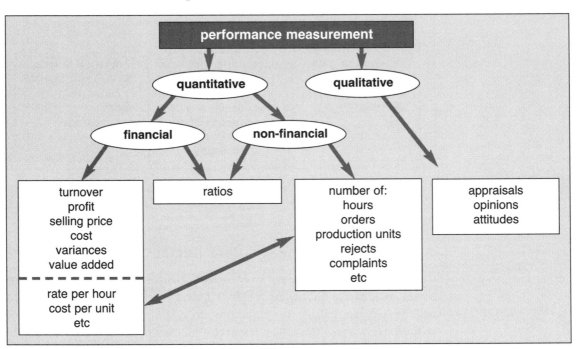

Quantitative data is data which can be stated in numbers, and this can be split into:

■ Financial or Monetary data which is in terms of money and

■ Non-financial or non-monetary data, which is in terms of units other than money, such as numbers of hours for example.

Qualitative data is data which cannot be put in numerical terms. It can consist of people's opinions or judgements, for example the views of students about a teacher. Such data is used for performance measurement, particularly in appraisal schemes for types of work where there is no clearcut numerical measure of performance. A combination of quantitative and qualitative data is often used.

The examples shown in the diagram on the previous page include variances as an example of financial data. You have seen in your earlier studies that variances are given in money terms. The other point to note about variances is that each variance comes from two pieces of information and is the difference between them. An alternative way of comparing two pieces of information is to calculate a ratio or percentage, and this is one of the most common ways of arriving at a useful measure of performance. Percentages are particularly useful when comparisons are being made.

---

tutorial note – dealing with percentages

In order to express a ratio as a percentage, it is necessary to multiply by 100. This can be done using the % function on a calculator.

In all the formulas which follow, we have shown 'x 100' as well as indicating that the answer is a percentage by using the % sign.

When using these formulas:

either multiply by 100

or   use the % button on your calculator.

| Case Study | LITTLE LIMITED AND LARGE LIMITED: PERFORMANCE INDICATORS AS PERCENTAGES |

Little Ltd and Large Ltd are companies which operate in the same industry. For a given period, we have the following data:

	Little Ltd	Large Ltd
	£000s	*£000s*
Turnover (Sales Revenue)	465	2,550
Gross Profit	185	895

At a glance, it is not easy to compare these figures because of the difference in size. If we calculate the gross profit as a percentage of sales revenue, we obtain more useful information for comparison:

Little Ltd   Gross profit percentage = $\dfrac{185}{465}$ x 100% = 39.8%

Large Ltd   Gross profit percentage = $\dfrac{895}{2,550}$ x 100% = 35.1%

We can then see that Little Ltd is translating a greater proportion of its sales revenue into gross profit than Large Ltd. This is an example of a performance indicator.

financial indicators: calculating averages

Although total amounts of money such as sales, profits and costs may be used for performance measurement, it is often more informative to calculate an average 'per employee', 'per hour', 'per unit of output' and so on. This is a simple calculation which relates the financial data to the size of the organisation in some way.

practical examples

1   If sales orders amount to £32million for the year and there are 16 sales representatives, then
    Average sales orders per representative = £32m ÷ 16 = £2m

2   If materials cost £87,000 in total for output of 29,000 units of a product, then
    Average cost of materials per unit = £87,000 ÷ 29,000 = £3

3   If training costs for the year total £171,000 and there are 450 employees, then
    Average expenditure on training per employee = £171,000 ÷ 450 = £380

RATIO ANALYSIS

Ratio analysis generally refers to the calculation of a set of ratios or percentages using data from the financial and management accounts of a business. The income statement (profit and loss account) and the statement of financial position (balance sheet) are used in the analysis, which can then be used to evaluate the performance of the business, particularly by:

■ comparing with budgets or targets

■ comparing with other periods of time

■ comparing with other similar organisations

In the case of limited companies, people outside the company can look at the final accounts and calculate ratios, for example when deciding whether to buy shares in the company. This analysis will add to the available information, but should not be used on its own.

In order to make meaningful comparisons between organisations or between time periods, the accounts must have been prepared on the same basis – applying the principle of consistency by comparing like with like. It is very difficult to achieve this, especially when using published accounts. In this case, it is essential to study the notes to the accounts, which may give important information about accounting policies and the breakdown of certain figures. Even so, details of the methods used may not be given and therefore the ratios calculated must be used with care.

The aim should always be to provide useful information for the purpose for which it is required. It is not sufficient to put figures into formulas (or into a computer program) without thinking of the factors that may affect them.

sources of data for ratios

In this chapter we consider the ratios which can be calculated from the statement of profit or loss (income statement) and the statement of financial position of a business. We will do this in a number of stages:

1 We will consider first the ratios calculated from the statement of profit or loss separately, before linking sales and profits with the statement of financial position.

2 The key measure of profit in relation to the assets shown on the statement of financial position is return on capital employed.

3 Our third section on ratio analysis will include ratios relating to the current assets and current liabilities of the organisation.

PROFITABILITY RATIOS

In the Case Study comparing Little Limited and Large Limited, the calculation of gross profit as a percentage of sales revenue gives useful information. It shows what proportion of the sales revenue remains as gross profit, after the cost of sales is taken out. Little Ltd's gross profit percentage of 39.8%, for example, means that, out of every £100 of sales revenue, there is £39.80 gross profit. Large Ltd keeps only £35.10 gross profit out of every £100 of sales revenue.

Similar percentages can be calculated comparing each of the figures on an income statement with the sales revenue. These show what proportion or 'slice' of sales revenue is being used for each type of cost and how big a slice is kept in profits.

Profit percentages are calculated on the basis of Sales Revenue. This can be done for Gross Profit and Net Profit. In the accounts of a company, several versions of profit are given, before and after interest and tax. To measure the performance of the company, the 'Operating Profit' or 'Profit before interest and tax' is used for many ratios, because this is the profit from the main trading activities of the company.

■ *gross profit margin (percentage)* = $\dfrac{gross\ profit}{sales} \times 100\%$

■ *net profit margin* = $\dfrac{net\ profit}{sales} \times 100\%$

■ *or operating profit margin* = $\dfrac{operating\ profit}{sales} \times 100\%$

Profit percentages are indicators of the profitability of the business.

It must be remembered that the choice of methods for depreciation of assets and for inventory valuation can make a difference to profit figures.

Any other figure from the statement of profit or loss can also be calculated as a percentage of sales, particularly if it appears to need investigation. For example, if selling expenses have increased from one period to the next, it may be useful to calculate for each period:

- *selling expenses as a percentage of sales = $\dfrac{\text{selling expenses}}{\text{sales}} \times 100\%$*

- ***or** any type of expense as a percentage of sales = $\dfrac{\text{expense}}{\text{sales}} \times 100\%$*

Similarly, if details of the costs of materials and wages are available, we can calculate, for any type of cost:

- *cost as a percentage of sales = $\dfrac{\text{cost}}{\text{sales}} \times 100\%$*

Whether costs behave as fixed or variable costs in relation to activity levels (see Chapter 1) makes a difference to how we would expect the ratios to behave. A higher revenue figure often results from a higher volume of sales, which would mean that total variable costs would also be higher. Total fixed costs, however, would not be expected to change with the volume. In percentage terms, this means that we would expect:

- a variable cost to remain relatively stable as a percentage of revenue
- a fixed cost as a percentage of revenue to decrease as revenue increases

  For example, the direct materials cost of a product may be expected to be 12% of the sales revenue and this percentage would stay approximately the same for different numbers of units. On the other hand, if a fixed cost is £90,000 per year:

  - compared with annual sales of £900,000, the fixed cost would be 10%
  - but compared with annual sales of £1,200,000, it would be only 7.5%.

Case Study

PERFORM LIMITED:
USING BENCHMARK RATIOS

Perform Limited is a manufacturing company that uses benchmark ratios based on a budget to compare with actual performance. The following operating statement has been compiled from actual data for the most recent period.

	£
Sales Revenue	9,400,000
Cost of Sales	6,080,000
Gross Profit	3,320,000
Selling and Distribution Expenses	1,415,000
Administration Expenses	1,170,000
Operating Profit	735,000

The following table shows the benchmark ratios for the company.

	Benchmark ratios	Actual ratios
Gross Profit Percentage	36.0%	
Operating Profit Percentage	9.0%	
Selling & Distribution Expenses as a percentage of Sales	14.5%	
Administration Expenses as a percentage of Sales	12.5%	

The sales revenue and the selling prices are in line with the budget.

required

- Calculate the ratios shown in the table relating to actual performance, rounded to one decimal place.
- Suggest possible areas of cost that could have contributed to the performance falling below expectations.

solution

	Benchmark ratios	Actual ratios
Gross Profit Percentage	36.0%	35.3%
Operating Profit Percentage	9.0%	7.8%
Selling & Distribution Expenses as a percentage of Sales	14.5%	15.1%
Administration Expenses as a percentage of Sales	12.5%	12.4%

The gross profit percentage and the operating profit percentage are both below benchmark.

Since the sales revenue and selling prices are in line with the budget, the volume of sales must also be as expected. This means that the reduced gross profit percentage must be due to increased costs of production. The difference in actual gross profit and

the benchmark ratio of 0.7% of sales represents additional cost of approximately £66,000. We do not have sufficient information to narrow the cause down within that category.

The reduced gross profit contributes to the reduced operating profit, which is 1.2% of sales (approximately £113,000) below benchmark. The other factor is the cost of selling and distribution expenses that are greater than expected. Since sales volume is in line with the budget, volume cannot have an impact on any variable costs within this category. The cause must therefore be cost increases which will need to be identified. The administration costs are slightly below benchmark and appear to be under control.

return on capital employed (ROCE)

By 'capital employed' we mean the money being used to finance the running of a business. This is normally represented by the owners' capital, together with any long-term liabilities such as loans that make more money available. We have seen above that the statement of financial position shows another way of looking at this, as the value of the non-current and current assets less the current liabilities.

Capital employed is the essential funding used by managers for the fixed assets, for keeping the business going and therefore for making sales and profits. It is important for investors to see that this funding is being put to good use. 'Return on Capital Employed' is a performance indicator that compares the profit with the amount of long-term finance being used by management.

Return on Capital Employed is a key ratio which therefore shows how well the management of an organisation has used the assets (or the resources shown on the statement of financial position) to generate profits.

To calculate ROCE, the profit is expressed as a percentage of the capital employed in the business.

Because there are alternative ways to express 'capital employed' we can use either of the following formulas to achieve the same result.

$$ROCE = \frac{operating\ profit}{non\text{-}current\ assets + net\ current\ assets} \times 100$$

$$ROCE = \frac{operating\ profit}{capital + long\ term\ liabilities} \times 100$$

A very similar performance indicator to ROCE is 'return on net assets'.

This is calculated as follows:

$$Return\ on\ net\ assets\ =\ \frac{operating\ profit}{net\ assets}\ x\ 100$$

Notice that in all of these ratios, the operating profit is used. This is the profit before interest and tax that arises from operations, and is usually shown in the operating statement. If you are asked to calculate one of these ratios you may be provided with a figure for 'capital employed' or net assets'.

<table>
<tr><td>Case Study</td><td colspan="3"># THICKE LTD AND THINN LTD: COMPARING PERFORMANCE</td></tr>
</table>

THICKE LTD AND THINN LTD: COMPARING PERFORMANCE

Thicke Ltd and Thinn Ltd are two companies that both operate in the DIY goods retail market. Thicke is a long established company that trades from several retail sites, but Thinn is a more recently opened company that operates online from a central distribution site. The companies have the following data for the last financial period.

	Thicke Ltd	Thinn Ltd
	£	£
Sales Revenue	15,150,000	6,950,000
Cost of Sales	12,500,000	5,940,000
Gross Profit	2,650,000	1,010,000
Distribution Costs	450,000	295,000
Administration Costs	600,000	95,000
Marketing Costs	150,000	380,000
Operating Profit	1,450,000	240,000
Net Assets	18,125,000	2,400,000

required

• Complete the following table to show performance ratios for both companies, rounded to two decimal places

	Thicke Ltd	Thinn Ltd
Gross Profit %		
Distribution Costs as % of Sales		
Administration Costs as % of Sales		
Marketing Costs as % of Sales		
Operating Profit %		
Return on Net Assets %		

• Comment on what the ratios reveal about the companies' performance.

solution

	Thicke Ltd	Thinn Ltd
Gross Profit %	17.49	14.53
Distribution Costs as % of Sales	2.97	4.24
Administration Costs as % of Sales	3.96	1.37
Marketing Costs as % of Sales	0.99	5.47
Operating Profit %	9.57	3.45
Return on Net Assets %	8.00	10.00

Thicke Ltd is maintaining a higher gross profit margin than Thinn Ltd, and this is also reflected in a higher operating profit margin. While Thinn Ltd has lower administration costs as a percentage of sales, all their other costs reveal higher percentages of sales than Thicke Ltd's. The result is that Thinn Ltd's operating profit as a percentage of sales is just over a third of that recorded by Thicke Ltd.

While this may seem to show poor cost control by Thinn Ltd, it could simply be in line with their business model. By selling online they are able to undercut traditional retailers (hence the lower gross profit percentage), but have higher distribution costs and invest more in marketing to increase customer awareness.

However, despite having higher operating costs than Thicke Ltd, Thinn Ltd has a higher return on net assets. This key measure shows that their method of operation needs fewer assets to produce profits. This makes sense as an online sales operation does not require expensive shops.

value added

Return on capital employed and return on net assets are performance indicators that measure profit by comparing it with the amount invested in the company's assets. 'Value added' is a way of showing how the inputs to the organisation have been changed into valuable outputs (the sales).

'Value added' as a financial measure refers to the difference between the value of outputs and the value of inputs. It shows the increase in monetary value which has resulted from the work done and the use of assets within the organisation. For the calculation of value added, 'inputs' are defined as 'materials and bought-in services'. These have been brought into the organisation *from outside*. The monetary value of outputs is sales revenue or turnover, which is their value as they go to *outside customers*.

Value added = Sales – (cost of materials used and bought in services)

The average value added per employee can also be used as an indicator of productivity within the organisation.

Case Study

TURNER LTD: VALUE ADDED

The following information is given for Turner Ltd for the year 20-5.

Sales	£475,000
Number of employees	22
Cost of materials used	£100,000
Total cost of bought-in services	£155,000

required

Calculate the total value added and the value added per employee for the year 20-5 for Turner Ltd.

solution

Value Added = £475,000 − (£100,000 + £155,000) = £220,000

Value Added per employee = £220,000 ÷ 22 = £10,000

asset turnover

Asset Turnover is another important ratio which links the statement of financial position with the income statement. It measures how well the assets have been used during a period to generate sales revenue.

Asset Turnover is the number of times the value of the assets has been obtained in Turnover (Sales).

For example, an asset turnover ratio of 3 times would mean that, for every £1 of value in the assets, there had been £3 of sales revenue. Any improvement in asset turnover means that more sales revenue is being obtained per £1 value of the assets used. This can lead to improvements in the amount of profit and in ROCE, provided that the profit margin is not cut too much. We see below how asset turnover, operating profit margin and ROCE are linked.

Again there may be different definitions of the value of the assets, but we will use the non-current assets plus net current assets as above.

$$asset\ turnover\ =\ \frac{turnover\ (sales\ revenue)}{non\text{-}current\ assets\ +\ net\ current\ assets}$$

The denominator could alternatively be shown as 'total assets − current liabilities'.

Depending on definitions, and the financial structure of the organisation, 'Net Assets' may be identical to 'Capital Employed'. In the following Case Study we will assume that 'non-current assets plus net current assets' is equal to 'net assets'.

Case Study

THICKE LTD AND THINN LTD: ASSET TURNOVER

The following abbreviated details refer to the previous Case Study.

	Thicke Ltd	Thinn Ltd
	£	£
Sales Revenue	15,150,000	6,950,000
Operating Profit	1,450,000	240,000
Net Assets	18,125,000	2,400,000

required

Calculate the asset turnover figures (rounded to two decimal places) for both companies and comment on what they reveal.

solution

	Thicke Ltd	Thinn Ltd
Asset Turnover	0.84	2.90

Workings:

| Thicke Ltd: | £15,150,000 / £18,125,000 | = 0.84 |
| Thinn Ltd: | £6,950,000 / £2,400,000 | = 2.90 |

Notice that these figures are not percentages. They are sometimes referred to as 'times' (for example '2.90 times').

The indicators show that Thinn Ltd is more successful at generating sales from its net assets than Thicke Ltd. As we already noted, Thicke Ltd has a number of expensive shops, whereas Thinn Ltd just has one distribution centre.

ROCE and operating profit margin

There is an important link between ROCE, Asset Turnover and the Operating Profit margin (ie Operating Profit as a percentage of Sales):

ROCE = operating profit margin x asset turnover

because:

$$\frac{Operating\ Profit}{Non\text{-}current\ \&\ net\ current\ assets} = \frac{Operating\ Profit}{\cancel{Sales}} \times \frac{\cancel{Sales}}{Non\text{-}current\ \&\ net\ current\ assets}$$

The sales (turnover) figure can be cancelled in the calculation of the right hand side of this equation (see lines).

The following diagram illustrates these connections:

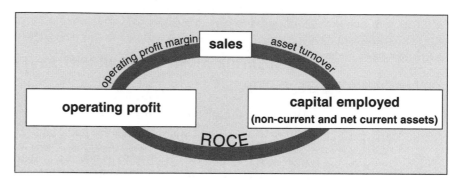

If we assume that for the companies in our Case Study 'non-current assets plus net current assets' is equal to 'net assets' (as previously mentioned) then the relationship shown in the above diagram will apply to 'return on net assets' as well as ROCE.

We can use the figures from the previous Case Study to illustrate this.

	Thicke Ltd	Thinn Ltd
Operating Profit %	9.57	3.45
Return on Net Assets %	8.00	10.00
Asset Turnover	0.84	2.90

Return on net assets = Operating profit margin x asset turnover

For Thicke Ltd:

$$8.00\% = 9.57\% \times 0.84$$

For Thinn Ltd:

$$10.00\% = 3.45\% \times 2.90$$

Both these are valid, subject to minor rounding errors.

This arithmetical connection emphasises that both operating profit % and asset turnover contribute to return on net assets (and return on capital employed).

Compared to Thinn Ltd, although Thicke Ltd has a higher operating profit %, it has a lower asset turnover (i.e. fewer sales generated from its net assets). The result is a return on net assets that is lower than that of Thinn Ltd.

non-current (fixed) asset turnover

In addition to calculating asset turnover, it is also possible to calculate the 'non-current asset turnover' by dividing sales by just the total of non-current assets. This can be useful if we wish to see how well these assets alone are being used to generate sales.

CALCULATION OF RATIOS: CURRENT ASSETS AND LIABILITIES

An important aspect of the management of a business is the control of the current assets of inventory, receivables and cash.

Usually a certain level of inventory is necessary in order to avoid running out of inventory and losing production and sales. Keeping too much inventory, however, incurs additional costs of storage and means that the money tied up in inventory cannot be used for other purposes. Offering customers credit may boost sales, but it is important to collect the money from receivables within a reasonable time. Similarly, cash is needed on a day-to-day basis, but surplus cash should be invested in order to earn extra income. In each case a suitable balance must be achieved.

Control of the current liability of payables means taking advantage of the credit terms offered by suppliers, but making sure they can be paid on time.

The ratios usually calculated relating to the control of current assets and current liabilities are often referred to as 'working capital ratios'.

Working Capital is the part of the capital of the business which circulates between the inventory, receivables, cash and trade payables. These current assets and liabilities are constantly changing, unlike the non-current assets which change only occasionally.

The circulation of working capital is often illustrated by the Cash Cycle:

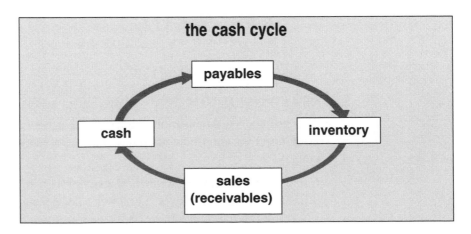

The diagram of the cash cycle on the previous page represents how suppliers provide inventory. When inventory is sold it results in an increase in receivables. When receivables pay, the cash increases. When suppliers are paid, the cash moves along to the payables. This decreases the payables' balance, but it will increase again when more inventory is provided . . . and so on.

calculation of working capital ratios: the current ratio

The current ratio compares the current assets with the current liabilities, to give an indication as to whether it should be possible to pay the current liabilities on time. We discuss below why it is important to consider how the balances of current assets and liabilities may be affected by the type of business, before drawing conclusions from the current ratio on its own.

The current ratio = $\dfrac{current\ assets}{current\ liabilities}$

This is kept as a ratio and written in the form x : 1, where x is the answer obtained above. It shows the **number of times that the current liabilities are covered by the current assets**. In your assessment you should show this (and other similar ratios) as straight numbers (without the ' : 1') unless the task states otherwise.

It is often said that the current ratio should be about 2 : 1, and this may be appropriate for some organisations. However, in certain types of business, the current assets are not expected to be so high in relation to the current liabilities. In a supermarket, for example, the level of receivables will be low in comparison to payables, and inventories are not held for long periods.

The ratio of 2 : 1 can be used as a guide for organisations where inventory does not sell so quickly and where sales as well as purchases are likely to be on credit. In a given case, look for comparisons (with other time periods or other similar organisations) rather than judging a single figure against this guideline.

Remember that the statement of financial position shows the current assets and current liabilities on a particular date. A single transaction may change them considerably. More cash may or may not come in before current liabilities fall due. The guideline ratio of 2:1 allows some leeway for these uncertainties of timing.

The current ratio is affected by the level of inventory included in the current assets. Inventory is usually considered to be the least 'liquid' of the current assets, because it is further from becoming cash in most businesses. In the diagram of the cash cycle above, it can be seen that trade receivables are one step nearer to cash. Cash itself is the most 'liquid' current asset, because it can be used immediately to pay the suppliers (trade payables). The measurement of 'Liquidity' is important, because it indicates the ability of the organisation to pay its current liabilities when they fall due.

A LTD, B LTD, C LTD: CURRENT RATIO

A Ltd, B Ltd and C Ltd are similar companies, which have current assets as shown:

	A Ltd £000	B Ltd £000	C Ltd £000
Inventory	170	100	50
Receivables	90	140	110
Cash at bank and in hand	40	60	140
	300	300	300

Each of the three companies has current liabilities of £150,000.

required

Calculate the current ratio for each of the three companies and compare the liquidity position of the three companies.

solution

For each company,
  current assets = £300,000 and current liabilities = £150,000.
  Each of the three companies therefore has a current ratio of 2 : 1.

However, A Ltd has built up inventory to a high level and we cannot be sure that these can easily be sold, in order to convert them into receivables and then into cash. When the inventory is taken out, A Ltd's current assets do not cover its current liabilities.

B Ltd has a better liquidity position, provided the receivables are well controlled.

C Ltd has the most liquid current assets and could pay most of its payables immediately.

calculation of working capital ratios: the quick ratio

The ratio which is usually used to measure liquidity compares the current assets *other than inventory* with the current liabilities, as follows:

$$Quick\ Ratio\ or\ Acid\ Test\ Ratio = \frac{current\ assets - inventory}{current\ liabilities}$$

This is based on the idea that inventory is the least liquid current asset. In some businesses such as supermarkets, however, inventory is very quickly turned into cash. As with all the ratios, the formula should not be applied as it stands without considering the particular situation.

As a guide, a level of 1 : 1 for the quick ratio is quoted, but a business with frequent cash inflows may operate satisfactorily on a lower quick ratio.

The aim is to check that the current liabilities are likely to be covered by cash or by current assets quickly convertible to cash.

Comparison with similar businesses gives more useful information, but it must be remembered that a single large transaction can alter the position significantly and the statement of financial position may not be typical.

In most cases, the timing of cashflows in and out will be a vital factor. The quick ratio only indicates whether enough cash should 'normally' be available to pay the current liabilities when they fall due.

Case Study

A LTD, B LTD, C LTD: CALCULATION OF THE QUICK RATIO

Referring to the data given for A Ltd, B Ltd and C Ltd in the last Case Study, we can calculate their quick ratios:

A Ltd: $\dfrac{300 - 170}{150}$ = 0.87, giving a quick ratio of   0.87 : 1

B Ltd: $\dfrac{300 - 100}{150}$ = 1.33, giving a quick ratio of   1.33 : 1

C Ltd: $\dfrac{300 - 50}{150}$ = 1.67, giving a quick ratio of   1.67 : 1

These calculations illustrate the discussion of the liquidity of the companies above.

RECEIVABLES, PAYABLES AND INVENTORY INDICATORS

We have seen above that an organisation needs to keep levels of receivables, payables and inventory that are appropriate for the type of business. Ratios used to measure these levels are usually calculated in terms of numbers of days or months, to estimate:

■ the average time taken to collect money from trade receivables

■ the average time taken to pay trade payables

■ the average time that goods or materials remain in inventory

The limitations of these estimates are discussed below. The usefulness of the ratios is in making comparisons and identifying trends. For example, if the average time taken to collect money from receivables decreases over several time periods, this suggests that control of receivables is improving.

receivable collection

In the last Case Study, B Ltd has a high proportion of receivables and we noted that these should be well controlled. This means that the cash should be received within the time allowed by the normal credit terms for customers. It is possible to *estimate* the time being taken for customers to pay, by using the formula:

receivables' collection period $= \dfrac{\textit{trade receivables}}{\textit{credit sales}}$ x *365 days*

A separate figure for 'Credit Sales' may not be available, and Total Sales would have to be used, although this is not appropriate if cash sales are a significant part of the total. Notice that the formula gives an average time, based on the closing receivables.

If customers are normally allowed two months' credit, for example, the receivables' collection period should not be much above 60 days (remembering that the closing receivables figure may not be typical). As usual, comparison over time is more useful and may show whether control of receivables is improving or not.

When making comparisons between organisations, remember that some businesses allow customers longer credit periods in order to increase sales.

In effect, customers are *borrowing from* the business, because sending goods without receiving payment is like lending money. Conversely, suppliers are *lending to* the business. It makes sense, therefore, to try to collect the money back from customers more quickly than paying amounts due to suppliers. However, suppliers who are not paid on time may refuse to supply goods or services in future.

payables' payment period

The **Payables' Payment Period** can be estimated in a similar way to the Receivables' Collection Period, but here it is credit purchases which are relevant.

payables' payment period $= \dfrac{\textit{trade payables}}{\textit{credit purchases}}$ x *365 days*

A separate figure for Credit Purchases may not be available, in which case Total Purchases or (less appropriately) Cost of Sales may have to be used.

Again, the formula gives an average, based on the closing trade payables figure, which may not be typical.

inventory holding ratios

Another step in the Cash Cycle can be estimated in terms of days: this is the length of time taken for inventory to be sold, or the average age of inventory. The inventory figure used in the formula may be the average of the opening and closing inventory, which is calculated in the usual way for an average (mean) of two items, by adding them together and dividing the total by 2:

average inventory = 0.5 x (opening inventory + closing inventory)

If the opening inventory is not known, the closing inventory figure is used.

$$\textit{average age of inventory} \; = \; \frac{\textit{average inventory}}{\textit{cost of sales}} \quad \textit{x 365 days}$$

or,

$$\textit{average age of inventory} \; = \; \frac{\textit{closing inventory}}{\textit{cost of sales}} \quad \textit{x 365 days}$$

It can be argued that the closing inventory gives an equally good estimate. The average based on the opening and closing inventory may not be a fairer reflection, especially if the trade is seasonal. (See the discussion below.)

Note the correspondence between the pairs of figures used in the last three ratios:

- trade receivables are related to credit sales
- trade payables are related to credit purchases
- inventory is related to cost of sales

As an alternative to calculating the average age of inventory, we can look at the number of times per year that the inventory is 'turned over' or sold. This is called **inventory turnover** or **inventory turn** and is calculated as:

$$\textit{Inventory Turnover} \quad = \frac{\textit{cost of sales}}{\textit{average inventory}} \quad \textit{or} \quad \frac{\textit{cost of sales}}{\textit{closing inventory}}$$

The result of this calculation gives the **Inventory Turnover as a 'number of times per year'**.

A higher inventory turn indicates that inventory is moving more quickly, and this corresponds to a lower average age of inventory. The speed with which inventory should be sold depends on the type of business. For example fresh fruit must be sold within a few days, whereas non-perishable goods may be kept for longer periods. In some businesses, such as manufacturing ice cream, toys or fireworks, the level of inventories will vary considerably with the seasons. The statement of financial position date may happen to coincide with particularly high (or low) inventories and the inventory turn will appear to be very slow (or fast) moving. Once more, we need more information about the business to be able to comment further.

working capital cycle

The combined impact of receivables, payables and inventory days can be shown by calculating the working capital cycle in days.

Working capital cycle = Inventory days + receivable days – payables days

Note that the inventory and receivable days are added together (as they represent current assets), but payables days are deducted because they relate to current liabilities. A greater number of working capital cycle days indicates a greater investment in working capital (or working capital requirement).

ratios: the whole picture

We now look at a Case Study which incorporates a number of the ratios described so far in this Chapter. It shows how ratios can be used in business decision making.

Case Study

TUBS AND POTS LIMITED: RATIO ANALYSIS

Tubs and Pots Ltd supply plant holders to local garden centres. The company has now been offered a contract to supply a national chain of home and garden superstores. The following information shows extracts from the statement of financial position and the income statement as forecast for the next year:

- on the basis of continuing with the current local trade ('Current Trade')
- on the basis of acceptance of the contract ('With Contract')

	Current Trade	With Contract
	£	£
Current Assets:		
Inventory	6,000	20,000
Trade Receivables	14,000	52,000
Cash at Bank	4,000	
	24,000	72,000
Current Liabilities		
Trade Payables	12,000	70,000
Bank Overdraft		7,000
	12,000	77,000
Sales (all Credit Sales)	70,000	204,000
Opening inventory	4,000	4,000
Purchases (all Credit Purchases)	40,000	140,000
Less: Closing inventory	(6,000)	(20,000)
Cost of Sales	38,000	124,000

required

Task 1

Using the above information, calculate the following indicators for the current trade and for the acceptance of the contract:

1 Current Ratio

2 Quick Ratio

3 Receivables' Collection Period

4 Payables' Payment Period

5 Average age of inventory (using the closing inventory)

6 Gross Profit

7 Gross Profit percentage (on Sales)

Task 2

Identify the changes which will take place in the business of Tubs and Pots Ltd if the contract is accepted and comment on the findings.

solution

Task 1: calculation of ratios

Check that you can carry out these calculations, before looking at the workings at the end of the solution.

		current trade	**with contract**
1	Current Ratio	2.0 : 1.0	0.9 : 1.0
2	Quick Ratio	1.5 : 1.0	0.7 : 1.0
3	Receivables' Collection Period	73 days	93 days
4	Payables' Payment Period	110 days	183 days
5	Average age of inventory	58 days	59 days
6	Gross Profit	£32,000	£80,000
7	Gross Profit percentage (on Sales)	45.7%	39.2%

Task 2: analysis of ratios

The forecasts show that, with the contract, **sales** would increase to nearly three times the current level and the management of the company would need to consider whether such expansion within one year is feasible. There would also be higher **inventory levels** and the company would go into an **overdraft** situation. Building up inventories means that **purchases** are increased to more than three times the current level, which could have contributed to the need for an overdraft. Another reason for the overdraft could be purchases of non-current assets.

The indicators we have calculated show that both the **current and quick ratios** would be adversely affected by the contract, such that the current liabilities are not covered by the current assets. The **Receivables' Collection Period** increases to about 3 months with the contract, and the Payables' Payment Period to about 6 months. The adjustment to inventory levels would keep the **average age of inventory** about the same. With the contract, there is a decrease in the **Gross Profit Margin** (Gross Profit as a percentage of Sales).

The managers of Tubs and Pots Ltd need to investigate the risks attached to acceptance of this contract. If non-current assets are purchased, longer-term finance would be more suitable than an overdraft. They also need more working capital to avoid the problems with liquidity. The increased collection period indicates that the national chain would take longer to pay for the goods than the current customers. It appears risky to plan for a 6 month payables' payment period <u>unless</u> such terms have been agreed with the suppliers.

It would be important to consider the length and security of the contract. The forecasts given are for one year only and show that Gross Profit Margin would decrease. This could be caused by the national chain insisting on paying lower prices for the goods. Over a number of years it may be possible to improve on this, by reducing costs. Expansion on this scale would not be worthwhile unless the contract was secure for the long term. The management of Tubs and Pots Ltd should also consider the effect on their current trade with their local customers.

Workings		**current trade**	**with contract**
1	$\dfrac{\text{Current assets}}{\text{Current liabilities}}$	$\dfrac{£24,000}{£12,000}$	$\dfrac{£72,000}{£77,000}$
2	$\dfrac{\text{Current assets} - \text{Inventory}}{\text{Current liabilities}}$	$\dfrac{£18,000}{£12,000}$	$\dfrac{£52,000}{£77,000}$
3	$\dfrac{\text{Receivables} \times 365}{\text{Credit sales}}$	$\dfrac{£14,000 \times 365}{£70,000}$	$\dfrac{£52,000 \times 365}{£204,000}$
4	$\dfrac{\text{Payables} \times 365}{\text{Credit purchases}}$	$\dfrac{£12,000 \times 365}{£40,000}$	$\dfrac{£70,000 \times 365}{£140,000}$
5	$\dfrac{\text{Closing inventory} \times 365}{\text{Cost of sales}}$	$\dfrac{£6,000 \times 365}{£38,000}$	$\dfrac{£20,000 \times 365}{£124,000}$
6	Sales – Cost of sales	£70,000 – £38,000	£204,000 – £124,000
7	$\dfrac{\text{Gross Profit} \times 100\%}{\text{Sales}}$	$\dfrac{£32,000 \times 100\%}{£70,000}$	$\dfrac{£80,000 \times 100\%}{£204,000}$

FINANCIAL STRUCTURE RATIOS

The final group of ratios that we need to examine in this chapter relate to the financial structure of a business. This is about the way that the business is funded – how much of the capital employed is funded by the 'equity' of the business and how much is funded by loans (or similar) from outside the business. The equity of a limited company is the value owned by the shareholders.

Equity is shown in the statement of financial position (balance sheet) as the total of:

- ordinary share capital (the nominal value of the ordinary shares), plus
- the accumulated profit and other reserves that are owned by the ordinary shareholders

On some statements this forms a sub-total shown as equity, but on others you may need to calculate it yourself.

Some businesses may be funded entirely by equity, and this provides a very safe form of finance. All the profits generated will be owned by the shareholders, and they don't have to share it with anyone else. If profits are good then dividends can be paid, but there is no compulsion to do so.

Other businesses may obtain some of their finance from short term and/or long term loans. While such loans may provide a cheap form of funding, interest will need to be paid regularly whether profits are made or not. Therefore too much finance in the form of loans can be a risky strategy, especially when profits are uncertain. Note that loans are also known as debts. Total debt includes both short and long term debt.

There are two ratios that help us to examine the financial structure of businesses.

If we think of the sources of finance in the form of a simple pie chart, this will help us understand both these ratios.

Suppose the capital employed by a company is £1m, made up of loans of £0.4m and equity of £0.6m, as follows:

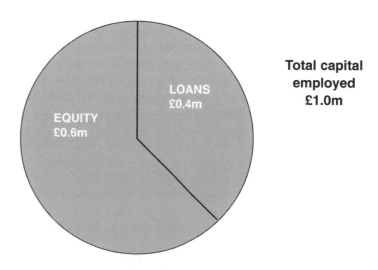

In the next two ratios the term 'debt' relates to the total debt, which can be defined as all non-current liabilities plus any overdrafts.

gearing ratio

This ratio (calculated as a percentage) shows how much of the total funding comes from sources that demand regular payments of interest or dividends.

It is calculated as: $\dfrac{Debt}{(Debt + Equity)} \times 100$

The higher the percentage, the higher the 'gearing' is said to be. A high gearing ratio will also mean that a low proportion of the capital employed is invested by the ordinary shareholders.

The gearing ratio based on the example above would be:

$$\frac{£0.4m}{£1.0m} \times 100 = 40\%$$

This means that 40% of the finance comes from loans (debt).

gearing (debt to equity) ratio

This ratio uses the same logic, but compares the loans or debt directly to the equity instead of the total capital employed. It is also calculated as a percentage.

It is calculated as: $\dfrac{Debt}{(Ordinary\ Share\ Capital + Reserves)} \times 100$

The debt to equity ratio based on the above example would be:

$$\frac{£0.4m}{£0.6m} \times 100 = 67\%$$

The debt to equity ratio will always result in a higher percentage than the gearing ratio when based on the same data.

For both these ratios, the higher the percentage the more debt is being used. While many businesses will want to use some finance of this type, if the amount becomes excessive then it will make the structure very risky. This is because if operating profits fell below a certain level then the company would find it difficult to pay the large amounts of interest, and this could ultimately result in the collapse of the company.

interest cover

Another useful ratio that helps show the impact of debt relates to interest coverage – how many times the organisation could pay its interest out of profit from operations. The lower the resulting figure, the more problematic the level of debt may be.

It is calculated as: *Profit from Operations*
                        ─────────────────────────
                        Finance Cost (i.e. interest)

VOLUMIZER LIMITED:
ADJUSTING VOLUMES AND PRICES

situation

Volumizer Limited is developing a new product and a colleague has prepared forecast information based upon two scenarios. The forecast operating statement and data from the statement of financial position for both scenarios is shown below.

- Scenario 1 is to set the price at £18 per unit with sales of 60,000 units each year.
- Scenario 2 is to set the price at £12 per unit with sales of 120,000 units each year.

Forecast Operating Statement	Scenario 1 £	Scenario 2 £
Sales	1,080,000	1,440,000
Cost of production		
Direct (Raw) Materials	300,000	600,000
Direct Labour	120,000	192,000
Fixed Production overheads	360,000	360,000
Total cost of sales	780,000	1,152,000
Gross profit	300,000	288,000
Selling and distribution costs	74,000	122,000
Administration costs	50,000	50,000
Operating profit	176,000	116,000
Other data:		
Total Net Assets	1,500,000	1,500,000
Inventory	130,000	192,000
Receivables	175,000	250,000
Payables (re raw materials)	63,000	126,000

required

Complete the table on the next page to show the performance indicators. Round percentages and values to two decimal places, and days to the nearest whole day.

	Scenario 1	Scenario 2
Gross profit margin		
Operating profit margin		
Return on net assets		
Direct materials cost per unit £		
Direct labour cost per unit £		
Fixed production cost per unit £		
Inventory days		
Receivables days		
Payables days		
Working capital cycle days		

Draft a report for the Finance Director covering the following:

(a) An explanation of why the gross profit margins are different, referring to the following:
- Sales price and Sales volume
- Materials cost
- Labour cost
- Fixed costs

(b) An explanation of why the net profit margins are different.

(c) The implications for liquidity of the two scenarios.

(d) A recommendation, with reasons, as to which course of action to take.

solution

	Scenario 1	Scenario 2
Gross profit margin	27.78%	20.00%
Operating profit margin	16.30%	8.06%
Return on net assets	11.73%	7.73%
Direct materials cost per unit £	5.00	5.00
Direct labour cost per unit £	2.00	1.60
Fixed production cost per unit £	6.00	3.00
Inventory days	61	61
Receivables days	59	63
Payables days	77	77
Working capital cycle days	43	47

| To: Finance director | Subject: Scenarios 1 & 2 |
| From: Accounting technician | Date: |

(a) Why are the gross profit margins different?

- Sales Price / Sales Volume

  The sales price is 50% higher under Scenario 1, which will result in an increase in the gross profit margin. The sales volume under Scenario 2 is double that of Scenario 1. This only affects the gross profit margin percentage because not all the production costs are variable.

- Materials

  The materials cost per unit is constant at £5.00 per unit, and therefore does not affect the gross profit margin. There is no economy of scale.

- Labour

  Labour cost per unit is £2.00 for Scenario 1 decreasing to £1.60 for Scenario 2. The more units that are produced, the lower the labour cost per unit. This will improve the margin for Scenario 2. The lower labour cost per unit may be because of economies of scale in production.

- Fixed costs

  Fixed costs are constant in total, and so as the volume of production increases, the fixed cost per unit decreases. This will increase the margin for Scenario 2.

(b) Why are the net profit margins different?

The net profit margins are different partly due to the reduction in gross profit for Scenario 2, and partly due to the increased sales and distribution costs in Scenario 2.

(c) Implications for liquidity

The working capital requirement for Scenario 2 is £74,000 greater than for Scenario 1. This is made up of increased value of inventory and receivables, less increased payables. This is in spite of only a modest increase in working capital cycle days. Since there is no change in total net assets under each scenario, this extra working capital will probably come from cash reserves or overdraft. This will put a strain on the resources.

(d) Recommendation, with reasons, as to which course of action to take

Based purely on the forecast information, Scenario 1 is the best option creating the largest return, and without the negative impact on working capital. However, the sales volume is lower than Scenario 2, and so the market share is lower. It may be worth considering what the demand level would be if the selling price were set somewhere between £12 and £18 per unit, and modelling that scenario before making a final decision.

LIMITATIONS OF RATIO ANALYSIS

In the introduction to this section, it was emphasised that one set of ratios alone does not give very useful information. Ratios for other time periods or other organisations are useful for comparison, as are target ratios.

The principle of **comparing like with like** should be applied in ratio analysis, but this is not always straightforward. Some of the ratios can be defined in different ways, so the particular definition used should be made clear. Even so, detailed information may not be given, for example to split sales into cash sales and credit sales.

When using the **published accounts of companies**, it is not possible to guarantee that we are comparing like with like, as different policies (including those regarding depreciation, inventory valuation and goodwill, for example) will affect the results.

For any organisation, there is also the possibility that the statement of financial position does not show a typical position, intentionally or otherwise. A single transaction the next day may make it look quite different. The statement of financial position reflects the conditions for a particular season of the year and in trades with seasonal variations, this can make a big difference to the ratios.

Discussion of a particular case may include looking for ways in which the ratios could have been distorted. For example, high levels of spending on research, training or marketing may reduce profits in one period, but bring much greater benefits in a later period. The reverse is also true: cutting these costs may improve the profit ratios in the short term, but in the long term sales and profits would suffer.

When making comparisons over different time periods, the ratios are based on historical costs as shown in the accounts. If there has been inflation during the time periods, a better comparison can be made by making adjustments for this before calculating the ratios.

Before drawing firm conclusions from ratio analysis, these limitations should be borne in mind. However, the analysis can give useful information, particularly in showing how items in the financial statements relate to each other and in identifying trends.

CALCULATING ACCOUNTS DATA FROM RATIOS

You may be tested on your understanding of ratios by being given various ratios and then asked to calculate figures from the financial statements.

worked example

For example, a task could say that a business has a gross profit of £80,000, a gross profit margin of 50% and an operating profit margin of 20%, you could then be asked to calculate sales revenue and the operating profit.

Taking a structured approach in these questions should enable the figures to be calculated. In this example the gross profit is 50% of sales revenue so the sales revenue must be £80,000 x 100/50 = £160,000. The operating profit is 20% of this: £160,000 x 20% = £32,000.

More complex examples can involve using receivables, payables and inventory days to calculate sales, purchases or cost of sales. The point to remember here is that the figures from the profit and loss account will represent 365 days of trading so you simply need to translate your days of sales (or costs) into a year of sales (or costs) to be able to move on.

worked example

To give an example, suppose that you are told that a firm holds 60 days of inventory valued at £75,000 and has a gross profit margin of 40%. Cost of sales will be 365 days of inventory so to calculate this we multiply £75,000 by 365/60 and get £456,250.

As the gross profit margin is 40%, cost of sales must be 60% of sales, so sales are: £456,250 x 100/60 = £760,417 (rounded). The gross profit is 40% of this which is £304,167 (rounded).

The figures would therefore appear as follows:

	£	
Sales	760,417	
Cost of Sales	456,250	(£760,417 x 60%)
Gross Profit	304,167	(£760,417 x 40%)

It's worth checking at this point that the percentages work and that the subtraction in the accounts is correct!

CONTROL RATIOS: EFFICIENCY, CAPACITY AND ACTIVITY

efficiency ratio

As we discussed earlier, efficiency takes the inputs of a process and assesses how economically they are used to produce the output.

One performance indicator to measure this is the Labour Efficiency Variance studied in Chapter 2. The variance shows the difference between the standard hours for actual production and the actual hours, valued at the standard labour rate. The same two figures in hours can be compared in percentage terms instead of calculating the difference. This gives the efficiency ratio:

efficiency ratio $=$ $\dfrac{standard\ hours\ for\ actual\ production}{actual\ hours\ worked}$ $\times\ 100\%$

If the ratio is exactly 100%, the employees have worked at the standard level of efficiency. If it is less than 100%, they have worked more slowly – this would result in an adverse variance. If it is more than 100%, they have worked more quickly than the standard – corresponding to a favourable variance.

Another ratio which links to efficiency is the idle time ratio. This measures the percentage of total hours that are lost due to idle time. It measures the same idle time that we saw reflected in the idle time variance. The formula is:

idle time ratio $=$ $\dfrac{idle\ hours}{total\ hours}$ $\times\ 100\%$

activity ratio and production volume ratio

The standard hours for actual production can also be compared with the original plan for the period, the budgeted hours. This is an indicator of how actual output compares with the budgeted output and is known as the **activity ratio**. The formula is:

$\dfrac{standard\ hours\ for\ actual\ production}{budgeted\ hours}$ $\times\ 100\%$

This can alternatively be expressed in terms of volume of output and is known as the **production volume ratio**:

$\dfrac{actual\ output}{budgeted\ output}$ $\times\ 100\%$

capacity ratio

This control ratio compares the actual 'capacity' which has been used with the planned amount.

Capacity (here being measured in terms of direct labour hours) is the amount of available resources being used. Full capacity would mean that all possible resources were being used. Budgeted capacity (probably less than full capacity) would be set in line with planned levels of production and sales.

The capacity ratio shows what proportion of the planned resources have actually been used. This is particularly important when there are significant fixed costs which have to be paid to make these resources available.

capacity ratio $=$ $\dfrac{actual\ hours\ worked}{budgeted\ hours}$ $\times\ 100\%$

EAC LTD: CONTROL RATIOS

EAC Ltd produces a single product, for which the standard direct labour time is 2 hours per unit. For a given period, EAC Ltd budgeted for a total of 68,000 hours. The actual results for the period showed that 34,600 units were produced and the actual total direct labour hours worked were 71,000 hours.

required

Calculate the standard hours for the actual production in this case and hence calculate the three control ratios.

solution

The standard hours for the actual production of 34,600 units would be:

34,600 x 2 = 69,200 hours.

Therefore, using the above formulas, the control ratios would be:

$$\text{Efficiency Ratio} = \frac{69,200}{71,000} \times 100\% = 97.5\%$$

$$\text{Activity Ratio} = \frac{69,200}{68,000} \times 100\% = 101.8\%$$

$$\text{Capacity Ratio} = \frac{71,000}{68,000} \times 100\% = 104.4\%$$

The control ratios for EAC Ltd, above, show that both the level of activity (output) and the resources used were more than planned in the budget, but the workforce were slightly less efficient than the standard. As in variance analysis, the reasons for the level of efficiency could be investigated and they may include external factors such as problems with supply of materials, not necessarily the fault of the employees.

NON-FINANCIAL INDICATORS

A **non-financial indicator** is a measurement which is expressed in numbers, but not in money terms, the possible units being very varied: for example hours, transactions, units of product, customers and so on.

Non-financial indicators can take many forms, because they can be designed to measure aspects of any kind of work. They are useful in both manufacturing and service industries and can be applied in both profit-making and non-profit making organisations. They are particularly useful for measuring quality, which will be discussed in Chapter 7.

Some examples of possible non-financial indicators are given below. Several indicators may be used together for the same activity. You may have other examples from the workplace.

In assessments, you may be asked to suggest how a particular aspect of the work of an organisation could be assessed.

Activity or aspect to be measured	Non-financial indicator
Automated production	Hours of machine down time
Absenteeism	Employee-days absence
Telephone helpline	Average time in seconds taken to answer calls
Quality of service	Number of customer complaints
Input of data to computer	Number of errors per 1000 inputs
Customer satisfaction	Number of repeat orders
Quality of output	Number of units rejected per 1000

QUALITATIVE (NON-NUMERICAL) MEASURES

Some aspects of work are very difficult to measure in terms of numbers, for example: motivation of others, team working, helpfulness to customers.

When numerical indicators are not suitable, **opinions** and **attitudes** have to be recorded, perhaps by customer surveys. Surveys often ask customers to give ratings, say on a scale of 1 to 5, but these are only an aid to obtaining an overall view, not an accurate measurement.

Appraisal schemes within an organisation may involve collecting feedback from colleagues. For example, those present at a meeting may be asked their opinion as to the how well the person chairing the meeting carried out that task. Work relationships can affect the judgements given (and vice versa), so the usefulness of this feedback may be limited.

PERFORMANCE MEASUREMENT IN SERVICE ORGANISATIONS

It is more difficult to measure the performance of a service organisation or department than one which produces tangible goods. Services cannot be checked before being provided in the same way as products can be inspected for faults.

The usual financial measures and ratios can be used for profit-making service organisations. (Non-profit-making organisations are considered in the next section of this chapter.)

Non-financial and qualitative measures, discussed earlier in this chapter, are often applicable to services. For example:

- Average waiting times for customers can be calculated and compared to a target.

- The number of customer complaints indicates the level of customer satisfaction.

The appropriate performance indicators to use depend on the type of service being provided and what its aims must be. From the organisation's point of view, financial indicators are likely to be important. If you then consider what features of the service would be important to customers, you can see which items of data are available to measure those features.

The **financial** and **customer** aspects or perspectives discussed in this section form part of the 'Balanced Scorecard', which can be applied to any kind of profit-making organisation, which is discussed later in this chapter.

PERFORMANCE MEASUREMENT IN NON-PROFIT MAKING ORGANISATIONS

Non-profit making organisations include charities and clubs as well as some public sector organisations. Without the objective of profit, there may be no single aim by which 'success' can be measured.

Performance indicators need to be designed to measure how well the organisation has achieved its aims. Much of the section on service organisations above applies to non-profit making organisations, many of which do provide services. Instead of profit, *value for money* is the main financial criterion. This is usually defined as:

- **economy**: controlling expenditure on costs
- **efficiency**: relating 'outputs' to inputs, meaning that obtaining more from the money spent shows greater efficiency
- **effectiveness**: relating 'outputs' to the aims of the organisation, so that achieving more of what it sets out to do shows greater effectiveness

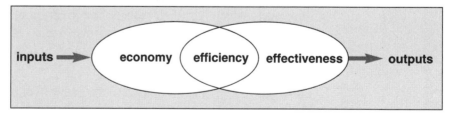

Economy can be measured in the same way as costs in businesses, by comparing with budgets and calculating variances for example.

A possible indicator for **efficiency** is the cost per unit, where units of output can be defined. For example, in a nursing home, the cost of a resident day could be calculated.

Effectiveness may be measured by comparison with targets or with other similar organisations.

Some aspects of non-profit-making activities can only be assessed by qualitative measures: opinions and judgements of experts, users or those who provide the funding. Representatives of government agencies or funding bodies may carry out observations or inspections, as in schools for example.

The general principles of performance measurement apply to these organisations as well as to businesses:

■ comparability – comparing like with like

■ comparison with standards, budgets or targets

■ comparison with similar organisations

■ comparison over time, to look for trends

ETHICAL CONSIDERATIONS

The choice of performance indicator to use in a particular situation can affect the way people approach their work. It is important to make sure that the measurement of performance motivates employees to work efficiently and in the best interests of the organisation as a whole.

If the particular measure being used can be manipulated by workers, so that their performance looks good, it may encourage behaviour that is not in fact beneficial to the organisation as a whole. We learned in our study of standard costing that responsibility for variances may be allocated to individual managers, and that this may cause unhelpful behaviour.

If people take action to improve particular measures of performance in the short term, their behaviour may have adverse effects for the organisation later on. For example, profits may be improved by cutting down on training costs. Eventually, the lack of training may result in inefficiencies or mistakes, which will then reduce the profits. Looking at ways in which a performance indicator can be manipulated may be part of its evaluation, because the results are not useful or meaningful if they can easily be changed by such behaviour.

If targets are set in terms of a particular measure of performance, they should be:

■ achievable, but encouraging improvement

■ within the area of responsibility of the person being measured

■ comparing like with like

■ seen to be fair and meaningful

A system for assessing people's work is more likely to motivate them as part of the organisation 'team' if they can see that it is fair and that they can attain the required level by being efficient. The result should be to encourage behaviour that benefits the organisation as a whole.

Sometimes using target indicators can encourage unethical behaviour. This would include manipulation of performance indicators to support an individual manager's apparent performance as already discussed. Unethical behaviour can also impact on those outside the organisation.

For example suppose a manager who is responsible for paying suppliers was assessed according to how high the 'payables days' indicator was. There would be a great temptation to delay payments, particularly to those suppliers who had little commercial leverage over the organisation. As well as being unethical, this practice could lead to difficulties negotiating new supplies contracts, and could even result in rumours circulating in the industry that the organisation was unable to make payments.

Unethical practices could arise from judging a credit control manager purely on the basis of reducing 'receivables days'. This could result in unacceptably aggressive tactics to chase money owed, which could also result in losing customers.

Great care must therefore be taken when using performance indicators as targets for individual managers that it does not encourage unethical behaviour.

THE BALANCED SCORECARD

The Balanced Scorecard is a way of viewing the performance of a profit-making organisation from four **perspectives**, relating to profits, customers, quality and development, as follows:

- **the financial perspective** is concerned with satisfying the shareholders or owners of a business and relates to profits. Suitable indicators include ROCE and profit margin

- **the customer perspective** is concerned with customer satisfaction and loyalty. It relates to customers' views of the business and suitable indicators include delivery times and numbers or amounts of orders from previous customers

- **the internal perspective** is concerned with technical excellence and consumer needs, which relate to quality. Suitable indicators are those which assess quality and value

- **the innovation and learning perspective** is concerned with the need for continual improvement of existing products and the ability to develop new products to meet customers' changing needs, so it is related to development. Suitable indicators may include the percentage of turnover attributable to new products or a measure of research and development expenditure

In a given case, you may be asked to identify ways of measuring these four perspectives. You will need to look for data available in the Case Study which you can connect with each aspect of the business and be prepared to develop new performance indicators. The next Case Study illustrates this type of task. Note particularly how the 'average delay in fulfilling orders' is calculated. The method is very similar to that used for the average age of inventory or receivables. You need to be able to apply general principles like this in different situations.

Sometimes, a task is set the other way round: you are asked to say which perspective is being measured by a given indicator. It is important to read the tasks carefully and make sure you answer the right question!

Case Study

HSB LTD: THE BALANCED SCORECARD

You are employed by HSB Ltd, a company with several subsidiaries and you have been asked to apply the balanced scorecard to monitor the performance of the subsidiaries. The following information relates to Subsidiary H for the period ended 31 December 20-3. You also have available the financial accounts of Subsidiary H for the same year. Extracts are given here.

	£000s
Gross sales	3,500
Less: returns	70
Sales	3,430
Operating profit	825
Analysis of sales by products:	
Sales of new products	1,350
Sales of existing products	2,080
Sales as above	3,430
Analysis of sales by customers:	
Sales to new customers	650
Sales to existing customers	2,780
Sales as above	3,430
Value of orders placed for delivery during the year	4,250

r e q u i r e d

Identify and calculate, from the available information, one performance indicator which you could use in monitoring each of the four perspectives in the balanced scorecard.

solution

Monitoring the balanced scorecard for subsidiary H for the year ended 31 December 20-3:

- The *financial* perspective could be measured by operating profit margin, which is (825 ÷ 3,430) x 100% = 24%.

- The *customer* perspective could be measured by repeat custom as a percentage of sales, which is (2,780 ÷ 3,430) x 100% = 81%.

- An alternative would be the average delay in fulfilling orders. The unfulfilled orders amount to £4,250,000 − £3,430,000 = £820,000 and this could be used as a fraction of turnover to calculate (820 ÷ 3,430) x 365 days, giving 87 days as the average delay.

- The *internal* perspective could be measured by the percentage of sales returns, which is (70 ÷ 3,500) x 100% = 2%.

- The *innovation and learning* perspective could be measured by the percentage of sales derived from new products, which is (1,350 ÷ 3,430) x 100% = 39%.

Chapter Summary

- ■ Data which is collected for performance measurement may be quantitative (numerical) data in terms of money or other units, or it may be qualitative data consisting of opinions or attitudes. A combination of quantitative and qualitative data can be used.

- ■ Comparisons are more useful than single sets of data, provided the data being compared has been prepared on a consistent basis, to compare like with like. Comparison may be made with standards, budgets or targets; with other periods of time; with other similar organisations, and to assess the viability of plans.

- ■ The methods and techniques used for performance measurement include Ratio Analysis – ie the calculation of percentages and ratios from the financial accounts.

- ■ Control ratios are based on direct labour hours and measure efficiency, capacity and activity in percentage terms.

- ■ Non-financial and qualitative measures of performance are useful for service organisations, and should be designed to measure the aspects of the service which are important to customers.

- ■ Financial performance measurement for non-profit making organisations is based on value for money, which is achieved through economy, efficiency and effectiveness.

■ Suitable performance indicators should be chosen to provide useful information and to motivate employees to improve efficiency. The choice of indicator should not encourage behaviour that is aimed at manipulating the figures, is not ethical and is not of benefit to the organisation.

■ The 'balanced scorecard' looks at an organisation from the financial, customer, internal and innovation and learning perspectives and identifies ways of measuring each of these aspects of its performance.

Key Terms

performance indicator	an individual measurement used to evaluate the performance of an organisation or part of an organisation
productivity	the aspect of the performance of an organisation which could be measured by the level of output
efficiency	the aspect of the performance of an organisation which could be measured by relating the value of the output to the inputs
benchmarking	the setting of standards or targets for the activities of an organisation
financial indicator	a performance indicator measured in money terms
ratio analysis	the analysis of the financial accounts of an organisation by calculating ratios and percentages
gross profit margin (percentage)	$\dfrac{\text{Gross Profit} \times 100\%}{\text{Sales}}$
net profit margin	$\dfrac{\text{Net Profit} \times 100\%}{\text{Sales}}$
operating profit margin	$\dfrac{\text{Operating Profit} \times 100\%}{\text{Sales}}$

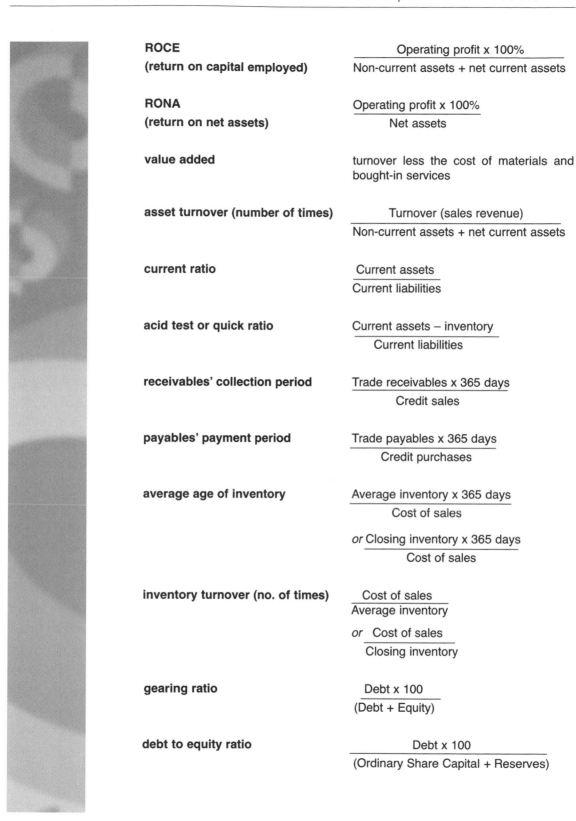

ROCE
(return on capital employed)

$$\frac{\text{Operating profit} \times 100\%}{\text{Non-current assets} + \text{net current assets}}$$

RONA
(return on net assets)

$$\frac{\text{Operating profit} \times 100\%}{\text{Net assets}}$$

value added

turnover less the cost of materials and bought-in services

asset turnover (number of times)

$$\frac{\text{Turnover (sales revenue)}}{\text{Non-current assets} + \text{net current assets}}$$

current ratio

$$\frac{\text{Current assets}}{\text{Current liabilities}}$$

acid test or quick ratio

$$\frac{\text{Current assets} - \text{inventory}}{\text{Current liabilities}}$$

receivables' collection period

$$\frac{\text{Trade receivables} \times 365 \text{ days}}{\text{Credit sales}}$$

payables' payment period

$$\frac{\text{Trade payables} \times 365 \text{ days}}{\text{Credit purchases}}$$

average age of inventory

$$\frac{\text{Average inventory} \times 365 \text{ days}}{\text{Cost of sales}}$$

$$or \frac{\text{Closing inventory} \times 365 \text{ days}}{\text{Cost of sales}}$$

inventory turnover (no. of times)

$$\frac{\text{Cost of sales}}{\text{Average inventory}}$$

$$or \frac{\text{Cost of sales}}{\text{Closing inventory}}$$

gearing ratio

$$\frac{\text{Debt} \times 100}{(\text{Debt} + \text{Equity})}$$

debt to equity ratio

$$\frac{\text{Debt} \times 100}{(\text{Ordinary Share Capital} + \text{Reserves})}$$

efficiency ratio

$$\frac{\text{standard hours for actual output}}{\text{actual hours worked}} \times 100\%$$

**activity
(or production volume) ratio**

$$\frac{\text{standard hours for actual output}}{\text{budgeted hours}} \times 100\%$$

capacity ratio

$$\frac{\text{actual hours worked}}{\text{budgeted hours}} \times 100\%$$

balanced scorecard

the concept of performance measurement from the point of view of four perspectives: financial, customer, internal and innovation and learning

Activities

5.1 The following income statements relate to a small retail shop selling stationery and gifts:

Toni Jones Statement of Profit or Loss for the year ended:

	31 May 20-3		31 May 20-2	
	£000s	*£000s*	*£000s*	*£000s*
Sales		525		450
Less: Cost of Sales				
Opening inventory	50		30	
Purchases	408		335	
Less: Closing Inventory	(80)	378	(50)	315
Gross Profit		147		135
Less: Expenses:				
Administration	25		24	
Selling	38	63	30	54
Net Profit		84		81

Required:

For Toni Jones for the given years, calculate:

(a) Gross Profit percentage.

(b) Net Profit percentage.

(c) Each expense as a percentage of Sales.

Comment briefly on the original figures and on the percentages calculated.

5.2 Using the following information, complete the performance indicators shown in the table below. Calculate percentages and values to two decimal places and days to the nearest day.

Sales volume (units)	84,000
	£
Sales	462,000
Cost of production	
Direct (Raw) Materials	193,200
Direct Labour	121,800
Fixed Production overheads	92,400
Total cost of sales	407,400
Gross profit	54,600
Selling and distribution costs	14,000
Administration costs	23,000
Operating profit	17,600
Other data:	
Total Net Assets	150,000
Inventory	21,200
Receivables	75,000
Payables (re raw materials)	33,000

Selling price per unit £	
Gross profit margin	
Operating profit margin	
Return on net assets	
Direct materials cost per unit £	
Direct labour cost per unit £	
Fixed production cost per unit £	
Full production cost per unit £	
Inventory days	
Receivables days	
Payables days	
Working capital cycle days	

5.3 Scinso Soft Ltd has developed a product that softens skin and is claimed to produce the appearance of a youthful complexion. The product competes with many other products in the marketplace. The market leader is Laurelle plc, which sells to over 60% of the market. You have been given the following information about Scinso Soft Ltd and Laurelle plc for the year ended 31 May 20-0.

Statements of Profit or Loss		Scinso Soft Ltd	Laurelle plc
		£000	£000
Sales revenue		4,500	22,000
Cost of Production:			
Direct materials		1,200	3,300
Direct labour		750	2,200
Fixed production overheads		600	3,000
Total cost of sales		2,550	8,500
Gross profit		**1,950**	**13,500**
Selling and distribution costs		500	1,000
Administration costs		375	750
Advertising costs		250	10,000
Net profit		**825**	**1,750**
Other Information		**Scinso Soft Ltd**	**Laurelle plc**
Number of units sold	Units	600	2,200
	000		
Net assets	£000	5,000	8,500

Calculate the performance indicators for Scinso Soft Ltd and Laurelle plc and complete the following table (give answers to two decimal places):

	Scinso Soft Ltd	Laurelle plc
Selling price per unit		
Material cost per unit		
Labour cost per unit		
Fixed production overheads per unit		
Gross profit margin		
Net profit margin		
Advertising cost as % of turnover		
Return on net assets		

5.4 Pacer is a company that manufactures deodorant that it sells through discount retailers. The market leader is Greenapple whose deodorant is sold through major supermarkets. Greenapple is able to take advantage of its market share to maintain its selling price, and invests heavily in advertising and promotion. The companies have the following data for the last financial period.

	Pacer	Greenapple
Sales volume (units)	23,500,000	280,000,000
	£000	£000
Sales Revenue	18,800	616,000
Cost of Sales:		
Direct materials	4,935	67,200
Direct labour	7,050	78,400
Fixed overhead	1,880	16,800
Gross Profit	4,935	453,600
Distribution Costs	1,410	19,600
Administration Costs	1,460	94,600
Marketing Costs	705	274,300
Operating Profit	1,360	65,100
Net Assets	16,850	812,000

Required:

- Complete the following table to show performance ratios for both companies, rounded to two decimal places

	Pacer	Greenapple
Sales price per unit £		
Direct materials per unit £		
Direct labour per unit £		
Fixed overhead per unit £		
Gross Profit %		
Distribution Costs as % of Sales		
Administration Costs as % of Sales		
Marketing Costs as % of Sales		
Operating Profit %		
Return on Net Assets %		

- Draft a report that explains the differences in the companies' strategies and the impact this has on their performance.

5.5 A business with receivables of £180,000 and receivables collection period of 60 days operates with a gross profit margin of 20% and an operating profit margin of 8%. Fixed production overheads constitute 30% of the cost of sales. The return on net assets is 10%.

Complete the following table to show the operating statement and total net assets.

	£
Sales	
Variable production costs	
Fixed production overheads	
Cost of sales	
Gross profit	
Sales and administration costs	
Operating profit	
Total net assets	

5.6 Wessit Housing Association is considering offering a contract for double-glazing its properties to one of two suppliers, Staylite Ltd and Temeglass Ltd. The following information has been extracted from the most recent annual report and accounts of the two companies.

	Staylite Ltd	Temeglass Ltd
	£000s	*£000s*
Sales	7,660	9,500
Gross Profit	3,467	4,522
Operating Profit	403	627
Interest charges	45	2
Non-current Assets (net book value)	600	800
Current assets	198	307
Inventory included in current assets	82	120
Current liabilities	182	156
Debentures	450	0
Share capital and reserves	166	951
Average number of employees	16	18

Required:

(a)   Calculate the following ratios for each of the two companies:
- gross profit margin
- operating profit margin
- return on capital employed
- current ratio
- quick ratio
- asset turnover
- sales per employee
- operating profit per employee

(b)   Using the given information and the ratios you have calculated, comment on the profitability and financial position of the two suppliers.

(c)   State which of the performance indicators you have calculated may be used to indicate how efficient the companies are.

(d)   State which of the performance indicators you have calculated may be used to indicate the productivity of the companies.

(e)   Explain the limitations of the above analysis, in particular from the point of view of Wessit Housing Association's decision about the contract.

(f)   Suggest one further indicator which Wessit Housing Association should seek to obtain (not necessarily from the report and accounts) before making this decision.

5.7   A company produces a single product which has a standard labour time of 0.5 hours per unit. During period 4, budgeted output was 80,000 units, actual output was 84,500 units and 41,800 hours were worked. Complete the following table to show the control ratios rounded to two decimal places.

Activity ratio %	
Efficiency ratio %	
Capacity ratio %	

5.8   CD Ltd makes a product which takes 6 hours per unit of direct labour time. In a given period it is planned (budgeted) that 14,700 direct labour hours will be worked.

During the period, the actual result is that 2,400 units of the product are made and the direct labour hours worked are 15,000 hours.

Calculate the Efficiency Ratio, the Capacity Ratio and the Activity Ratio for this period.

5.9 Use ticks to complete the following table to show which perspective of the balanced scorecard is being measured by each performance indicator.

	Financial perspective	Customer perspective	Internal perspective	Innovation and learning perspective
Average delivery time				
Gross profit margin				
% sales to existing customers				
Return on capital employed				
% of rejects				
Number of new products				
Research and development expenditure as % sales				

5.10 The following information is given for Exe Ltd for the year 20-3.

Turnover	£972,000
Output (product units)	67,500
Number of employees	54
Cost of materials used	£216,000
Total cost of bought-in services	£324,000
Total cost of inputs	£540,000

Required:

Calculate for Exe Ltd for the year 20-3:

(a) Total value added.

(b) Value added per employee.

(c) Material cost per unit.

(d) Total cost of inputs per unit.

6 Decision making techniques

this chapter covers...

We will start this chapter by examining which costs are relevant for decision making and how this fits in with marginal costing. We will illustrate this by looking at minimum pricing for special orders, and using incremental costs to evaluate the impact of innovations.

The next specific situation that we will examine concerns the 'make or buy' decision. Here we will use our knowledge of marginal costing to develop our plans, and also consider some of the other important non-financial issues.

We then consider limiting factor decisions and will learn how to deal with:

■ *more than one constraint for a single product, and*

■ *product choice when there is a limiting factor*

In the next section we examine the marginal costing tools of contribution, break-even point and margin of safety. We will also see how an understanding of risk can be developed by examining the cost structure and using these indicators.

Next we will see how closure of a business segment can be analysed. This has some issues in common with the 'make or buy' decisions examined earlier.

Automation is then considered and the techniques that are applicable to this situation are illustrated. These are:

■ *redrafting an income statement*

■ *using discounted cash flow*

Finally we will review some of the ethical implications that apply to decision making and how corporate social responsibility should be considered.

RELEVANT COSTS FOR DECISION MAKING

In this chapter we are going to examine various techniques and situations related to decision making. When looking at costs and benefits for any kind of decision making the key is to only use relevant costs (and sometimes income) in the calculations.

What is relevant will depend on the decision that is being considered, but will always be simply the costs or income that will change depending on the outcome of the decision. There is no point in thinking about costs that will be the same no matter what decision is made. For example, if a machine replacement is being considered, but both the new and the existing machines have the same maintenance costs, then these maintenance costs are not relevant to the decision.

Since relevant costs will always be those that can be affected by the decision, they must always be costs that can occur in the future. Costs that have already been incurred cannot be changed whatever is decided, and so should be ignored. These past costs that are not relevant are sometimes known as 'sunk costs'.

We must also be careful not to be swayed by notional costs, like depreciation, that are based on past activities. We are really only interested in income and costs that are based on future flows of cash.

One way to think of relevant costs is to use the idea of them being 'future incremental cash flows'. Let's look at that phrase in more detail.

Future	**not past** transactions that cannot be changed
Incremental	the **extra** cost or income that derives directly from the decision being considered
Cash flows	movements of **real money**, not notional book entries

Suppose a company has a machine that is no longer in day to day use, but is only used for special orders that occur about once a year. A decision is being made about whether to keep the machine, or to sell it and hire in a machine to deal with the special orders when necessary. Here the only **relevant** figures are:

■ the amount that the machine could be sold for, and

■ the cost of hiring a machine to deal with the special orders.

Notice that both these figures pass our test of being 'future incremental cash flows'.

The following amounts are irrelevant and can be ignored for the purposes of the decision:

- original cost of the machine, since it is a sunk cost
- the depreciation being changed on the machine and it's written down value
- any costs that do not change whichever machine is used

An idea that fits neatly within this concept is opportunity cost. This is the income avoided by the course of action taken, and is a relevant cost. This means that the relevant cost that should be applied when considering using a resource is the income that could otherwise be generated from that resource. If the resource could be used in various alternative ways then the opportunity cost would be the highest amount of income that it could generate – because logically that is the best use.

For example, suppose a company has a material in stock that could be used for the project that we are trying to evaluate. There are no plans to use the material for anything else. The material originally cost £1,000, but could be returned to the supplier in exchange for £500. Alternatively, it could be sold to another organisation for £700.

In this situation, the relevant cost of using the material in the project would be £700, since this is the highest income that we would be avoiding by using the material. We would not logically choose to return it to the supplier for less than we could sell it for. The figure of £1,000 is not relevant since it is sunk cost.

The same idea could be applied to labour. If a project that is being evaluated involves taking labour away from an existing job, then the contribution that is being lost will form an opportunity cost that is part of the relevant cost.

The general concept of relevant costs fits in with the application of marginal costing, and can be applied to various situations. These will be illustrated in the rest of this chapter.

special order pricing

One type of situation that uses the concept of relevant costs together with marginal costing is the pricing of special orders. These may be offers made to purchase output that are in addition to normal sales. The price offered may be below the normal selling price, and even below the absorbed 'full' cost of the product. In these situations it is important to be able to calculate the minimum price that can be applied without incurring a loss on the transaction.

These calculations can involve the application of relevant costing to several elements of cost, as the following Case Study will illustrate.

Case Study

EXTRAS LIMITED: MINIMUM PRICING

Extras Limited manufactures vinyl flooring and sells it to various wholesalers and retail outlets. The company is able to budget its level of output quite accurately and uses absorption costing for planning and control.

Each roll of flooring normally sells for £200, and has the following cost data:

		£
Direct materials	40 kgs x £1.30	52.00
Direct labour	4 hours x £12.00	48.00
Fixed overheads	4 hours x £5.00	20.00
Total absorbed cost		120.00

Expo, a company that is not a current customer wishes to purchase 100 rolls of a special flooring to use in an exhibition. The company is unwilling to pay more than £115 per roll.

The following additional information is available:

Extras Limited is already manufacturing and selling at the budgeted level.

The contract from Expo would involve using different materials than is used in the current range. There is sufficient of this material in the inventory of Extras Limited to fulfil this contract, with the following details.

Extras Limited has no current use for this material. It originally cost £1.50 per kilo. It could be returned to the supplier, who would pay £0.90 per kilo.

Direct labour is a variable cost. The contract would involve paying overtime rate of £18.00 per hour to the direct labour force.

required

Calculate the minimum cost per roll that Extras Limited would incur if they accepted this contract, and recommend whether the contract should be undertaken at the price offered.

solution

The following shows the relevant costs for one roll of the special contract flooring, with explanations.

		£
Direct materials	40 kilos x £0.90	36.00
Direct labour	4 hours x £18.00	72.00
		108.00

Since there is no alternative use for the direct materials, it is costed at £0.90 per kilo as this is the alternative amount that it could be sold for (the opportunity cost).

The direct labour force would need to be paid at overtime rate, so this is used.

The fixed overheads are already covered by the normal output level, so there are no additional costs that would be incurred.

Note that all the relevant costs are future incremental cash flows.

The contract would therefore be profitable at £115 per roll.

calculating the impact of innovations

Decisions sometimes have to be made about changes that will have lasting effects. These decisions will often relate to changes to products or to improved ways of working. If we need to compare profitability under the current situation and the proposed innovation then there is often no need to recalculate the whole expected statement of profit or loss. We can simply just look at the aspects that change to be able to calculate the net change to profit based on the proposals. In other words we are examining just the incremental changes and their net effect.

Since we are calculating changes to accounting profit, it is worth noting that we will incorporate any changes to depreciation charges where appropriate.

The following Case Study will illustrate the type of situation where this approach can be used.

Case Study

INCREMENTAL LIMITED: MAKING COMPARISONS

The company manufactures shoe cleaning polish that is currently sold in tins. It is considering changing to a modified product that will be sold in tubes. The following information is available.

- Current sales volume is 4.0 million units and this is not expected to change.
- Current fixed production costs are £0.85 million per year.
- Current labour cost per unit is £0.15, which is completely variable.
- Current material cost per unit is £0.11, which is completely variable.
- Current selling price is £1.00 per unit.

The revised product would have variable material costs £0.02 higher than the current product.

The revised product would require less labour, and so the variable labour cost would reduce by £0.015 per unit.

The fixed costs per year would increase by £0.13 million.

Selling price would increase by £0.05 per unit.

required

Complete the following table to calculate the changes in revenue and costs if the new product were to be produced.

	Units	Per Unit £	Total £
Additional revenue			
Increased material cost			
Reduced labour cost			
Increase fixed costs			
Net increase / (reduction) in profit			

solution

	Units	Per Unit £	Total £
Additional revenue	4,000,000	0.05	200,000
Increased material cost	4,000,000	0.02	(80,000)
Reduced labour cost	4,000,000	0.015	60,000
Increase fixed costs			(130,000)
Net increase / (reduction) in profit			50,000

MAKE OR BUY DECISIONS

One of the situations where decisions need to be made concerns the possible outsourcing of production. This means having products made for you by an outside organisation instead of making them in-house.

If production was outsourced savings would normally be made of various manufacturing costs, but of course the cost of buying in a ready made product would be much greater than simply buying raw material. Great care must be taken to calculate which costs would be saved and which would remain.

variable costs

The general rule would be that any variable costs relating to the production that would not be taking place in-house would be saved, although any variable non-production costs (for example selling costs) would remain.

fixed costs

It is possible that some fixed costs may also be saved if they relate entirely to the production of the products to be made elsewhere. However fixed production costs that relate to several products, some of which continue to be made on site would not be saved in the short term. This is because if one product was no longer made on site these shared fixed costs would not change in total and would then need to be covered by the existing products.

other issues to consider

If a decision is to be made about outsourcing then various other commercial issues will need to be considered. These include:

- price – the agreed price must be guaranteed for an acceptable period of time, with any future increases within agreed limits
- quality – there needs to be sufficient reassurance that quality will be maintained when the production is in the control of another organisation

- supply – the manufacturing company must be able to offer guaranteed continuity of supply and timely deliveries
- commercial sensitivity – some products may be made to a 'secret' formula, or companies may wish to protect its brand by implying that its products are not made by anyone else

Once a decision has been made to cease manufacture of a product in-house it may be difficult to reverse in the future, especially if skilled staff and / or specialised equipment are required.

TOUCAN LIMITED: MAKE OR BUY DECISION

situation

Toucan Limited, a soft drink manufacturer, currently makes two products in its factory. The first product is 'Wings', a high energy drink, and the second is 'SSSh', a calming and relaxing drink.

The following budgeted operating statement relates to the next year, and assumes that both products will be manufactured in-house. It is based on making and selling 1,000,000 units of Wings, and 1,000,000 units of SSSh.

	£000	£000	£000
	Wings	**SSSh**	**Total**
Sales	750	500	1,250
Variable costs of production	200	230	430
Direct fixed costs of production	150	110	260
Shared fixed costs of production	150	100	250
Gross profit	250	60	310
Administration costs			80
Selling and Distribution costs			100
Operating profit			130

Consideration is being given to an option to buy in ready made SSSh units at £0.30 per unit. This would save both the variable costs of production and the direct fixed costs of production of that product. Shared fixed costs of production would remain the same in total. The number of units of SSSh sold would be unchanged.

If the decision were made to buy in the SSSh units, then the released manufacturing space could be used to increase the manufacture and sales of Wings to 1,200,000 units. The direct fixed costs of Wings production would be unchanged by this. Additional selling and distribution costs of £20,000 would be incurred by this increase in volume of Wings.

required

(a)   Calculate the following data for each product, based on the current plan to manufacture both products in-house:

- Selling price per unit
- Variable production cost per unit
- Gross profit per unit

(b)   Draft a revised budgeted Operating Statement, based on buying in ready made units of SSSh and increasing the volume of Wings units made and sold.

(c)   Recommend whether, on the basis of your figures, the decision should be made to buy in SSSh. Note any factors that may risk the future business remaining in line with the budget if your recommendation were to be followed.

solution

(a)

Selling price per unit

Wings	£750,000 / 1,000,000	= £0.75 per unit
SSSh	£500,000 / 1,000,000	= £0.50 per unit

Variable costs per unit

Wings	£200,000 / 1,000,000	= £0.20 per unit
SSSh	£230,000 / 1,000,000	= £0.23 per unit

Gross profit per unit

Wings	£250,000 / 1,000,000	= £0.25 per unit
SSSh	£60,000 / 1,000,000	= £0.06 per unit

(b)

Revised Operating Statement

	£000	£000	£000
	Wings	**SSSh**	**Total**
Sales	900	500	1,400
Variable costs of production / buy-in	240	300	540
Direct fixed costs of production	150		150
Shared fixed costs of production	250		250
Gross profit	260	200	460
Administration costs			80
Selling and Distribution costs			120
Operating profit			260

(c)

Recommendation

From the calculations, the total operating profit would increase from £130,000 to £260,000, and therefore the units of SSSh should be outsourced. However, factors that may make the business more risky in future include:

• whether sales of Wings can be increased by 20% as assumed

• whether the quality of SSSh can be assured

• whether the long term continuity of supply and price of SSSh can be assured

LIMITING FACTOR DECISIONS

You may need to deal with situations where production is reduced because of one or more 'limiting factors'. These could be, for example:

■ shortage of materials – a short or longer term issue that may restrict production; tactics for dealing with this situation range from changing supplier to using up inventories, or even changing the product that is being made

■ shortage of labour – this could restrict production, especially if the labour force is skilled; this could be tacked by overtime working, sub-contracting or outsourcing

■ limited production capacity – based on the size or maximum throughput of the organisation's manufacturing plant; while long term solutions include outsourcing or investing in property and equipment, short term issues can sometimes be resolved by shift working or manipulating inventory levels

Dealing with one factor alone is relatively straightforward if there is only one product, and a given scenario should contain clear information on the calculations required. The next two topics to examine are:

■ more than one constraint for a single product

■ product choice when there is one limiting factor

dealing with a combination of limitations

There may be occasions when there is a limit on not just one resource, but a combination of two or more. This can also form the basis for an examination task, so you should make sure that you are able to carry out the necessary calculations.

The technique that we are going to use is quite logical. We will calculate which one of the limitations on our output is going to limit production most severely, and concentrate on that problem.

For example if we originally planned to make 5,000 units, but find that we only have sufficient labour for 4,800 units, and enough materials for 4,000 units, then materials is the most pressing problem. It would not make sense to bring in temporary staff while there was still a material shortage. If we can solve the material shortage problem, only then should we turn our attention to the labour limitation. The issue that most constrains the output (as materials does in this example) is sometimes known as the binding constraint.

product choice when there are limited resources

The final situation that we must be able to deal with when there are limited resources concerns selecting the most profitable products. The situation arises when it was originally planned to make a number of different products, but a shortage of some resource now makes the plan impossible. The resource that is preventing normal output is known as the limiting factor. The most common limiting factors are either materials or labour.

What we must do in these circumstances is to calculate which of our products gives us the most profitable use of the limited resources. The technique relies on marginal costing techniques, and even if the data is provided in a different form, you must first identify the variable costs for each product.

The full procedure to be adopted is as follows:

- Using marginal costing, calculate the contribution per unit that each different product generates. This is carried out by subtracting the variable costs per unit from the selling price per unit. Fixed costs are ignored.

- Identify the resource that is in short supply (the limiting factor), and how much of that resource is needed to make one unit of each different product. Divide the contribution per unit already calculated by the quantity of limited resource required to make a unit. This gives the contribution per unit of limiting factor.

- Rank the possible products according to the value of the contribution per unit of limiting factor. Starting with the product ranked highest, schedule the production so that the expected demand is met for this product. Then schedule the next highest-ranking product, and so on until the limited resources are used up.

The procedure is based on the idea of opportunity cost. By concentrating on the products that have the highest contribution per unit of limited resource we are ensuring that the opportunity cost is minimised. This is because we are continually avoiding income from less profitable uses of that resource.

This technique will ensure that the quantities of different products manufactured will make the most profit from the limited resources. This does mean that some products will be made in reduced quantities, or not made at all. This will leave the demand from some customers unsatisfied, and the technique does not address any further implications of this policy. For example, a customer of a product that may have production suspended could also be a valuable customer of other products. Suspension of manufacture could result in the customer cancelling their orders and finding an alternative supplier for all their requirements.

The two Case Studies that follow show how the technique is used to schedule production so that the profit from using limited resources is maximised.

Case Study

THE THREE COUNTIES COMPANY: CONTRIBUTION PER UNIT OF LIMITING FACTOR

The Three Counties Company manufactures three products, each using the same material. The budget data for quarter 2 (the next quarter) is as follows. (There is no budgeted finished goods inventory at the beginning or end of any quarter.)

Product	Demand (units)	Costs per unit		
		Materials	Labour	Overheads
Gloucester	10,000	£25.00	£30.00	£60.00
Worcester	15,000	£50.00	£30.00	£60.00
Hereford	12,000	£15.00	£20.00	£40.00

The material costs £5.00 per kilo. Due to its short shelf life it must be used in the period that it is bought. The labour force is employed on a fixed contract that entitles them to a weekly pay of £350 for a guaranteed 40-hour week. The contract prohibits any overtime working. The overheads are a fixed cost.

The Gloucester sells for £125 per unit, the Worcester for £150 per unit, and the Hereford for £90 per unit.

It has just been discovered that there is a limit on the quantity of material that can be purchased in quarter 2 of 180,000 kilos.

required

Produce a revised production budget in units for quarter 2 that maximises profit.

solution

Since the labour force is paid a guaranteed week the cost of labour behaves as a fixed cost in this Case Study. Because overheads are also fixed, the only variable cost is material. This gives contributions per unit calculations as follows:

	Gloucester	Worcester	Hereford
	£	£	£
Selling Price per unit	125	150	90
less variable costs	25	50	15
contribution per unit	100	100	75

The quantity of material used for each product can be calculated by dividing the cost of material for a unit by the cost per kilo of £5.00. This quantity is then used to calculate the contribution per kilo of material (the limiting factor).

	Gloucester	Worcester	Hereford
Quantity of material per unit	5 kg	10 kg	3 kg
Contribution per kilo of material	£100 / 5	£100 / 10	£75 / 3
	= £20	= £10	= £25
Ranking	2	3	1

The ranking is derived directly from the contribution per kilo of material. Note that this ranking is different from both the contribution per unit and from the profit per unit if calculated under absorption costing. We now use the ranking to produce up to the demand level of first the Hereford, followed by the Gloucester, and finally the Worcester, using up the material until there is none left.

Product	Ranking	Production (units)	Material Required (kilos)		
Hereford	1	12,000	12,000 x 3 kg	=	36,000
Gloucester	2	10,000	10,000 x 5 kg	=	50,000
Worcester	3	9,400*	9,400 x 10 kg	=	94,000
					180,000

* The quantity of Worcester that can be produced is calculated as follows:
First, the remaining quantity of material is calculated in kilos:
(180,000 – 36,000 – 50,000 = 94,000)
Then the number of units of Worcester that can be produced with that material is calculated: (94,000 kg / 10 kg each unit = 9,400 units).

In the next Case Study we will see how labour can be a limiting factor, and how we will tackle the problem.

THE TWO CITIES COMPANY:
CONTRIBUTION PER UNIT OF LIMITING FACTOR

The Two Cities Company manufactures two products, each using the same material and the same direct labour force.

The original budget data for month 6 is as follows. There is no budgeted finished goods inventory at the beginning or end of any month.

Product	Demand	Costs per unit		
	(units)	Materials	Labour	Overheads
Bristol	2,000	£70.00	£18.00	£80.00
Cardiff	2,500	£60.00	£12.00	£40.00

The material costs £10.00 per kilo. The labour force is paid on an hourly basis at £6 per hour, and can be called in to work as appropriate. They have no minimum agreed working week, and will be sent home if there is no work available. Because of the nature of the contract there is no overtime premium payable. The overheads are a fixed cost.

The Bristol sells for £178 per unit, and the Cardiff for £150 per unit.

Following negotiations with the company management regarding conditions of employment, a number of the direct labour workers have decided to withdraw their labour. This leaves a reduced number of employees willing to work normally. It is estimated that the maximum number of working hours available from those working normally is 7,100 hours in month 6.

required
Produce a revised production budget in units for month 6 that maximises profit.

solution
Due to the conditions under which the labour force operates, the labour cost behaves as a variable cost. The material cost is also a variable cost, since it will always vary in proportion to production levels. Note that even though there is no shortage of material, its cost is still used to determine the contribution figures. This gives contributions per unit calculations as follows:

	Bristol	Cardiff
	£	£
Selling price per unit	178	150
less variable costs:		
materials	70	60
labour	18	12
contribution per unit	90	78

The amount of labour time used for each product can be calculated by dividing the cost of labour for a unit by the labour hourly rate of £6.00. The direct labour time is then used to calculate the contribution per hour of direct labour (the limiting factor).

	Bristol	Cardiff
Labour time per unit	3 hours	2 hours
Contribution per direct labour hour	£90 / 3	£78 / 2
	= £30	= £39
Ranking	2	1

We now use the ranking to produce up to the demand level of first the Cardiff, followed by the Bristol, using up the labour hours until there is none left.

Product	Ranking	Production (units)	Labour Hours Required		
Cardiff	1	2,500	2,500 x 2 hours	=	5,000
Bristol	2	700	700 x 3 hours	=	2,100
					7,100

BREAK-EVEN ANALYSIS AND MARGIN OF SAFETY

You will be familiar with the use of marginal costing to calculate contribution, break-even point and margin of safety from your earlier studies. All these are important techniques for scenario planning and decision making.

In this section we will first remind ourselves of the calculations of these indicators, and then go on to see how they can help us understand the risk that a business is exposed to.

contribution

The contribution is:

Sales Revenue – Variable Costs

It can be calculated per unit or per period of time. The contribution can also be calculated as a percentage of the sales revenue – this is sometimes known as the PV (profit-volume) ratio.

worked example

Suppose a company sells 3,000 units per month for £6 each. Variable costs are £3.50 per unit, and fixed costs are £4,000 per month.

The contribution per unit is £6 − £3.50 = £2.50 per unit.

The contribution per month is 3,000 x £2.50 = £7,500 per month.

This can also be calculated as:

Monthly Sales	3,000 x £6	£18,000
Monthly Variable Costs	3,000 x £3.50	£10,500
Monthly Contribution		£7,500

The contribution as a percentage of sales revenue will be the same whether calculated per unit or per month:

Per unit (£2.50 / £6) x 100	= 41.67%
Per month (£7,500 / £18,000) x 100	= 41.67%

break-even point

The break-even point is the number of units, or the value of sales that would result in zero profit. It is calculated as follows:

$$\text{Break-even point (in units)} \qquad \frac{\text{Fixed Costs}}{\text{Contribution per Unit}}$$

$$\text{Break-even point (in sales value)} \qquad \frac{\text{Fixed costs}}{\text{Contribution per £ of Sales}}$$

The contribution per £ of sales is the same as the contribution as a percentage of sales, but expressed as a decimal.

To return to our example; a company sells 3,000 units per month for £6 each. Variable costs are £3.50 per unit, and fixed costs are £4,000 per month.

Break-even point (in units)   £4,000 / £2.50   = 1,600 units
Break-even point (in sales value)   £4,000 / 0.4167   = £9,600 sales value

Note that these two break-even figures are completely compatible; 1,600 units sold for £6 each gives a sales value of £9,600.

target profit

In addition to determining the break-even point, the calculations can be modified to calculate the units or sales value needed to reach a predetermined target profit. This is done by simply adding the required profit to the fixed costs in the equation before dividing by the contribution (per unit or per £ of sales), as follows:

$$\text{Sales units to reach target profit} \; = \; \frac{\text{(Fixed Costs + Target Profit)}}{\text{Contribution per unit}}$$

$$\text{Sales value to reach target profit} \; = \; \frac{\text{(Fixed Costs + Target Profit)}}{\text{Contribution per £ of Sales}}$$

Using the figures from the example, if we had a target profit of £2,500, then the sales units to achieve this could be calculated as:

(£4,000 + £2,500) / £2.50 = 2,600 units

The calculation could alternatively be carried out using contribution per £ of sales to give an answer in sales value:

(£4,000 + £2,500) / 0.4167 = £15,600 sales value (after rounding adjustment)

margin of safety

This measures how far the expected sales level is from the break-even sales level. It is often calculated as a percentage of the current sales level – showing what percentage drop in expected sales would result in a zero profit.

This calculation would be:

$$\frac{(Budgeted\ Sales - Break\text{-}even\ Sales)}{Budgeted\ Sales} \quad x\ 100$$

It can be calculated using sales values or units, and the percentage results will be identical.

Using our example again; a company sells 3,000 units per month for £6 each. Variable costs are £3.50 per unit, and fixed costs are £4,000 per month.

Margin of safety (in units)

    (3,000 – 1,600) / 3,000 x 100   = 47%

Margin of safety (in sales value)

    (£18,000 – £9,600) / £18,000 x 100 = 47%

understanding risk

The margin of safety is a clear indicator of the risk that a business will fail to make a profit, by showing how far its sales would have to fall. In the above example the business has a low risk, since its sales would have to fall by 47% to reduce its profit to zero. The expected monthly profit in this example is:

Monthly contribution	£7,500
Less monthly fixed costs	£4,000
Monthly profit	£3,500

A business with different levels of fixed and variable costs might have a very different exposure to risk.

worked example

Suppose a business sells 3,000 units per month for £6 each. Variable costs are £1 per unit, and fixed costs are £11,500 per month.

Contribution would be £5 per unit x 3,000 units = £15,000 per month

Profit would be £15,000 contribution, less £11,500 fixed costs = £3,500 per month – the same as the last example.

Break-even point (in units) is £11,500 / £5   = 2,300 units

Margin of safety (in units) is (3,000 – 2,300) / 3,000 x 100   = 23%

This is much lower than the previous example, as this business has a riskier cost structure, with higher fixed costs and lower variable costs. The higher fixed costs need to be covered to break-even. If sales levels fall each unit lost will reduce profit by its contribution of £5, so that the profit is very sensitive to changes in sales level.

DELTA LIMITED:
USING MARGINAL COSTING

Delta Limited manufactures a skin cream and is considering how it can be more environmentally friendly. Scientists have developed a new product to replace Alpha's existing skin cream; the new product is a gel and takes up less than 10% of the volume and weight of the existing product.

You have been given the following information.

- current sales volume is 1.0 million units per annum and this is not expected to change
- current fixed production costs are £0.8 million
- current labour cost per unit is £1.25 which is completely variable
- current material cost per unit is £2 and is completely variable
- assume inventory levels are kept at zero
- variable material cost of the new product will be £0.50 less per unit than the current cream
- selling price will be increased from £7.50 to £8.50
- fixed selling and distribution costs will reduce from £800,000 to £300,000
- additional investment in assets will be £4 million which will be depreciated at £400,000 per annum
- all other costs will remain the same

required

(a) Calculate the total annual increase in profit by completing the table below.

	Units	Price/cost	Total *(£)*
Additional revenue			
Savings on materials			
Reduction in selling and distribution costs			
Additional depreciation			
Additional annual profit			

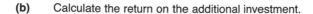

(b) Calculate the return on the additional investment.

(c) The marketing department is concerned that the volume of sales may not reach 1.0 million. The Finance Director has asked for the break even sales volume.

Calculate:

• the fixed costs

• the contribution per unit

• the break even sales volume in units

• the percentage margin of safety

solution

(a)

	Units	Price/cost	Total *(£)*
Additional revenue	1,000,000	£1	1,000,000
Savings on materials	1,000,000	£0.50	500,000
Reduction in selling and distribution costs			500,000
Additional depreciation			−400,000
Additional annual profit			1,600,000

(b) Return on investment:

£1,600,000 (as above) / £4,000,000 (investment)   x 100   = 40%

(c) Fixed costs:

	Production	£800,000
	Selling & Distribution	£300,000
	Depreciation	£400,000
	Total	£1,500,000

Contribution per unit:

	Selling Price	£8.50
Less	Labour	£1.25
Less	Materials	£1.50
	Contribution	£5.75

Break-even sales volume in units:

$$\frac{\text{Fixed Costs}}{\text{Contribution per unit}}$$

£1,500,000 / £5.75　= 260,870 units

Percentage margin of safety:

$$\frac{\text{(Budgeted Sales} - \text{Break-even Sales)} \times 100}{\text{Budgeted Sales}}$$

(1,000,000 – 260,870) / 1,000,000　x 100

= 73.91%

CLOSURE OF A BUSINESS SEGMENT

The closure of an uneconomic part of a business requires careful planning. Particular attention must be paid to the cost savings that will be made, especially if there are costs which are currently apportioned to more than one part of the business. It will often be the case that all or part of these costs will continue after closure, and therefore need to be set against the income of the remaining part of the business.

If closure is undertaken then redundancy costs of employees will need to be calculated and taken into consideration. As these are a 'one-off' cost, the exact way that these are accounted for in the management accounts would depend on the company policy.

It is possible that the operation could be relocated overseas to make it more economic. This could relate to a manufacturing activity, and the products could then be transported to be sold to the same or new markets. This could either be based on outsourcing to an established foreign business, or by setting up an in-house operation in the new location.

The outsourcing model would be similar to the 'make or buy' decision that was discussed earlier in this chapter. The added risk factor would be currency exchange movements that could rapidly change or eliminate any profits.

Setting up a new operation in a foreign country would be a complicated project, although the planning would follow the normal procedures. The added complications of language, legal systems, tax and currency would have to be considered carefully.

MINUTEMAN LIMITED:
CLOSURE OF A BUSINESS SEGMENT AND MAKE OR BUY

Minuteman Limited is a watch manufacturer located in the UK. It currently manufactures two ranges of watches; a craftsman made traditional precision watch that sells to the premium market for £450, and an electronic fashion watch that is assembled from bought-in components and sells for £40.

The manager is concerned about the lack of profitability of the electronic watch division.

The current factory is used for the manufacture of both watch ranges, and there is no likelihood of another use for the part currently used for assembly of the electronic watches.

The operating statement for the last quarter was as follows:

	Premium Watch	Electronic Watch	Total
	£000	£000	£000
Sales	225	160	385
Materials and components	15	64	79
Direct labour	75	60	135
Fixed Factory Costs	45	32	77
Administration Costs	20	20	40
Selling and Distribution Costs	10	20	30
Operating Profit / (Loss)	60	(36)	24

The following information has been established:

- Materials and components and direct labour are variable costs
- Fixed factory costs relate to the whole factory, and have been apportioned based on sales value
- Administration costs are fixed costs and would remain if the electronic watches were no longer made
- Selling and distribution costs are variable costs
- Redundancy costs can be ignored
- This level of sales of both watches is expected to continue

required

CLOSURE OF A BUSINESS SEGMENT

- Restate the operating statement in a marginal costing format, showing clearly the contribution of each division to company fixed costs.

- Recommend whether the electronic watch division should be closed in the short term.

MAKE OR BUY DECISION

- The manager has obtained quotations from the Far East where these watches could be made for £15 each (including delivery). The existing variable selling and distribution costs would apply to the bought in watches.

- Prepare a budgeted operating statement in a marginal costing format based on ceasing to manufacture the electronic watches in the factory, but buying them in ready made from the Far East.

solution

CLOSURE OF A BUSINESS SEGMENT

Operating Statement – Marginal Costing Format

	Premium Watch £000	Electronic Watch £000	Total £000
Sales	225	160	385
Variable Costs:			
Materials and components	15	64	79
Direct labour	75	60	135
Selling and distribution costs	10	20	30
Contribution	125	16	141
Fixed Costs:			
Fixed Factory Costs			77
Administration Costs			40
Operating Profit / (Loss)			24

The operating statement in this format clearly shows that the electronic watch division is making a contribution to overall fixed costs of £16,000. If the electronic watches were to be discontinued the overall profit would therefore be reduced to £8,000.

MAKE OR BUY DECISION

Budgeted Operating Statement – Marginal Costing Format

	Premium Watch £000	Electronic Watch £000	Total £000
Sales	225	160	385
Variable Costs:			
Materials and components	15		15
Bought in watches		60	60
Direct labour	75		75
Selling and Distribution Costs	10	20	30
Contribution	125	80	205
Fixed Costs:			
Fixed Factory Costs			77
Administration Costs			40
Operating Profit / (Loss)			88

The contribution from the Electronic Watch Division would increase from £16,000 to £80,000. The overall profit would increase from £24,000 to £88,000.

However additional risks in terms of currency movements, price stability and quality control would need to be considered.

AUTOMATION

Automation of a production operation usually involves:

■ spending considerable amounts of money on buying (or leasing) non-current assets, and subsequently maintaining and operating them

■ reducing labour costs

This may mean that fixed costs increase (eg the operating costs and depreciation of the plant or machinery, and variable costs decrease (eg if labour costs are variable). This can therefore change the cost structure to a more risky one which is more sensitive to changes in the volume of output. This is the same idea that we examined in the section on break-even and margin of safety earlier in this chapter.

There are two main types of task relating to automation:

■ redrafting of an income (or operating) statement to determine the impact on profit

■ using discounted cash flow (DCF) to establish the net present value of the automation

redrafting an income statement

This type of task can use similar techniques and logic to the Case Studies that we have already seen in this chapter. Remember that depreciation is a proper cost to show in an income statement, so the additional depreciation change related to the non-current assets will need to be accounted for.

You may also be asked to carry out some contribution calculations and work out the break-even point and margin of safety as illustrated earlier.

The following Case Study will illustrate this type of task.

Case Study

EDDY'S READIES:
MARGINAL COSTING AND AUTOMATION

situation

Eddy's Readies Limited makes a range of prepared meals that are ready to be heated and eaten. The operation is currently labour intensive, and a large number of people are employed to prepare the meals in the factory, using traditional cooking techniques. These employees are brought in to work according to demand, and are therefore treated as a variable cost.

The manager has been investigating the purchase of automated production line equipment that would eliminate the need for the majority of employees. The purchase and installation of the equipment would cost £1,000,000, and would be depreciated at £200,000 per year.

The following income statement is based on the next year's operation, assuming the current working practices, and production of 1 million meals.

	£000
Sales	3,950
less:	
variable material cost	1,800
variable labour cost	700
Contribution	1,450
less:	
fixed production costs	150
fixed administration costs	320
Operating profit	980

The net operating assets of the business are currently £1,500,000.

If the automated production line is installed:

• labour costs will reduce to £250,000 per year, regardless of the production level
• fixed production costs will increase by £160,000 per year, in addition to the depreciation expense
• other costs will be unchanged

required

(a) Calculate the current

- break-even point (in units)
- margin of safety as a percentage of sales
- return on net assets

(b) Show the revised income statement based on the installation of the automated production line.

(c) Calculate the revised

- break-even point (in units)
- margin of safety as a percentage of sales
- return on net assets

(d) Briefly comment on whether the automated production line would make the cost structure more or less risky.

solution

(a) Current position:

Break-even point

£470,000 / £1.45   = 324,138 meals

Working:

Fixed Costs: £150,000 + £320,000 = £470,000

Contribution per unit £1,450,000 / 1,000,000 meals = £1.45 per meal

Margin of safety as percentage of sales

$$\frac{(1,000,000 - 324,138) \text{ meals}}{1,000,000 \text{ meals}} \quad \times 100 \qquad = 67.6\%$$

Return on net assets

$$\frac{£980,000}{£1,500,000} \quad \times 100 \qquad = 65.3\%$$

(b) Revised income statement

	£'000
Sales	3,950
less:	
variable material cost	1,800
Contribution	2,150
less:	
fixed labour costs	250
fixed production costs	510
fixed administration costs	320
Operating profit	1,070

(c) Revised position:

Break-even point

£1,080,000 / £2.15 = 502,326 meals

Working:

Fixed Costs: £250,000 + £510,000 + £320,000 = £1,080,000

Contribution per unit £2,150,000 / 1,000,000 meals = £2.15 per meal

Margin of safety as percentage of sales

$$\frac{(1,000,000 - 502,326) \text{ meals}}{1,000,000 \text{ meals}} \times 100 = 49.8\%$$

Return on net assets

$$\frac{£1,070,000}{(£1,500,000 + £1,000,000)} \times 100 = 42.8\%$$

(d) Although the profit would be greater with an automated production line, the break-even point is higher, leading to a reduced margin of safety. Therefore if sales fell below the expected level the profit would fall more rapidly than under the existing cost structure. This makes the revised cost structure more risky. However if sales were to rise above the 1m expected meals then the revised cost structure would mean that profits would increase more rapidly due to the increased contribution per meal.

USING DISCOUNTED CASH FLOW

Discounted cash flow (DCF) techniques can be used to establish the net present value of a project to automate a manufacturing activity.

When using DCF to make a comparison – for example automation or no automation, we can:

- ignore costs that are the same in both cases
- ignore non-cash costs like depreciation
- include both capital and revenue receipts and payments

Contrast this with the technique that we have just examined where we were calculating a profit figure – here we are only concerned with cash flows.

We can use the same data as the last Case Study to contrast the techniques.

Case Study

EDDY'S READIES:
DISCOUNTED CASH FLOW AND AUTOMATION

situation

Eddy's Readies Limited makes a range of prepared meals that are ready to be heated and eaten. The operation is currently labour intensive, and a large number of people are employed to prepare the meals in the factory, using traditional cooking techniques. These employees are brought in to work according to demand, and are therefore treated as a variable cost.

The manager has been investigating the purchase of automated production line equipment that would eliminate the need for the majority of employees. The purchase and installation of the equipment would cost £1,000,000, and would be depreciated at £200,000 per year.

The following income statement is based on the next year's operation, assuming the current working practices, and production of 1 million meals.

	£000
Sales	3,950
less:	
variable material cost	1,800
variable labour cost	700
Contribution	1,450
less:	
fixed production costs	150
fixed administration costs	320
Operating profit	980

The net operating assets of the business are currently £1,500,000.

If the automated production line is installed:

• labour costs will reduce to £250,000 per year, regardless of the production level

• fixed production costs will increase by £160,000 per year, in addition to the depreciation expense

• other costs will be unchanged

The company's cost of capital is 5%, and discount factors over the five year life of the project are as follows:

Year	Discount factor 5%	Year	Discount factor 5%
0	1.00	3	0.864
1	0.952	4	0.823
2	0.907	5	0.784

The automated production line will be paid for immediately and have no value at the end of the five year project. Assume that sales and costs remain at the same level for each of the five years, and occur at the end of each year.

required

Using the following table, calculate the net present value of the automation project.

Year	Cash outflow £000	Cash savings £000	Discount factor	Present value £000
0				
1				
2				
3				
4				
5				
	Net Present Value			

solution

Working:

Annual cash savings	Labour £700,000 – £250,000	£450,000
	Less additional production costs	£160,000
	Net cash savings	£290,000

Year	Cash outflow £000	Cash savings £000	Discount factor	Present value £000
0	1,000		1.000	(1,000)
1		290	0.952	276
2		290	0.907	263
3		290	0.864	251
4		290	0.823	239
5		290	0.784	227
	Net Present Value			256

The net present value is a positive amount of £256,000, which means that based on these figures the automation project appears to be worthwhile.

Note that in the calculation only cash figures which arise directly from the decision to automate (or not) are used. The Case Study therefore provided lots of data that was not needed for this technique. You may need to carefully select the data that you need to use in a DCF calculation.

CORPORATE SOCIAL RESPONSIBILITY AND ETHICAL CONSIDERATIONS

Although profitability is a main driver for many of the type of decisions that we have examined in this chapter, it is not the only consideration. Organisations are increasingly becoming aware of their responsibility to all stakeholders (not just shareholders) and to society as a whole. For example, while the Case Studies that we have looked at often refer to savings in labour cost, in the real world these would mean job losses for individuals and hardship for families.

Consumers are also becoming aware of the impacts that businesses have on social and environmental issues, and many will boycott those who do not appear to be acting fairly. Acting ethically and with social responsibility is therefore often in the best interests of organisations as well as for society as a whole.

Make or buy situations will have consequences for the current labour force if a decision is taken to outsource. The loss of local jobs will affect the community as well as the local businesses that rely on the organisation and its employees for trade. Where sites are closed there must be regard given to clean-up costs and environmental factors where appropriate.

Where a decision is made to manufacture overseas there may be ethical considerations regarding the working conditions that the employees are operating under and whether they are being paid fairly.

Automation will also have implications for employees, but there could also be considerations regarding energy consumption and sustainability.

All corporate decisions have wide ranging consequences and it is not sufficient to only consider the financial implications of decisions.

Chapter Summary

■ Decision making is often carried out by examining relevant costs. These are the financial changes that arise directly out of the decision being considered.

■ Make or buy decisions involve using marginal costing to examine all costs and establish which ones would remain if the goods were outsourced. Other non-financial issues would also need to be considered.

■ There may be limiting factors (eg lack of resources) that prevent manufacturing or selling the desired quantities. Techniques are available for establishing the 'binding constraint' and for making choices when there are several products.

■ The marginal costing indicators of contribution, break-even and margin of safety can be used to analyse situations. These indicators can also be used to help assess the risk of a business plan.

■ The consideration of the closure of a business segment involves examining all relevant costs as well as non-financial risks.

■ Automation can be tackled by using one or more techniques. These include redrafting an income statement, and discounted cash flow.

■ As well as financial considerations, decisions must also take account of ethical, social and environmental issues.

Key Terms	**relevant cost**	a cost that arises directly from a decision; these are often future incremental cash flows
	contribution	the difference between sales and variable costs; this can be calculated per period or per unit
	break-even point	the number of units or sales value that results in a profit of zero
	margin of safety	a measure of how far the expected position is from the break-even point; it is often measured as a percentage drop in sales
	net present value	the net result of cash inflows and outflows at different points in time, converted into present value terms by using discount factors
	net present cost	the net result of cash inflows and outflows at different points in time, converted into present cost terms by using discount factors; net present cost is always a net outflow
	corporate social responsibility	the concept that organisations have ethical responsibilities to all their stakeholders and to the wider community

Activities

6.1 A manufacturing company that is operating at budgeted level, but has sufficient spare capacity has been approached regarding a special order. The order would need to be priced competitively, but the company must not lose money on the transaction. From the following list of costs, select those that are relevant when calculating the cost of undertaking the special order.

Cost:	
(a) Standard mark-up of 35% on cost	
(b) Additional direct materials to be purchased for this order	
(c) Fixed overhead absorption cost per unit	
(d) Incremental cost of additional direct labour required	
(e) Depreciation of production machinery	
(f) Fees for consultant to work on design of special order	
(g) Cost of salaried factory manager	
(h) Original cost of materials needed for this order that are in stock and have no other use and no resale value	
(i) Delivery costs of special order	

6.2 A company produces and sells premium baked beans in 400 gram cans. It is considering also producing and selling the same product in 200 gram cans. The smaller cans will be sold at more than half the current price, although there will be an impact on the sales volume of the current product. The following information is available.

- Current sales volume is 7.0 million units of the 400 gram cans and this is expected to reduce to 6.0 million units if the smaller cans are also produced.
- Current fixed production costs are £0.85 million per year.
- Current labour cost per unit is £0.05, which is completely variable.
- Current material cost per unit is £0.11 (including can), which is completely variable.
- Current selling price is £0.80 per unit.
- The new product would have variable material costs (including can) of £0.07 per unit.
- The new product would have a variable labour cost of £0.03 per unit.
- The total fixed costs per year would increase by £0.11 million.
- Selling price of the existing product would be unaffected, but the new product would sell for £0.55 per unit, with expected sales of 2.2 million units.

Required:

Complete the following table to calculate the changes in revenue and costs if the new product were to be produced alongside the existing product. Show negative amounts in the total column with minus signs.

	Units	Per Unit £	Total £
Lost contribution on 400 gram can sales			
200 gram can sales:			
Additional revenue			
Material cost			
Labour cost			
Increase fixed costs			
Net increase / (reduction) in profit			

6.3   The following shows the standard data of one unit of product RIC:

	£
Selling price	15
Variable production costs	9
Fixed overheads based on production of 7,000 units per week	4
Total production cost	13
Profit	2

The product currently has UK sales of 7,000 units per week and no overseas sales. Capacity is 8,000 units per week.

A customer from Argentina has offered to buy 1,500 units per week at a discounted price of £14 per unit, but will not accept a lower quantity.

Finished RICs could be purchased from a competitor at £16 per unit.

Complete the following table based on accepting the order by buying in the units that cannot be made in-house. Insert zeros if appropriate. Make a recommendation as to whether or not to accept the order.

	Total per Week £	
Incremental revenue		
Incremental costs:		
Variable production costs		
Purchase of finished goods		
Fixed production costs		
Incremental profit / (loss)		
Recommendation	**Accept**	**Reject**

6.4 A company produces two products, the Shiver and the Shake from the same material, with revenues, variable costs and weekly demand as follows:

	Shiver	Shake
Selling price	£50	£60
Direct materials (at £10 per kg)	£20	£25
Direct labour	£12	£16
Demand	12,000 units	15,000 units

Weekly production capacity is restricted to a maximum of total 25,000 units.

(a) Assuming that there is no shortage of resources, complete the following table to show the optimum production level for each product and the resulting contribution.

	Shiver	Shake	Total
Production (units)			
Total contribution £			

(b) In the coming week there is a shortage of raw materials and only 36,000 kg will be available. Complete the following table to show the various contributions, and the optimum production and material usage quantities for the week.

	Shiver	Shake	Total
Contribution per kg of material			
Production (units)			
Material usage (kg)			
Total contribution £			

6.5 A company is planning to launch a new product and is considering two possible selling prices. Forecasts for revenues and costs for each strategy are shows below.

	Strategy 1	Strategy 2
Selling price per unit	£49.00	£39.00
Demand	5,000 units	8,000 units
Material cost per unit	£10.00	£10.00
Labour cost per unit	£12.00	£12.00
Fixed production cost per unit	£10.00	£6.25
Total cost per unit	£32.00	£28.25

Complete the following table, rounding to the nearest unit and the nearest whole percentage where appropriate:

	Strategy 1	Strategy 2
Contribution per unit £		
Total fixed production costs £		
Forecast profit £		
Breakeven point (units)		
Margin of safety (units)		
Margin of safety %		

6.6 A business operates with two separate departments, each producing a different product. The following information has been provided for the last month.

	Dee	Eff
Sales volume (units)	70,000	60,000
Selling price per unit £	10.00	10.00
Variable production costs per unit £	5.00	2.00
Fixed overheads £	175,000	360,000

(a) Calculate the relevant figures to complete the following table.

	Dee	Eff
Contribution per unit £		
Total contribution £		
Break-even point (units)		
Margin of safety %		

(b) Draft a report that provides an analysis of the figures, under the following headings:

- An evaluation of the difference in the total contribution and profit between the two departments.
- The implications of the different break-even points and margins of safety.
- An evaluation of the risk of each department.

6.7   Duo-active is a manufacturer located in the UK. It currently manufactures two products in its factory, Aye and Bee.

The manager is concerned about the lack of profitability of the Bee product.

The current factory is used for the manufacture of both products, and there is no likelihood of another use for the part currently used for the manufacture of the Bee product.

The operating statement for the last quarter was as follows:

	Aye £000	Bee £000	Total 000
Sales	320	160	480
Direct materials	40	35	75
Direct labour	115	60	175
Fixed Factory Costs	85	75	160
Selling and Distribution Costs	10	5	15
Administration Costs	10	10	20
Operating Profit / (Loss)	60	(25)	35

The following information has been established:
- Materials and direct labour are variable costs.
- Fixed factory costs relate to the whole factory, apart from £25,000 which relates specifically to supervision costs in production of Aye and £15,000 which relates to supervision costs in production of Bee. The remaining costs have been apportioned equally.
- Administration costs are fixed costs and would remain if either of the products were discontinued.
- Selling and distribution costs are variable costs.
- Redundancy costs can be ignored.
- This level of sales of both products is expected to continue.

Required:

Complete the table on the next page to show the performance of each product in marginal costing format.

	Aye £000	Bee £000	Total £000
Sales			
Total variable costs			
Fixed costs related to products			
Product contribution			
Whole business fixed costs			
Operating Profit			

Recommend whether the Bee product should be discontinued.

7 Cost management techniques

this chapter covers...

In this chapter we examine various cost management techniques, many of which have been developed or refined over the last 50 years.

We start by looking at cost reduction, and learn that there are ways that this can be planned and implemented, as well as pitfalls to be avoided. This leads to an examination of value engineering and value analysis which was created out of issues caused by shortages. In these techniques every aspect of a product or component is examined to establish whether it is necessary and if so whether the function can be achieved more efficiently.

Target costing is considered next, which takes the selling price as a starting point for design to ensure that costs are planned to ensure profitability.

The chapter then goes on to provide an overview of quality and 'total quality management,' which provides a background to various ideas within cost management.

The final section in this chapter deals with lifecycle costing as it applies to products. The use of discounted cash flow in this context is also explored.

COST REDUCTION

cost reduction programmes

Ever since there have been manufacturing businesses, managers have sought to ensure that they are using the most appropriate inputs (materials, labour and expenses) and using them in the most efficient way.

The aim of standard costing and budgetary control is to keep costs within pre-determined targets. By contrast, the aim of a cost reduction programme is to reduce costs from their previously accepted levels without reducing the value of the product or service.

For example, the value to the customer of the packaging of plain biscuits is that it prevents deterioration or breaking of the biscuits. It may be possible to achieve this with cheaper materials. On the other hand, the superior packaging of expensive chocolates may be important to consumers as chocolates are often given as a gift and the packaging is a sign of perceived quality. Cutting the costs here could reduce the value of the product.

To succeed, cost reduction programmes need the full support of senior management and the co-operation of all other employees. It is essential to plan for cost reduction throughout all areas of the organisation. It may be possible to reduce certain costs with no effect on the product or service at all, for example by reducing the wastage of power for lighting and heating.

approaches to cost reduction

In planning for cost reduction, it is important to ensure that the measures taken will reduce costs in the long term.

Initially, the costs to be considered are likely to be variable costs, because most fixed costs will already have been paid or contracted for a time period.

The only fixed costs which it may be possible to reduce immediately are the 'discretionary' fixed costs. Discretionary fixed costs are those which can be changed by managers. They are the costs of items where there is a choice about the level of expenditure, so that the level can be reduced within a shorter timescale. Examples of discretionary fixed costs include:

- advertising
- non-essential training and staff development
- research and development.

Cutting discretionary costs may increase profits in the short term, but could be damaging in the long term. Reducing spending on advertising and product development may lead to loss of market share. Cutting down on training and staff development will result in a less skilled workforce, inefficiency and possibly a high labour turnover. Care must be taken to plan cost reduction programmes, so that the savings are not outweighed by the loss of profits in future.

There is a great danger if managers are allowed to reduce discretionary costs that the overall result may be inconsistent with the aims of the business. This would be an example of lack of goal congruence, as discussed previously. Particularly where managers are judged solely on the cost reduction in their own area of control they may be tempted to cut costs which have an adverse impact elsewhere.

In general, long-term cost reduction can be achieved by improving productivity and efficiency and making better use of all resources. Changes may be made to working practices in all sections of the organisation, in order to make procedures, and hence the use of materials and of people's time, more cost-effective.

methods of assessing possible cost reductions

Methods which may be applied include:

- **Work Study**
  This is used in manufacturing to determine:
  - the most efficient methods and procedures
  - the best layout of the factory or production line to reduce costs
  - the most efficient ways to use materials, labour and machinery to reduce waste

- **Organisation and Methods**
  This is used in administration to determine ways to improve office methods and procedures, including:
  - form design, office layout, workflows and communication
  - the benefits of computerisation
  - elimination of unnecessary procedures and paperwork

- **Variety reduction**
  This may involve:
  - reducing the product range
  - standardising the components used in different products.

Variety reduction means reducing the number of different products or components which pass through the system. Standardising the components used in different products can be very cost-effective. It can allow for greater use of automation and also economies through bulk purchasing. Cutting the range of products, however, must be balanced with customer needs. The value of all the products to the user must be maintained, or sales and goodwill will be lost.

For example:

■ customers expect a range of cars with different features, but the majority of the components can be standardised

■ domestic products such as kitchen appliances are produced in different colour finishes and different sizes, but the working parts can be standardised.

other methods of cost reduction

Other aspects of an organisation where planned cost reduction should be considered are:

■ **finance costs**: the interest payable on loans and overdrafts, foreign exchange, the cost of capital tied up in inventory and the timing of capital expenditure may offer scope for cost reduction

■ **energy costs**: savings may be made by energy conservation

■ **staffing**: numbers of staff needed and the skill levels required should be considered

■ **consumables**: the control of purchases and of stocks of items such as stationery may need to be tightened to make savings

■ **authorisation of expenditure**: all expenditure should be subject to proper authorisation at a sufficiently high level of management

Cost reduction programmes should involve all staff and hence draw on each person's specialist knowledge of their own job. Production staff can suggest changes in processing to reduce waste, human resource managers can assist with analysing staffing costs, accountants can look at finance costs and so on. Additional specialists may be brought in from outside to solve specific problems or to carry out work study for example.

examples of employee suggestions . . .

• In a small factory, where production of sports cars is not automated, workers noticed that they were spending unnecessary amounts of time fetching small items such as nuts and bolts from central bins. Placing stocks of these items nearer to the actual work speeded up production.

• In a large factory, one employee operated a machine to screw two parts of a component together. He realised that one of the four screws used did not actually contribute any strength or have any purpose. By modifying the process and eliminating this screw, both time and materials were saved. The suggestion earned the employee a bonus.

VALUE ENGINEERING AND VALUE ANALYSIS

Whereas general cost reduction programmes concentrate on producing existing products more efficiently and cheaply, a more focussed approach can be used. This technique was developed during the resource shortages during the Second World War, and examines each component to ensure that it contributes to the value of the product. Components that can be made from cheaper materials or in different ways without compromising the value to the user of the final product will be changed.

In order to ensure that value is maintained, what constitutes that value must be analysed:

- before production starts (this is **value engineering**)
- or when the product or service is already on the market (**value analysis**).

definitions of value engineering and value analysis

value engineering	Ensuring that new products or services are designed for quality but at low cost, by analysing how every part of the design enhances value.
value analysis	Analysing the value of every part of the design of an existing product or service, and questioning whether its function can be achieved some other way at lower cost.

The aim of both these processes is to build quality into the design of the product or service, while keeping the costs down. Relevant specialists in engineering, design and technology will be consulted.

Clearly it is easier to make alterations at the design stage than afterwards, the aim being to build in value but at lower cost. At the design stage, each part or feature of the product or system is looked at to check that it is necessary and that it contributes value.

In existing products or services, it is possible to analyse the value provided to the customer, and decide whether that level of quality can be kept or improved, when costs are reduced.

For example, the exact colour of a disposable razor may be of no importance to customers, whereas the exact colour of a sofa may be part of its value. Cheaper raw materials which may show colour variations may be acceptable for some products but not others.

The term 'value added' is used to describe activities or manufacturing processes that create an aspect of the product that customers are willing to pay for. Some writers describe value added activities as those that change the 'form, fit, or function' of a product.

Value engineering and value analysis attempt to eliminate activities that are 'non-value added'. These are the wasteful activities that do not contribute to the value of the product. As well as more obvious examples like idle time while waiting for materials, or moving part finished products to the next stage in production, it can also include the inspection activity if it doesn't contribute to the quality of the product.

Businesses that have mainly eliminated non-value added activities may be said to be 'lean' organisations.

Ethical values should also be considered when making changes to the design of products. Packaging should be minimised and made environmentally friendly. The end life of the product should be considered so that the maximum amount of components can be recycled efficiently. Ethical and commercial considerations will converge when a component which is found to be unnecessary can be entirely eliminated.

practical aspects of value engineering and value analysis

Value engineering and value analysis must look at each product or service in great detail. Typical questions to be asked include:

- Can the function of this product or component be achieved some other way?

- Are all the functions of the product or service essential?

- Can the product be made lighter or smaller, thus using less material? (This may enhance its value.)

- Can components be standardised across a range of products?

- Can the design of the product or the processes involved in a service be modified to save time?

advantages of value engineering and value analysis

The potential advantages of these techniques to the producer or provider are:
- continuous improvements in design and methods
- more efficient use of resources
- higher profits
- enhanced reputation
- extended product life

■ improved customer service through standardisation of components

■ improved employee motivation

The potential advantages of these techniques to the customer are:

■ prices may be reduced without loss of quality

■ better design based on satisfying users' needs

■ improved performance and reliability

■ quicker delivery

■ standard components for servicing

We have seen that cost reduction programmes should be planned for the long term. Value engineering and value analysis can be used as part of these programmes, so that the value of products or services to users is maintained or increased, even when costs are reduced.

examples of cost reduction and value analysis

· In a hospital outpatients' clinic, the original system meant that each consultant remained in one room, seeing a succession of patients. Time was wasted while patients were prepared for the consultation. The system was changed to one in which two rooms were used and the consultant moved between them. While the consultant saw one patient, the next could be prepared in the other room. The service to patients was improved at reduced cost.

· In a factory manufacturing cheap pottery mugs, the handles for the mugs were made separately and attached to the mugs before firing. A moulding process was then developed which allowed the mug to be produced with the handle. This speeded up production and reduced the number of rejects.

· Products such as radios and telephones are often produced in a range of exterior designs but offering the same functions. The basic product can then be exactly the same, but housed in different casings. Costs can be reduced by manufacturing the working parts in large numbers, and the value to customers is maintained. This is an example of 'variety reduction'.

TARGET COSTING

During the 1960s many new management and cost management techniques were developed, particularly by the Japanese. One of these was the concept of 'target costing'.

Where selling prices are determined by market forces it is often possible to anticipate what an ideal selling price is before the product is designed. In this way the whole design can be driven by the target price, so that all the materials, labour and expenses meet the requirements of the product and its profitability.

The steps involved in **target costing** are:

■ decide the level of **market share** the organisation wants to achieve for the product and the level of **profit** expected

- estimate the target **selling price** at which the product would be expected to achieve the desired market share
- subtract the organisation's required level of profit from the target selling price to give the **target cost**
- compare the actual costs with the target. For a product in the design stage, the projected cost would be compared with the target cost. If the costs are too high, then cost reductions must be found in order to meet the target. Alternative methods of production may have to be considered. Value engineering and value analysis may be used
- if it is impossible to reduce costs to the target level without affecting quality, then it can be seen that the product is not viable at the chosen selling price and profit level

Target costing can only be used in situations where there is sufficient information available about the market for the product or service. It must be possible to link selling prices with market share. The organisation must also have a specific target for contribution or profit as a percentage of sales.

Target costing may be used with Activity Based Costing (see Chapter 1). In Activity Based Costing, overheads are charged to a specific product according to how much use it makes of the activities within the organisation. Required cost reductions would be concentrated on the activities most used by the product in question. This method should result in real cost savings for that product. In contrast, charging overheads to products using apportionment and absorption does not give a realistic view of how the costs (and therefore any reductions in those costs) relate to a particular product.

Target costing should take account of ethical considerations in the design process. For example, it may be possible to use board created from wood waste as an alternative to plastic in the construction of some products. This may be of equivalent cost and yet meet the requirements of being sourced sustainably and have the ability to be recycled easily at the end of the product's life.

advantages of target costing

The potential advantages of target costing to the producer or provider are:

- improved sales volumes and market share through competitive pricing
- good relationships with customers through consultation and a team-based approach
- achievement of a planned level of profit
- more efficient use of resources
- improvements in production methods
- involvement of all sections of the organisation, resulting in better coordination of functions

The potential advantages of target costing to the customer are:

■ the required product or service obtainable at the right price

■ more reliable service from the supplier resulting from better relationships

■ prices reduced without loss of quality

All the advantages of value engineering and value analysis are relevant if these methods are being used to achieve the target cost.

Case Study

METTLE PLC: TARGET COSTING

situation

Mettle plc is a manufacturer of components for heavy goods vehicles. The market for these products is limited to a small number of large companies, which manufacture the vehicles. Mettle plc currently supplies only three customers and the loss of a single customer would therefore be a serious problem. Mettle plc will lose sales if its prices for components are not competitive.

The sales manager of Mettle plc has established a maximum price for a particular component, C34, above which the vehicle manufacturers will not buy from Mettle plc. This price is £350 per unit of C34. At this price, sales demand for the next year is expected to be 6,000 units of C34. Mettle plc has a target level of 18% operating profit on sales.

Note: here we are using target 'operating profit', which means that the 'total costs' will include non-production costs. In other cases, the 'target profit' may be based on a required level of contribution or of gross profit, depending on the costing method being used in the organisation.

required

Calculate:

(a) The expected total sales revenue from component C34 for the next year.

(b) The target operating profit required by Mettle plc from the total sales of C34.

(c) The total target cost for C34 for the next year.

(d) The target operating profit per unit of C34.

(e) The target cost per unit of C34.

solution

(a) Expected total sales revenue from C34 = £350 x 6,000 = £2,100,000

(b) Target operating profit from C34 = 18% x £2,100,000 = £378,000

(c) Total target cost for C34 = £2,100,000 − £378,000 = £1,722,000

(d) Target operating profit per unit of C34 = £378,000/6,000 = £63

(e) Target cost per unit of C34 = £350 − £63 = £287

target costing and value engineering

We have seen that value engineering is used to ensure that quality is built into the design of new products without incurring unnecessary costs. Unnecessary costs are those which do not add value to the product. As a result of value engineering, the lowest cost for a particular design should be established. This technique is clearly a useful tool if target costing is being used. If the lowest cost for the design meets the target cost, then that design is acceptable. If not, then it is necessary to re-think the whole design and carry out value engineering again or to reconsider the original product specifications. Care must be taken to avoid wasting resources on a lengthy design process in which too many alternatives are considered.

Success is achieved using a combination of target costing and value engineering if the resulting product satisfies the needs of both the customer and the producer:

- the product satisfies the user's requirements (value in use and prestige value)
- the selling price is at a level that customers are prepared to pay
- the selling price attracts sufficient customers to meet the producer's target market share
- the costs are reduced to the target level, so that the producer's target profit level is reached

The following diagram illustrates the links between value engineering and the steps of target costing.

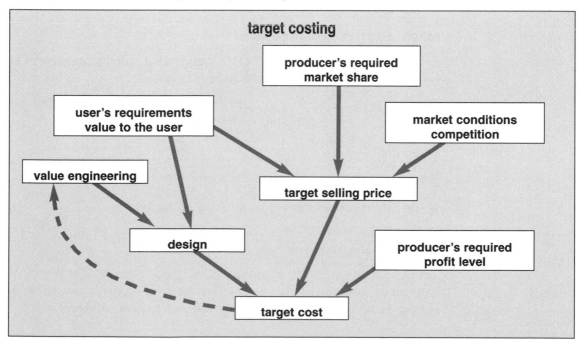

QUALITY AND TOTAL QUALITY MANAGEMENT

Throughout the second half of the 20th Century there were further developments in cost management techniques. One of these, 'Total Quality Management' became popular in the 1980s. It starts from an understanding that the quality of a product or service can be defined as 'its fitness for the customer's purpose'. This is important as it emphasises the purpose that the customer will have for the item.

For a product or service to be of high quality, it does not necessarily mean that it uses very expensive materials or highly skilled staff to provide it. What is important is that it **satisfies the customer**. This means that the product or service must:

- be fit for the purpose for which it is purchased
- represent value for money to the customer.

In modern consumer-led societies, customers have access to a wide choice of products and services and make greater demands on suppliers. It is therefore increasingly important for businesses to pay more attention to the requirements of consumers. For example, there is fierce competition for market share between the main supermarket chains in the UK. If they all sell similar products at similar prices, the quality of the service they provide becomes a factor. Attention turns to reducing queues at the tills, providing in-store restaurants and other ways of increasing customer satisfaction.

total quality management

Total Quality Management (TQM) means that quality management becomes the aim of every part of an organisation.

The basic principle is one of continuous improvement, in order to eliminate faulty work and prevent mistakes. Mistakes carry a cost:

- wastage of materials
- idle time
- the cost of reworking
- the loss of customer goodwill, resulting in lost sales
- the cost of replacements
- the cost of dealing with customers' complaints

The concept of continuous improvement and getting more 'right first time' will reduce these costs. Other costs will be incurred in quality management, but the intention is that in the long term the organisation will benefit.

implementing TQM

If TQM is to be introduced, it must become the philosophy of everyone in the organisation, and apply to every activity, including administration, purchasing, sales, marketing and distribution, as well as production. Training and motivation of staff is essential, so that an attitude of seeking improvement is encouraged. Everyone should be allowed to put forward ideas. Groups of employees may form 'quality circles' and have regular meetings to discuss their ideas for quality improvements.

Each person within an organisation has customers. These may be *internal* users of his/her work – ie colleagues – as not everyone deals directly with the external customers. If the quality of the work for the next immediate user is monitored, mistakes will be reduced throughout the organisation.

The involvement of all staff of an organisation means that many different types of knowledge and skills are being used. These may be in engineering, design, information technology, materials handling, office management and many other areas. Specialist consultants may also be needed from outside the organisation.

the costs of quality

The costs relating to quality management can be grouped under four headings:

Prevention costs	The costs associated with preventing faulty output, for example training employees in quality control
Appraisal costs	The costs of checking quality, like inspection costs
Internal failure costs	The costs of rectifying problems within the organisation, for example having to scrap sub-standard products
External failure costs	The costs incurred when sub-standard products reach the customer, including repairs and loss of goodwill

the benefits of Total Quality Management

Organisations which develop a culture of TQM and continuous improvement expect that the costs will be outweighed by the benefits. The benefits include:

- reduction of Internal Failure Costs
- reduction of External Failure Costs

- improved reputation and goodwill of customers
- increased sales
- better motivated staff due to improved job satisfaction
- reduction of staffing costs in some areas (typically in middle management, as senior management develops closer links to the operational workforce)
- improve ethical standards or behaviour

TOGS: THE ACTUAL COST OF QUALITY

situation

Togs manufactures clothes for a number of UK retail stores. The company has unfortunately allowed its quality systems to slip in recent years.

The fabric supplies are not inspected before cutting and making up the garments.

The finished garments are inspected, and on average 120 items per month are found to have fabric faults. Of these, 20 have to be scrapped. The remainder are sold as seconds at a discount of £15 on the normal price.

A further 40 garments per month are returned by retailers because of fabric faults, which have been missed by the inspectors in the factory. The retailers do not pay for these and they are not replaced. Some retailers do not reorder from the company.

The returned garments are all sold as seconds at the reduced price.

The variable cost of manufacture is £48 per garment.

A management consultant suggests that Togs should:

1   Identify the costs of quality, in money terms where possible and state in which of the four types of cost of quality each cost should be categorised.

2   Think about and suggest ways in which improvements could be made.

solution

1   **The costs of quality and types of cost**

- The cost of scrapping 20 garments is the cost of making them, which is:

  20 x £48 = £960 per month.

  This is an internal failure cost.

  Note: We use the variable cost of making the garments, because the fixed costs (by definition) are not increased by making additional items.

- The cost of selling the faulty goods as seconds is £15 per garment, as this is the reduction in contribution from the discounted selling price. The cost of seconds found on inspection is:

100 x £15 = £1,500 per month.

This is an internal failure cost.

- The cost of selling the other faulty goods, which are returned by retailers, as seconds is:

40 x £15 = £600 per month.

This is an external failure cost, because the faulty goods went out of the factory. Additional external failure costs will result from the lost orders from retailers and loss of reputation amongst customers, but we do not have sufficient information to measure these.

2 how can improvements be made?

The situation could be improved by inspection of the fabric as it is received. This would give rise to appraisal costs. An alternative would be to negotiate contract terms with the supplier to include guarantees regarding the quality of the fabric. Immediate action could be taken to improve the inspection of finished goods and avoid sending faulty goods to retailers. Although this alone would not reduce the total number of substandard goods, it would avoid the external failure cost of lost goodwill and future sales.

LIFE CYCLE COSTING

The life cycle of a product is a sequence of stages through which it passes, from the start of its development to the point at which it is no longer sold or supported by customer services. We use the term 'product life cycle' throughout this section, but all the ideas could equally well be applied to services.

Products typically go through a number of distinct stages between conception and finally being withdrawn from sale. The stages are:

- development
- launch
- growth
- maturity
- decline

These stages are shown on the graph at the top of the next page.

Life cycle costing can also be applied to decisions relating to non-current assets (for example machinery). In that situation we would examine costs and savings over the life of the asset.

The length of a product life cycle can vary from a few years to 50 years or more. For example, products and services in hi-tech industries have short life cycles, whereas standard food products sell for many years.

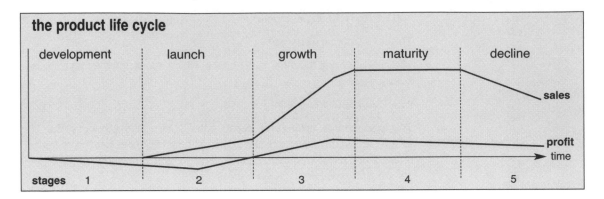

Life cycle costing involves considering costs for the whole life cycle of a product instead of the usual short time periods. Target selling prices and target costs may result from a planning process covering the life cycle of the product.

As the product life cycle progresses, costs are accumulated in:

■ research, development and design
■ production
■ selling and distribution
■ customer services

When all these costs are considered, for many products, the costs of production represent a small proportion of the total. Research and development, followed by the detailed design of the product, may build up a very large part of the costs. Examples of such products include medicines, computer software and cars. In some cases, heavy costs are incurred at the end of the life cycle, when sales have ceased, for example in decommissioning nuclear power stations.

Life cycle costing aims to collect together the costs of a single product over its entire life cycle. This means accounting for costs over a period of several years instead of a single year or less. Life cycle budgeting similarly involves planning for all the costs and revenues associated with the whole life cycle of the product.

life cycle costing and decision making

Research, development and design take place before the product goes into production. They also have a major influence on the other life cycle costs. Money spent on value engineering at the design stage can reduce production, marketing and customer service costs. On the other hand, a badly designed product will be more difficult to make, to sell and to maintain. This interdependence between the different stages of the life cycle is the main argument in favour of looking at the total cost of all the stages, rather than concentrating on just the production costs.

Budgeted life cycle costs and forecast sales volumes may be used for pricing decisions. The demand for a product will vary over its life cycle and the total sales revenue must cover the total life cycle costs. Forecasts of sales demands at different possible selling prices and expected costs for several years in advance are necessary to carry out the calculations for deciding on the best selling price. The chosen selling price, together with a required profit percentage, may be used for target costing. On the other hand, life cycle budget calculations may show that the product will not be profitable and therefore that expensive research and development work should not be carried out.

Economies of scale will need to be considered alongside pricing decisions. Generally, the lower the selling price, the higher the sales volume that can be sustained. Higher sales volume will result in fixed costs being shared over a greater number of units and sometimes variable costs can be reduced by bulk discounts. The learning effect may also have an impact as practice improves efficiency. The degree of mechanisation will also depend partly on the expected volumes and whether it is worthwhile to incur heavy capital costs in exchange for lower production costs. This idea is explored later when we examine the use of Discounted Cash Flow techniques.

The proportion of costs that are fixed and variable will change over the product life cycle. At the initial stages of development, launch and growth the majority of costs will be fixed costs (for example costs of design and product development and of marketing). As the life cycle continues, a lower level of fixed costs will usually be needed to sustain the product through maturity as customers are aware of the product and marketing can be reduced to a certain extent.

If life cycle budgeting and costing is being used, the accounting systems of the organisation must be designed to collect the relevant information. The costs of:

- research, development and design
- production
- selling and distribution
- customer services

must be collected separately for each product over its life, rather than being split down into monthly totals, for example. Of the costing methods studied in this book, activity based costing is likely to be the most appropriate. It can be seen that the four stages listed above represent groups of activities. Each one could be broken down into a number of separate activities, each with an appropriate cost driver. A particular product could then be charged for its usage of each activity (see Chapter 1).

Once the life cycle of a product is completed, the actual costs and revenues can be compared with the life cycle budget in order to obtain information to help with future planning and decision making.

AEROCAR PLC: LIFE CYCLE COSTING

situation

The managers of Aerocar plc are considering the possible development of a revolutionary kind of engine. The following forecasts have been made for the life cycle of this engine:

- research, development and design would take 3 years and cost £3million per year

- production and sales would take place over the following 4 years

- production costs would be £2million per year for 4 years plus £3,000 per engine

- selling and distribution costs would be £1million per year plus £1,000 per engine

- customer services would have to continue for 6 years and would cost £1.2million per year

- the total sales demand for the engine over the whole of its life cycle has been estimated for two possible selling prices:

    Case 1: 12,000 engines at a selling price of £7,000 each

    Case 2: 15,000 engines at a selling price of £6,000 each

required

(a) Calculate the total life cycle sales revenue at each of the possible selling prices.

(b) Calculate the total life cycle costs for:

    Case 1: 12,000 engines

    Case 2: 15,000 engines

(c) Calculate the total profit from the engine and the percentage profit on sales over its life cycle for each of the two possible selling prices.

    Hint: Set out your answer in £millions, correct to 1 decimal place.

solution

(a) Sales revenue

12,000 engines at a selling price of £7,000 each gives sales revenue of
12,000 x £7,000 = £84,000,000 or £84.0million.

15,000 engines at a selling price of £6,000 each gives sales revenue of
15,000 x £6,000 = £90,000,000 or £90.0million.

(b) Life cycle costs

Case 1: 12,000 engines

	£million	£million
Research, development and design		
£3million per year for 3 years		9.0
Production		
£2million per year for 4 years	8.0	
12,000 engines at £3,000 each	36.0	44.0
Selling and distribution		
£1million per year for 4 years	4.0	
12,000 engines at £1,000 each	12.0	16.0
Customer services		
£1.2million per year for 6 years		7.2
		76.2

Case 2: 15,000 engines

	£million	£million
Research, development and design		
£3million per year for 3 years		9.0
Production		
£2million per year for 4 years	8.0	
15,000 engines at £3,000 each	45.0	53.0
Selling and distribution		
£1million per year for 4 years	4.0	
15,000 engines at £1,000 each	15.0	19.0
Customer services		
£1.2million per year for 6 years		7.2
		88.2

(c) Life cycle summary and profit calculation:

Selling price per engine	£7,000	£6,000
Total sales demand	12,000	15,000
	£million	£million
Total sales revenue	84.0	90.0
Life cycle costs	76.2	88.2
Life cycle profit	7.8	1.8
Profit percentage on sales	9.3%	2.0%

Notes:

It can be seen that, according to these forecasts, the selling price of £7,000 per engine would be the more profitable option.

Suppose Aerocar plc uses target costing in conjunction with life cycle budgeting and costing, with a required profit percentage of 15% on sales. If the decision were made to use the selling price of £7,000 per engine, then the required profit would be 15% of the total sales revenue.

15% x £84million = £12.6million

Target total cost = £84million – £12.6million = £71.4million

Forecast total cost = £76.2million

The managers of Aerocar plc would have to look for £4.8million in cost reductions in order to meet this target. They would have to bear in mind that, if they cut back on the research phase, for example, the engine might cost more to produce. New forecasts for all the costs would need to be prepared.

LIFE CYCLE COSTING AND DISCOUNTED CASH FLOW

We were reminded in Chapter 1 how discounted cash flow (DCF) can be used to help make decisions regarding future costs and revenues. Since life cycle costing often relates to a substantial period of time (typically several years) it makes sense to make use of DCF techniques where appropriate.

Life cycle costing using DCF can be applied to decisions about products by using the product life cycle.

When we use DCF to make decisions we are usually making comparisons between two situations. In order to make valid comparisons we must bring the appropriate cost figures into our calculations. These are often called relevant costs, as discussed in Chapter 6. One way to remember what costs are relevant to any decision is that they are future incremental cash flows.

This means the costs are:
- future (not those costs that have already been incurred and cannot be changed by our decision),
- incremental (these are just the extra costs or savings resulting from the decision), and
- cash flows (always ignore non-cash items like depreciation).

Sometimes we can use just one DCF calculation to make our decision. This approach often suits situations where we are deciding to simply do something or not to do it. The Case Study that follows takes this approach, and is based on developing (or not developing) a new product.

The alternative approach is to use two DCF calculations. This is useful when we want to compare doing something in one of two ways.

Examine the following Case Study carefully and make sure that you can understand the logic that is being used.

LIFE CYCLE PRODUCT COSTING

A company is considering developing and launching a new product into a fast moving market. The following data has been estimated, based on the project going ahead.

- Product development and testing would cost £6m immediately and a further £6m in one year's time.

- Marketing would cost £0.5m in one year's time, and a further £0.2m for each of the next two years.

- Variable unit costs would be £4, and each unit would sell for £10.

- Fixed production costs that relate only to this product would be £0.5m for each year of production. Production and sales will take place in the same year.

- The company already incurs fixed costs of £5m related to other products and these costs will continue.

- Sales will be as follows (based on the start of the project being year 0):

Year 2	1m units
Year 3	2m units
Year 4	0.5m units

There will be no sales after year 4.

The company's cost of capital is 5% and relevant discount factors are:

Year	Discount Factor
0	1.000
1	0.952
2	0.907
3	0.864
4	0.823

required

Using DCF, calculate whether the new product is worthwhile. Carry out calculations in £ thousands.

solution

The cash flows and present values are set out in the following table.

Year	Details	Cash inflow £000	Cash outflow £000	Discount factor	Present value £000
0	Product development		6,000	1.000	(6,000)
1	Product development		6,000		
	Marketing		500		
	Net total year 1		6,500	0.952	(6,188)
2	Marketing		200		
	Sales Revenue	10,000			
	Variable costs		4,000		
	Fixed costs		500		
	Net total year 2	5,300		0.907	4,807
3	Marketing		200		
	Sales Revenue	20,000			
	Variable costs		8,000		
	Fixed costs		500		
	Net total year 3	11,300		0.864	9,763
4	Sales Revenue	5,000			
	Variable costs		2,000		
	Fixed costs		500		
	Net total year 4	2,500		0.823	2,057
				Net Present Value	4,439

Notice that the fixed costs that are already incurred are not relevant and are therefore not brought into the calculation. This is because they would not be altered by the decision on the new product – they remain the same regardless.

Based on the data given, the net present value is positive, so the project appears to be worthwhile.

Chapter Summary

■ Cost reduction involves examining current products and processes in order to see if savings can be made. It includes the application of work study to increase efficiency and approaches like variety reduction to utilise common components.

■ In value engineering (for new designs) and value analysis (for existing designs), the question: 'Can the same (or better) value to the user be achieved some other, cheaper way?' is asked about every part of the design. If this can be done, then:
  – the organisation should be able to increase its sales and profitability
  – customers will benefit from the availability of more efficiently designed products and services

■ Target costs are calculated by starting from the chosen selling price for the product and deducting the organisation's required profit. If it proves impossible to plan costs at the target level without affecting quality, then the product is not viable at this selling price.

■ When using target costing, the chosen selling price for the product may be decided by considering the market value, taking into account the market share that the producer hopes to obtain.

■ The quality of a product or service can be considered as its fitness for the customer's purpose.

■ The intention of quality management is that the additional costs of getting more 'right first time' will be outweighed by the benefits.

■ There are costs attached both to poor quality and to making improvements. These costs are grouped under the headings:
  – Prevention costs
  – Appraisal costs
  – Internal failure costs
  – External failure costs

■ Life cycle costing can be used to examine and quantify the costs throughout the life cycle stages of a product. At various stages during the life cycle the proportion of fixed and variable costs will alter considerably.

■ Discounted cash flow techniques can be used in conjunction with life cycle costing. It can be used to analyse the net present value (or cost) of products.

cost reduction	a positive approach to reducing costs in all departments of an organisation, without affecting the quality of output
value	a product or service has value to the customer and also to the producer or provider: . . . *for the customer:* – value in use – esteem or prestige value . . . *for the producer/provider:* – the cost to produce or provide – exchange or market value
value engineering	ensuring that new products or services are designed for quality but at low cost, by analysing how every part of the design enhances value
value analysis	analysing the value of every part of the design of an existing product or service, and questioning whether its function can be achieved some other way at lower cost
value added activities	those activities that create an aspect of a product or service that customers are willing to pay for
non-value added activities	wasteful activities that do not contribute to the value of the product or service
lean organisations	those organisations that have mainly eliminated non-value added activities
target costing	setting targets for costs as *selling price less required profit* and if necessary using cost reduction to meet the target cost
quality	the quality of a product or service can be considered as its fitness for the purpose for which it is to be used by the customer
total quality management (TQM)	a concept that means that continuous improvement is sought in every part of an organisation, attempting to get everything right first time and eliminate mistakes and defects
life cycle costing	accounting for the costs of a product over its entire life from the start of development to the end of customer support

Activities

7.1 The following statements relate to cost reduction programmes. Select the statements that are true.

		True
(a)	Cost reduction is only concerned with finding the cheapest materials	
(b)	Cost reduction could involve capital expenditure on machinery to reduce material wastage	
(c)	Cost reduction could include changing the factory layout to increase efficiency	
(d)	Variety reduction can never save costs and is therefore not part of cost reduction	
(e)	There is a danger that if costs are reduced by a manager in one area without consultation the organisation may lack goal congruence	

7.2 The following table shows activities in separate manufacturing organisations. Identify which activities add value to the end product and which are non-valued added.

		Added value	Non-added value
(a)	Moving engines made in one location to another factory for installing in cars		
(b)	Holding meeting to decide on the colour of paint to use on new range of products		
(c)	Applying several coats of paint to prestige products		
(d)	Fitting strings to electric guitars by a musical instrument manufacturer		
(e)	Waiting by production workers for materials to be delivered		
(f)	Clearing waste materials away from production area		

7.3   The managers of Snaps plc expect to achieve sales next year of 25,000 units of a digital camera, the Digisnap. They have established a market price of £480 per unit. Snaps plc has a target level of 22% operating profit on sales.

Required:

Calculate:

(a)   The expected total sales revenue from the Digisnap for the next year.

(b)   The target operating profit required by Snaps plc from the total sales of Digisnap.

(c)   The total target cost for Digisnap for the next year.

(d)   The target operating profit per unit of Digisnap.

(e)   The target cost per unit of Digisnap.

7.4   Delta Limited is considering designing a new product, and will use target costing to arrive at the target cost of the product. You have been given the following information and asked to calculate the target cost for materials so that the purchasing manager can use this as a target in her negotiations with suppliers.

- The price at which the product will be sold is £50

- The company has firm orders for 20,000 units at a price of £50

- The fixed costs per unit are £16 per unit

- The labour requirement is 20 minutes at a cost of £18 per hour

- The required profit margin is 40%

- The material requirement is 200 grams per unit (ie 0.2 kilogram)

(a)   Calculate the target cost per kilogram for the materials component of the product.

	£
Sales price per unit	
Profit margin	
Total costs	
Fixed cost per unit	
Labour cost per unit	
Maximum material cost per unit	
Target cost per kilogram	

(b)   Complete the following statement:

The trade price per kilogram quoted on the supplier's price list is £50 per kilogram. The purchasing manager has negotiated a discount of 15%. The discount should be **accepted / rejected** because the £50 reduces to £ [   ] which is **above / below** the Target cost.

(c)   The minimum percentage discount needed to achieve the Target cost is:

[   ]

7.5   The costs of quality are divided into four categories:

1   Prevention costs

2   Appraisal costs

3   Internal failure costs

4   External failure costs

Required:

State the category to which each of the following types of cost belongs:

(a)   Investigation of faults.

(b)   Training production staff to use new equipment.

(c)   The loss of customer loyalty due to poor quality goods.

(d)   Costs resulting from loss of production due to machine breakdown.

(e)   Inspection of raw materials when received.

(f)   The cost of scrapping output.

(g)   Claims from customers relating to defective products.

7.6 Clever Technologies Ltd is considering developing a new product. It will consist of a mobile phone charger that will use a combination of solar power and generated kinetic energy. Through wireless technology the device will enable any phone within range to be kept fully charged continually.

The following data has been collected regarding this new product.

Development costs (including creating prototypes) are expected to be £1,900,000 in each of years 0, 1 and 2.

Production unit numbers and sales numbers are planned as follows:

	Production	Sales
Year 2	50,000	0
Year 3	90,000	80,000
Year 4	100,000	110,000
Year 5	0	50,000

No production or sales are expected after year 5.

Variable costs of production are budgeted at £15 per unit. Fixed production costs are budgeted at £2,000,000 for each of the years 2 to 4.

Selling prices are planned at £70 per unit.

The company's cost of capital is 10%, and this is reflected in the discount factors given below.

Complete the following table to calculate both the non-discounted and discounted life-cycle cash flows for the product. Round to nearest £000.

Year	Cash Inflow £000	Cash Outflow £000	Net Cash Flow £000	Discount Factor	Present Value £000
0				1.000	
1				0.909	
2				0.826	
3				0.751	
4				0.683	
5				0.621	
	Totals				

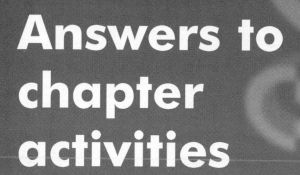

Answers to chapter activities

CHAPTER 1: MANAGEMENT ACCOUNTING TECHNIQUES

1.1 (a) (1)   **Profit Statements Using Absorption Costing**

	Week 1		Week 2	
	£	£	£	£
Sales		24,000		40,000
Less cost of sales:				
Opening Inventory	–		5,000	
Cost of Production:				
Direct Materials	5,000		5,000	
Direct Labour	9,000		9,000	
Fixed Overheads	6,000		6,000	
Less				
Closing Inventory	(5,000)		–	
		15,000		25,000
Profit		9,000		15,000

(2)   **Profit Statements Using Marginal Costing**

	Week 1		Week 2	
	£	£	£	£
Sales		24,000		40,000
Less cost of sales:				
Opening Inventory	–		3,500	
Variable Cost of				
Production:	14,000		14,000	
Less Closing Inventory	(3,500)		–	
		10,500		17,500
Contribution		13,500		22,500
Less Fixed Costs		6,000		6,000
Profit		7,500		16,500

(b)

	Week 1	Week 2
	£	£
Profit under absorption costing	9,000	15,000
Less:		
Fixed costs absorbed into closing inventory	(1,500)	
Add:		
Fixed costs absorbed into opening inventory		1,500
Profit under marginal costing	7,500	16,500

The inventory valuation using absorption costing includes £6,000 ÷ 4,000 units = £1.50 per unit of fixed overheads, which is not included when using marginal costing. This means that the inventory of 1,000 units at the end of week one is valued at £1,500 more using absorption costing, and the profit recorded in week one is also £1,500 more. Marginal costing records a profit higher by £1,500 in week two, as the inventories fall by 1,000 units. Both systems show identical profits for the two weeks added together because the inventory level at the start of week one is the same as at the end of week two.

1.2   Fixed overhead absorption rate (using budgeted figures):
£126,500 / 55,000   = £2.30 per unit

Amount of fixed overheads absorbed:
£2.30 x actual output of 56,000   = £128,800

Under or over absorption:
Fixed overheads absorbed – actual fixed overheads
£128,800 – £129,000   = –£200

The actual overheads exceed the overheads absorbed, therefore this is under absorption.

1.3   Fixed overhead absorption rate (using budgeted figures):
£282,600 / 36,000   = £7.85 per unit

Amount of fixed overheads absorbed:
£7.85 x actual output of 34,500   = £270,825

Under or over absorption:
Fixed overheads absorbed – actual fixed overheads
£270,825 – £279,500   = –£8,675

The actual overheads exceed the overheads absorbed, therefore this is under absorption.

1.4

Situation	Absorption costing	Marginal costing	Activity based costing
(a) A company that has restricted capacity and needs to choose which products should be given priority		✔	
(b) A hotel that wishes to sell some rooms on a 'last minute' basis at the minimum price without incurring losses		✔	
(c) A company that makes a wide range of different products using advanced manufacturing technology. Design costs are significant. In the competitive market place it is important that unit costs are as accurate as possible.			✔
(d) A company that builds large commercial premises that take a considerable time to complete. Most costs can be attributed to specific buildings.	✔		
(e) A company that makes an established range of products where volumes can be accurately predicted. All products are made in similar size batches.	✔		

1.5   Variable cost at 900 units:
        900 x £5   = £4,500
Fixed cost:
        £6,200 – £4,500   = £1,700
At 1,050 units:
        Variable cost   (1,050 x £5)   £5,250
        Fixed cost   £1,700
        Total cost   £6,950

1.6   Variable cost at 1,450 units:
  £9,650 - £5,590   = £4,060

  Variable cost per unit:
   £4,060 / 1,450   = £2.80 per unit

  Total cost at 1,200 units:

Variable cost	(1,200 x £2.80)	£3,360
Fixed Cost		£5,590
Total cost		£8,950

1.7   At the output level of 30,000 units we know the fixed costs and can therefore calculate the variable costs as follows:

Variable cost per unit = (£380,000 − £200,000) / 30,000 = £6.00.

Fixed costs account for the difference between the variable costs and the total costs.

At 36,000 units:

Total costs	£466,000
Variable costs (36,000 x £6)	£216,000
Therefore stepped fixed costs are	£250,000

The fixed costs therefore rise from £200,000 to £250,000 when the production level exceeds 31,000 units.

1.8   Since we know the variable cost per unit we can calculate the fixed costs at each given production level:

At 12,000 units:

Total costs	£136,000
Variable costs (12,000 x £3)	£36,000
Therefore stepped fixed costs are	£100,000

At 17,000 units:

Total costs	£186,000
Variable costs (17,000 x £3)	£51,000
Therefore stepped fixed costs are	£135,000

1.9

	Year 0	Year 1	Year 2	Year 3
Net cash flows £	−60,000	25,000	25,000	25,000
Discount factor	1.000	0.909	0.826	0.751
Present values £	−60,000	22,725	20,650	18,775
Net present value £				2,150

1.10

	Year 0	Year 1	Year 2	Year 3
Cash inflows £	0	38,500	38,500	39,500
Cash outflows £	74,500	1,500	9,500	1,500
Net cash flows £	−74,500	37,000	29,000	38,000
Discount factor	1.000	0.909	0.826	0.751
Present values £	−74,500	33,633	23,954	28,538
Net present value £				11,625

1.11   Discount has reduced total cost at 7,500 units by 7,500 x £1.50 = £11,250. Therefore without discount, total cost at 7,500 units would be £72,500.

Using this data to calculate variable cost (ignoring discount):

	Cost	**Units**		
High	£72,500	7,500		
Low	£48,500	4,500		
Difference	£24,000	÷ 3,000		= £8.00 per unit

Variable cost after discount is £8.00 - £1.50 = £6.50

Using 7,500 units: Fixed cost = £61,250 – (£6.50 x 7,500 units) = £12,500

1.12   Here we use the data at 5,000 and 8,000 units, since this does not cross the point at which discount starts to apply. This will give us the variable cost after discount.

	Cost	**Units**		
High	£162,000	8,000		
Low	£108,000	5,000		
Difference	£54,000	÷ 3,000		= £18.00 per unit

Using 5,000 units: Fixed cost = £108,000 – (£18.00 x 5,000 units) = £18,000

Variable cost before discount is £18.00 x 100 / 90 = £20.00

Total costs for production at 3,000 units uses variable cost without any discount, as follows:

Variable Cost: 3,000 x £20.00 =	£60,000
Fixed Costs	£18,000
Total Costs	£78,000

CHAPTER 2: STANDARD COSTING – DIRECT COSTS

2.1   The following statements are true: (b), (c), (d), (f). All the other statements are false.

2.2   The following comments are valid: (b), (c), (e), (f), (g), (h), (i), (j).
The remaining comments are false.

2.3 **(a)**

One Unit of X	Quantity	Cost per unit of input £	Total cost £
Direct Materials	0.75 (kg)	10.00	7.50
Direct Labour	0.20 (hr)	13.00	2.60
Fixed Overheads	1	7.00	7.00
Total			17.10

(b)   20,000 units x £17.10 = £342,000

2.4   Using the budget data to calculate the standard data for one unit:

Direct Materials   40,000 kg ÷ 20,000   = 2 kg
                        @ £300,000 ÷ 40,000   = £7.50 per kg.
                                                  = £15.00 per unit

Direct Labour   10,000 hrs ÷ 20,000   = 0.5 hrs
                        @ £60,000 ÷ 10,000   = £6.00 per hr
                                                  = £3.00 per unit

Direct Material Price Variance: (37,000 kg x £7.50) − £278,000 = £500 A

Direct Material Usage Variance: £7.50 x ([2 kg x 19,000 units] − 37,000 kg) = £7,500 F

Direct Labour Rate Variance: (9,800 hrs x £6.00) − £58,600 = £200 F

Direct Labour Efficiency Variance: £6.00 x ([0.5 hr x 19,000 units] − 9,800 hrs) = £1,800 A

Reconciliation:
Standard Cost for Actual Production Level
            19,000 x (£15.00 + £3.00)   £342,000
Add: Direct Material Price Variance   £500   A
Less: Direct Material Usage Variance   (£7,500)   F
           Direct Labour Rate Variance   (£200)   F
Add: Direct Labour Efficiency Variance   £1,800   A
Actual Cost of Actual Production   £336,600

2.5   **(a)**   Direct material price variance
                      (610 sq metres x £25) − £15,400   = £150 Adverse
       (b)   Direct material usage variance
                      ((300 windows x 2 sq metres) x £25) − (610 sq metres x £25)   = £250 Adverse
       (c)   Direct labour rate variance
                      (145 hours x £8) − £1,220   = £60 Adverse
       (d)   Direct labour efficiency variance
                      ((300 windows x 0.5 hours) x £8) − (145 hours x £8)   = £40 Favourable

2.6   Using the budget data to calculate the standard data for one unit:

Variable Materials 3,000 kg ÷ 30,000   = 0.1 kg
                    @ £75,000 ÷ 3,000   = £25 per kg
                                               = £2.50 per unit

Variable Labour 15,000 hrs ÷ 30,000   = 0.5 hrs
                 @ £150,000 ÷ 15,000   = £10.00 per hr
                                              = £5.00 per unit

Variable Material Price Variance: (3,100 kg x £25.00) − £81,000 = £3,500 A
Variable Material Usage Variance: £25 x ([0.1 kg x 32,000 units] − 3,100 kg) = £2,500 F
Variable Labour Rate Variance: (15,900 hrs x £10.00) − £155,000 = £4,000 F
Variable Labour Efficiency Variance: £10.00 x ([0.5 hr x 32,000 units] − 15,900 hrs) = £1,000 F

Reconciliation:

Standard Marginal Cost for Actual Production Level

	32,000 x (£2.50 + £5.00)	£240,000	
Add:	Variable Material Price Variance	£3,500	A
Less:	Variable Material Usage Variance	(£2,500)	F
	Variable Labour Rate Variance	(£4,000)	F
	Variable Labour Efficiency Variance	(£1,000)	F
Actual Marginal Cost of Actual Production		£236,000	

2.7   Direct Material Price Variance: (71,500 kg x £9.45) − £678,700 = £3,025 A
Direct Material Usage Variance: £9.45 x ((96 kg x 700 units) − 71,500 kg) = £40,635 A
[**Note:** 5 hours 6 minutes = 5.1 hours.]
Direct Labour Rate Variance: (3,850 hrs x £6.30) − £24,220 = £35 F
Direct Labour Efficiency Variance: £6.30 x ([5.1 hr x 700 units] − 3,850 hrs) = £1,764 A

Reconciliation:
Standard Cost for Actual Production Level

	700 x ((96 x £9.45) + (5.1 x £6.30))	£657,531	
Add:	Direct Material Price Variance	£3,025	A
	Direct Material Usage Variance	£40,635	A
Less:	Direct Labour Rate Variance	(£35)	F
Add:	Direct Labour Efficiency Variance	£1,764	A
Actual Cost of Actual Production (£678,700 + £24,220)		£702,920	

2.8   (c)   £3,000 A

2.9   (d) 1,000 This is an adverse variance.

2.10 (a) £148,500

2.11   Standard cost of actual material used is £900 + £168 = £1,068.

Actual quantity of material is £1,068 / £12 = 89 kilos.

2.12   Standard cost of labour is £12,560 − £536 = £12,024.

Standard rate of labour per hour = £12,024 / 668 hours = £18.00.

2.13

Email	
To:	Production Manager
From:	Accounting Technician
Subject:	Reasons for Direct Cost Variances

The following are likely reasons for the variances shown in the recent report.

Direct Material Price Variance £2,960 Favourable

This variance appears to be the result of the new contract that was agreed with the material supplier. This is effectively a bulk discount which was able to be negotiated due to the additional requirements for material due to the increased production level.

Direct Material Usage Variance £5,350 Adverse

The most likely cause of this variance is the excess material wastage created when the machine was not working correctly.

Direct Labour Rate Variance £9,260 Adverse

This variance has occurred despite the anticipated pay increase not having been paid (which would normally have led to a favourable variance). The most likely reason is the additional overtime worked which would have resulted in enhanced pay for the hours concerned. Some overtime was due to catching up with production following the machine problems, but overtime may also have been used to increase production above the budgeted level. This should be investigated to determine whether this was the case.

Direct Labour Efficiency Variance £5,150

This variance relates to the labour time taken to produce the output. The problem with the machine working slowly would have contributed to this, as would the extra idle time that occurred when the machine broke down and had to be repaired.

2.14   Labour efficiency variance (excluding idle time):

(5,000 units x 0.75hr x £10) − (3,850 hrs x £10)   = £1,000 A

Labour idle time variance:

(150 hrs x £10)   = £1,500 A

2.15

	£	Adverse / Favourable
Labour rate variance	36.00	Favourable
Labour efficiency variance (excluding idle time)	75.00	Adverse
Idle time variance	300.00	Adverse

2.16

Standard labour cost of 5,800 units			£191,400
Direct labour rate variance		£3,538	
Direct labour idle time variance	£990		
Direct labour efficiency variance	£2,200		
Direct labour idle time + efficiency variances		£3,190	
Total direct labour variance			£6,728
Actual labour cost of 5,800 units			£198,128

CHAPTER 3: STANDARD COSTING – VARIABLE AND FIXED OVERHEADS

3.1 **(a)** Variable overhead expenditure variance:
(2,420 direct labour hours x £1.50) – £3,910 = £280 Adverse

(b) Variable overhead efficiency variance:
(5 hours x 500 units x £1.50) – (2,420 hours x £1.50) = £3,750 – £3,630 = £120 Favourable

3.2 **(a)** Variable overhead expenditure variance:
(1,900 machine hours x £20*) – £38,600 = £600 Adverse
* Standard hourly rate = £30 / 1.5

(b) Variable overhead efficiency variance:
(1.5 hours x 1,250 units x £20) – (1,900 hours x £20) = £37,500 – £38,000 = £500 Adverse

3.3 **(a)** Absorption rate = Budgeted overheads / budgeted output
= £500,000 / 25,000 units   = £20 per unit

Fixed overhead volume variance:
Actual output x absorption rate – Budgeted output x absorption rate
= (30,000 x £20) – (25,000 x £20)   = £100,000 F
The volume variance is favourable because actual volume is greater than budgeted.

(b) Fixed overhead expenditure variance:
Budgeted cost of fixed overheads – Actual cost of fixed overheads
= £500,000 – £480,000   = £20,000 F
The expenditure variance is favourable because actual costs are less than budgeted.

3.4 **(a)** Fixed overhead expenditure variance:
£60,000 – £58,000 = £2,000 F

(b) Fixed overhead volume variance
£12 per unit* x (3,500 units – 5,000 units) = £18,000 A
*Absorption rate = £60,000 / 5,000 units = £12 per unit

3.5 **(a)** Fixed Overhead Expenditure Variance
£440,000 – £428,000 = £12,000 F

Fixed Overhead Volume Variance
(2,150 x £200) – (2,200 x £200)   = £10,000 A

(b) One disadvantage of absorbing overheads on a per-sofa basis is that each sofa will absorb an identical amount of overheads. This may not be appropriate if different types of sofa use different amounts of resource – for example, some sofas may take longer to manufacture.

(c)

Budgeted / Standard fixed cost for actual production (2,150 x £200)			£430,000
Variances	**Favourable**	**Adverse**	
Fixed overhead expenditure	£12,000		
Fixed overhead volume		£10,000	
Total variance	£2,000		–£2,000
Actual fixed cost for actual production			£428,000

3.6 **(a)** £94,600 ÷ 2,200   = £43 per hour

(b) Exp = £94,600 – £99,000   = £4,400 A
Vol = £43 x (2,500 – 2,200)   = £12,900 F
Total = (2,500 x £43) – £99,000   = £8,500 F

(c) Valid: 3 and 4.

3.7 **(a)** £448,000 ÷ 14,000 = £32 per hour

(b) 14,000 ÷ 2,000 = 7 hours each

(c) 7 x 1800 = 12,600 hours

(d) Exp = £448,000 – £455,000 = £7,000 A
Vol = £32 x (12,600 – 14,000) = £44,800 A

(e) Reconciliation:

Overhead Absorbed	£403,200
Expenditure Variance	£7,000 A
Volume Variance	£44,800 A
Actual Overhead	£455,000

3.8 **(a)** (5,100 desks x 5 std hrs) + (7,000 chairs x 2 std hrs) = 39,500 std hrs for actual production

(b) £600,000 / 40,000 standard direct labour hours = £15 per standard direct labour hour

(c) Variances:
Fixed Overhead Expenditure Variance
£600,000 – £603,500 = £3,500 A
Fixed Overhead Volume Variance
(39,500 std hrs x £15) – (40,000 bud std hrs x £15) = £7,500 A
Total Fixed Overhead Variance
(39,500 std hrs x £15) – £603,500 = £11,000 A

3.9 **(a)** (1) Standard usage of steel is 20,000 sq mt / 5,000 radiators = 4 sq mt per radiator
Standard price of steel is £30,000 / 20,000 sq mt = £1.50 per sq mt
direct material (steel) usage variance:
(5,200 radiators x 4 sq mt x £1.50) – (21,320 sq mt x £1.50) = £780 A

(2) Standard labour rate is £27,500 / 2,500 hours = £11.00 per hour
direct labour rate variance:
(2,650 hours x £11) – £31,800 = £2,650 A

(3) Standard labour hours per radiator is 2,500 hours / 5,000 radiators = 0.5 hours per radiator
direct labour efficiency variance:
(5,200 radiators x 0.5 hours x £11.00) – (2,650 hours x £11.00) = £550 A

(b) 'An adverse variance is **a debit to** the statement of profit or loss (income statement), and a favourable variance is **a credit to** the statement of profit or loss.'

(c)

Budgeted / Standard variable cost for actual production			£62,400
Budgeted fixed costs			£60,000
Variances	**Favourable**	**Adverse**	
Direct materials (steel) price	£1,066		
Direct materials (steel) usage		£780	
Direct materials (paint) price		£75	
Direct materials (paint) usage	£75		
Direct labour rate		£2,650	
Direct labour efficiency		£550	
Fixed overhead expenditure	£1,500		
Total variance		£1,414	£1,414
Actual cost of actual production			£123,814

Workings:
Budgeted / standard variable cost for actual production
(£30,000 + £2,500 + £27,500) x 5,200 / 5,000 = £62,400
Fixed overhead expenditure variance
(£60,000 − £58,500) = £1,500 F

3.10

Standard cost for actual production*			£15,015
Variances	**Favourable**	**Adverse**	
Direct materials (liquid soap) price	£700		
Direct materials (bottles) price	£113		
Direct materials (liquid soap) usage		£150	
Direct materials (bottles) usage		£30	
Direct labour rate	£262		
Direct labour efficiency		£110	
Fixed overhead expenditure		£250	
Fixed overhead volume	£350		
Total variance			£885 F
Actual cost of actual production			£14,130

* calculated as £13,650 x 5,500 units ÷ 5,000 units

3.11

Situation	Fixed Overhead Expenditure Variance			Fixed Overhead Volume Variance		
	Adverse	Favourable	No impact	Adverse	Favourable	No impact
Production manager awarded a pay increase	✔					✔
Unplanned additional day's holiday shut down			✔*	✔		
Additional direct labour staff used to increase production			✔		✔	
Unplanned pay rise given to direct labour staff			✔			✔**
New maintenance contract implemented with reduced costs		✔				✔
Additional shift working (including supervisors) used to increase production	✔				✔	

*Unless there are heating and lighting savings that would result in a favourable variance.
**Unless pay rise increases motivation and speed of working

CHAPTER 4: STATISTICAL TECHNIQUES

4.1

Period	1	2	3	4	5
Sales (units)	212,800	210,600	208,400	206,200	204,000

4.2

Period	1	2	3	4	5	6	7
Sales (units)	123,400	123,970	124,525	125,085	125,640	126,200	126,760

Average change (125,640 − 123,400) / 4 = 560

4.3

Month	Jan	Feb	March	April	May
Actual Price £	6.80	6.40	7.00	6.40	6.40
Seasonal Variation £	+0.40	−0.10	+0.40	−0.30	−0.40
Trend £	6.40	6.50	6.60	6.70	6.80

4.4 500 units   Total cost   (£13.20 x 500) + £480.00 = £7,080

800 units   Total cost   (£13.20 x 800) + £480.00 = £11,040

The total cost behaves as a semi-variable cost.

4.5 August 20-9 will be month 37

Forecast sales   1,200 + (13 x 37)   = 1,681 units

4.6 (a) and **(b)**

Period	Actual data	3 point moving averages (Trend)	Seasonal variations
30	3,500		
31	3,430	3,460	-30
32	3,450	3,470	-20
33	3,530	3,480	+50
34	3,460	3,490	−30
35	3,480	3,500	−20
36	3,560		
37	3,490	3,520	−30
38	3,510	3,530	−20
39	3,590	3,540	+50
40	3,520	3,550	−30

4.7

Material	Old price £	New price £	New price as index number with old price as base	% increase in price
A	2.13	2.16	101.41	1.41%
B	10.25	11.00	107.32	7.32%
C	3.60	3.75	104.17	4.17%
D	240.00	252.00	105.00	5.00%
E	68.00	84.32	124.00	24.00%

4.8

	January	February	March
Total cost £	20,000	24,000	25,000
Total quantity	2,000 kilos	2,200 kilos	2,140 kilos
Cost per kilo £	10.00	10.91	11.68
Cost index	100	109	117

4.9

	Amount £	Adverse / Favourable
Material price variance	13,500	Adverse
Part of variance explained by change in index	7,070	Adverse

CHAPTER 5: PERFORMANCE INDICATORS

5.1 (a) - (c)

	31 May 20-3	31 May 20-2
Gross Profit % of Sales	28%	30%
Net Profit % of Sales	16%	18%
Administration expense as % of Sales	4.8%	5.3%
Selling expense as % of Sales	7.2%	6.7%

Comments: Looking at the original figures, it can be seen that Sales Revenue, Purchases and Expenses have all increased in the second year. Administration, which would probably be expected to be a fixed cost, has remained relatively stable. Inventory levels have built up in both years. Profits have also increased.

Looking at the ratios, the percentage Gross Profit has decreased slightly, which could be due to increased purchase costs or having to reduce selling prices, or both. The expenses together still represent 12% of Sales, and as would be expected for a fixed cost, the administration percentage has gone down slightly. The selling expense, however, has increased as a proportion of sales, possibly due to increased advertising to generate more sales. The reduction in Net Profit percentage results from the decreased Gross Profit margin.

Toni Jones should consider whether there is a problem with the build-up of inventory – are there goods which do not sell? Also the reasons for the decrease in Gross Profit margin and increase in selling expenses should be investigated.

5.2

Selling price per unit £	5.50
Gross profit margin	11.82%
Operating profit margin	3.81%
Return on net assets	11.73%
Direct materials cost per unit £	2.30
Direct labour cost per unit £	1.45
Fixed production cost per unit £	1.10
Full production cost per unit £	4.85
Inventory days	19
Receivables days	59
Payables days	62
Working capital cycle days	16

5.3

	Scinso Soft Ltd	Laurelle plc
Selling price per unit	£7.50	£10
Material cost per unit	£2.00	£1.50
Labour cost per unit	£1.25	£1.00
Fixed production overheads per unit	£1.00	£1.36
Gross profit margin	43.33%	61.36%
Net profit margin	18.33%	7.95%
Advertising costs as % of turnover	5.56%	45.45%
Return on net assets	16.50%	20.59%

5.4

	Pacer	Greenapple
Sales price per unit £	0.80	2.20
Direct materials per unit £	0.21	0.24
Direct labour per unit £	0.30	0.28
Fixed overhead per unit £	0.08	0.06
Gross Profit %	26.25	73.64
Distribution Costs as % of Sales	7.50	3.18
Administration Costs as % of Sales	7.77	15.36
Marketing Costs as % of Sales	3.75	44.53
Operating Profit %	7.23	10.57
Return on Net Assets %	8.07	8.02

Report

Strategies and Performance of Pacer and Greenapple

Both companies sell a similar product with similar costs per unit. Greenapple uses a slightly more expensive material, but this is offset by economies of scale that bring down the direct labour and fixed overhead costs per unit. Despite the similar unit costs, Pacer sells its deodorant at just over a third the price of Greenapple's product. This is the reason for the large difference in gross profit percentages.

While Pacer has other costs totalling just over 19% of sales value, Greenapple's other costs are over 63% of sales value. This is mainly due to the marketing costs which appears to be necessary to maintain the high quantity of sales despite the high selling price.

The result is operating profit percentages that are 7.23% for Pacer and 10.57% for Greenapple. However the return on net assets for both companies are very similar at just over 8%.

5.5

	£
Sales	1,095,000
Variable production costs	613,200
Fixed production overheads	262,800
Cost of sales	876,000
Gross profit	219,000
Sales and administration costs	131,400
Operating profit	87,600
Total net assets	876,000

5.6   Wessit Housing Association

(a)   The ratios for each of the two companies are:

	Staylite Ltd	Temeglass Ltd
Gross profit margin	45.3%	47.6%
Operating profit margin	5.3%	6.6%
Return on capital employed	65.4%	65.9%
Current ratio	1.09 : 1	1.97 : 1
Quick ratio	0.64 : 1	1.20 : 1
Asset turnover	12.44 times	9.99 times
Sales per employee	£478,750	£527,778
Operating profit per employee	£25,188	£34,833

(b)   Indicators of the profitability of the two companies include the profit margins and ROCE. Temeglass Ltd appears to be more profitable using any of these indicators. The financial position of the two suppliers can be seen partly from the original figures, in that Temeglass Ltd has no long-term liabilities, whereas Staylite Ltd has significant long-term loans (debentures). Also Temeglass Ltd has a better liquidity position, as can be seen from the current and quick ratios.

(c)   The main performance indicators which may be used to indicate efficiency are ROCE and operating profit margin. (Profit per employee may also be significant).

(d)   The performance indicator which may be used to indicate the productivity of the companies is sales per employee, although this is not ideal because comparative selling prices and volumes of output are not known. Output per employee would be a better indicator. Profit per employee could also be used here.

(e)   The limitations of the above analysis are:

When using the published accounts of companies, it is not possible to guarantee that we are comparing like with like, as different policies (including those regarding depreciation, inventory valuation and goodwill, for example) will affect the results. Also there is the possibility that the statement of financial position does not show a typical position. In this case, only one year's results are available for each company, so it is not possible to see whether there are any significant trends.

(f)   A further indicator which Wessit Housing Association should seek to obtain would be some measure of quality or value for money. Suggestions include selling prices, product specifications, or some indication of customer satisfaction. The companies may be able to show their previous work and it would be particularly useful to the housing association to obtain opinions or references from previous customers. Numbers of customer complaints would be another possible measure, if available.

5.7

Activity ratio %	105.63
Efficiency ratio %	101.08
Capacity ratio %	104.50

Workings: Activity ratio   ((84,500 x 0.5) / (80,000 x 0.5)) x 100
            Efficiency ratio   ((84,500 x 0.5) / 41,800) x 100
            Capacity ratio   (41,800 / (80,000 x 0.5)) x 100

5.8   Efficiency ratio = (Standard hours of actual output ÷ Actual hours) x 100%

Standard hours of actual output = 2,400 units x 6 hours = 14,400 hours

Actual hours = 15,000 hours

Therefore Efficiency ratio = (14,400 ÷ 15,000) x 100% = 96%

Capacity Ratio = (Actual hours ÷ Budgeted hours) x 100%

= (15,000 ÷ 14,700) x 100% = 102%

Activity Ratio = (Standard hours of actual output ÷ Budgeted hours) x 100%

= (14,400 ÷ 14,700) x 100% = 98%

5.9

	Financial perspective	Customer perspective	Internal perspective	Innovation and learning perspective
Average delivery time		✔		
Gross profit margin	✔			
% sales to existing customers		✔		
Return on capital employed	✔			
% of rejects			✔	
Number of new products				✔
Research and development expenditure as % sales				✔

5.10   Exe Ltd, for the year 20-3,

(a)   Value Added = £972,000 – (£216,000 + £324,000)

= £972,000 – £540,000 = £432,000

(b)   Value Added per employee = £432,000 ÷ 54 = £8,000

Output = 67,500 product units.

Therefore the Unit Cost is calculated as follows:

(c)   Materials used: £216,000 ÷ 67,500 = £3.20 per unit

(d)   Total cost of inputs: £540,000 ÷ 67,500 = £8.00 per unit

CHAPTER 6: DECISION MAKING TECHNIQUES

6.1

Cost:	
(a) Standard mark-up of 35% on cost	
(b) Additional direct materials to be purchased for this order	✔
(c) Fixed overhead absorption cost per unit	
(d) Incremental cost of additional direct labour required	✔
(e) Depreciation of production machinery	
(f) Fees for consultant to work on design of special order	✔
(g) Cost of salaried factory manager	
(h) Original cost of materials needed for this order that are in stock and have no other use and no resale value	
(i) Delivery costs of special order	✔

6.2

	Units	Per Unit £	Total £
Lost contribution on 400 gram can sales	1,000,000	0.64	−640,000
200 gram can sales:			
Additional revenue	2,200,000	0.55	1,210,000
Material cost	2,200,000	0.07	−154,000
Labour cost	2,200,000	0.03	−66,000
Increase fixed costs			−110,000
Net increase / (reduction) in profit			240,000

6.3

	Total per Week £	
Incremental revenue	21,000	
Incremental costs:		
Variable production costs	9,000	
Purchase of finished goods	8,000	
Fixed production costs	0	
Incremental profit / (loss)	4,000	
Recommendation	**Accept**	**Reject**
	✔	

6.4   **(a)**

	Shiver	Shake	Total
Production (units)	10,000	15,000	25,000
Total contribution £	180,000	285,000	465,000

(b)

	Shiver	Shake	Total
Contribution per kg of material £	9.00	7.60	
Production (units)	12,000	4,800	16,800
Material usage (kg)	24,000	12,000	36,000
Total contribution £	216,000	91,200	307,200

6.5

	Strategy 1	Strategy 2
Contribution per unit £	27.00	17.00
Total fixed production costs £	50,000	50,000
Forecast profit £	85,000	86,000
Breakeven point (units)	1,852	2,942
Margin of safety (units)	3,148	5,058
Margin of safety %	63	63

6.6   **(a)**

	Dee	Eff
Contribution per unit £	5.00	8.00
Total contribution £	350,000	480,000
Break-even point (units)	35,000	45,000
Margin of safety %	50	25

(b)   **Report**

- An evaluation of the difference in the total contribution and profit between the two departments:

  Dee has a lower total contribution than Eff, mainly because its contribution per unit is only £5 compared with Eff's £8. Even though Dee's sales volume is a little higher than Eff the total contribution of Dee is less than three quarters of the other department.

  However, since Dee's fixed costs are less than half those of Eff, it has a much greater profit at £175,000 compared with £120,000.

- The implications of the different break-even points and margins of safety:

  Dee's current sales volume is twice the volume needed to break-even, mainly because it has low fixed costs. Eff's volume would only need to fall by 25% to reach its break-even point.

- An evaluation of the risk of each department:

Dee is in a much safer position due to its low fixed costs and its high margin of safety. If sales of both departments were to fall, Eff would become loss making much more quickly.

However, for every unit sold above its break-even point, Eff will generate greater contribution per unit than Dee, so if sales were to rise sufficiently it would overtake Dee in terms of profit.

6.7

	Aye £000	**Bee** £000	**Total** £000
Sales	320	160	480
Total variable costs	165	100	265
Fixed costs related to products	25	15	40
Product contribution	130	45	175
Whole business fixed costs			140
Operating Profit			35

Since the Bee product is making a contribution of £45,000 to the overall profitability, this would be lost if the product were discontinued. Therefore the product should not be discontinued.

CHAPTER 7: COST MANAGEMENT TECHNIQUES

7.1

	True
(a) Cost reduction is only concerned with finding the cheapest materials	
(b) Cost reduction could involve capital expenditure on machinery to reduce material wastage	✔
(c) Cost reduction could include changing the factory layout to increase efficiency	✔
(d) Variety reduction can never save costs and is therefore not part of cost reduction	
(e) There is a danger that if costs are reduced by a manager in one area without consultation the organisation may lack goal congruence	✔

7.2

	Added value	Non-added value
(a) Moving engines made in one location to another factory for installing in cars		✔
(b) Holding meeting to decide on the colour of paint to use on new range of products		✔
(c) Applying several coats of paint to prestige products	✔	
(d) Fitting strings to electric guitars by a musical instrument manufacturer	✔	
(e) Waiting by production workers for materials to be delivered		✔
(f) Clearing waste materials away from production area		✔

7.3 (a) Expected total sales revenue from Digisnap = £480 x 25,000 = £12,000,000

(b) Target operating profit from Digisnap = 22% x £12,000,000 = £2,640,000

(c) Total target cost for Digisnap = £12,000,000 – £2,640,000 = £9,360,000

(d) Target operating profit per unit of Digisnap = £2,640,000/25,000 = £105.60

(e) Target cost per unit of Digisnap = £480 – £105.60 = £374.40

7.4 **(a)**

	£
Sales price per unit	50.00
Profit margin (40% of £50)	20.00
Total costs (£50 – £20)	30.00
Fixed cost per unit	16.00
Labour cost per unit	6.00
Maximum material cost per unit	8.00
Target cost per kilogram (£8 x 1,000/200)	40.00

(b) The trade price per kilogram quoted on the supplier's price list is £50 per kilogram. The purchasing manager has negotiated a discount of 15%. The discount should be **rejected** because the £50 reduces to **£42.50** which is **above** the Target cost.

(c) The minimum percentage discount needed to achieve the Target cost is **20%**.

7.5   Prevention Cost: (b)
Appraisal Cost: (e)
Internal Failure Costs: (a) (d) (f)
External Failure Costs: (c) (g)

7.6

Year	Cash Inflow £000	Cash Outflow £000	Net Cash Flow £000	Discount Factor	Present Value £000
0	0	1,900	−1,900	1.000	−1,900
1	0	1,900	−1,900	0.909	−1,727
2	0	4,650	−4,650	0.826	−3,841
3	5,600	3,350	2,250	0.751	1,690
4	7,700	3,500	4,200	0.683	2,869
5	3,500	0	3,500	0.621	2,174
	Totals		1,500		−735

Index

for your notes